CW01023451

NEVER A DULL MOMENT

NEVER A
DULL MOMENT

THE AUTOBIOGRAPHY OF

JOHN MILLARD

ADMINISTRATOR
SOLDIER *&* FARMER

SILENT BOOKS

FOR CORINNE

First published in Great Britain in 1996
by Silent Books Ltd
Swavesey, Cambridge CB4 5QG

© Copyright 1996 John Millard

ISBN 1 85183 096 0

British Library Cataloguing-in-Publication Data
A catalogue record of this book is available
from the British Library

Printed in Great Britain by St Edmundsbury Press
Bury St Edmunds, Suffolk

Portrait of Tshekedi Khama by Neville Lewis
by kind permission of the
permanent collection
of the
National Museum, Monuments & Art Gallery,
Botswana

CONTENTS

CHAPTER 1 Childhood & School   9

CHAPTER 2 Chariots of Fire   22

CHAPTER 3 The Lake Rudolf Expedition   34

CHAPTER 4 Basutoland, South Africa and Tanganyika   56

CHAPTER 5 Nairobi to Addis   78

CHAPTER 6 The Italian Defeat   113

CHAPTER 7 Madagascar   133

CHAPTER 8 North Africa, Italy and Europe   140

CHAPTER 9 Tanganyika Again   163

CHAPTER 10 Bechuanaland   185

CHAPTER 11 Kilimanjaro   207

ACKNOWLEDGEMENTS

I WRITE this on the eve of my eighty fifth birthday. But for the kindness of my family and assistance of some special friends, I would never have had the courage to produce a book about what has been a long and happy life. In particular I am indebted to the late Sir Michael Blundell, David Coulson, Tom Heaton, Ian and Chris Parker and many others who read my script, commented on it and helped with the editing.

INTRODUCTION

T H E past eighty years cover a fascinating period in which to have worked, fought, farmed and lived mostly in Africa. It covers a time in history during which the world has advanced at an unprecedented pace, and many nations including those in Africa have emerged from obscurity to take their place and contribute each in its own way to the changes involving mankind as a whole since I was born on 8th of March 1911.

To an old-timer like myself, change is sometimes difficult to accept. One is tempted to look back over one's shoulder and brood upon the past when the tempo of living was slower, and when, in the Africa I knew as a young man, wild animals for example, roamed freely and unmolested in many regions, and when parts of the continent were still unexplored and unblemished by over-population, soil erosion, and tribal warfare, and when our horses, the ox-wagon, and the Cape cart were the only forms of transport.

I remember very vividly much that was important to me as a child, and later as a young man, when life seemed to be full opportunities and adventure free from the restrictions and complexities of the age in which we now live. However, change and the march of time is inevitable, and I think I have succeeded in adapting and moving along with the tide. There are fewer backward glances, and the changes taking place world-wide are full of interest and very much part of the life I lead and love.

For me Africa is, and always will be home, and in this story I shall endeavour to capture something of its wonder and ever present mystery, and remember journeys made, and stories told of an age gone by.

Some of the romance of the continent has disappeared, but if you know where to look and where to go on the dusty ever changing face of Africa, with its great isolated mountains and endless savannah plains, its deserts and lakes, there are parts still as they were in the beginning of time, their magic intact.

Mine has been a superbly happy life full of interest and action. I thank my parents for this and the sacrifices they made on my behalf. Anything I have achieved, and my approach to life generally has been due to their guidance and example.

Sadly there are limits to what one can remember or place on record. Eighty years is a long, long time – almost forever – and inevitably I have omitted some journeys to remote and far away places. Neither have I told of all the individuals of different colours and creeds I have met, many of them better men than I, and aspects of whose characters and attitudes I have endeavoured to emulate. Also missing are some great friendships and never-to-be-forgotten experiences: fishing expeditions to Labrador, Iceland, Scotland, Ethiopia, Chile and elsewhere, as well as great mountains and climbs. Yet despite these deficiencies I hope what follows is at least interesting and perhaps enjoyable. After all, the last licence left the elderly is to tell of things as they were.

CHAPTER I

CHILDHOOD AND SCHOOL

IT WAS during the winter when much of the North Eastern Cape and the Orange Free State lay under a freezing blanket of snow. The war declared by the Boers on 11th October 1899 was giving the British, as Kipling put it, "no end of a lesson". It was all supposed to have been over by Christmas but, that had been many months ago, and now the end still seemed to be a very long way off.

Captain Philip Millard MD was on the march with a mounted detachment of the Connaught Rangers. They crossed the Orange River from the Free State at Kiba Drift. The river was in spate and by the time they got their horses and gear across, darkness was falling. However, they pressed on as far as Herschel, a small native reserve on the border with Basutoland, and bivouacked on high ground above the village. My father told me he woke next morning to a cold cloudless day, and the sheer beauty of the snow-covered mountains and the vast views from that point made such an impression on him that he vowed to return some day to this very place, start up a practice, and build a home and a hospital.

Meanwhile, the war dragged on. As medical officer with the Connaught Rangers he was continually on the move until he took charge of the military hospital at Aliwal North. From there he covered, mostly on horseback, a line of strong points known as blockhouses along the railway between the Stormberg Mountains, Burgersdorp, and the surrounding countryside.

My father's letters at this time sharply reflect the character of the man and how he lived and worked. In a letter to his brother he wrote:

> I am seeing a little of warfare just now. In fact, as I write, 10 p.m., we are all on the "qui vive" as this camp can scarcely be called well protected. I think I told you that the Boers have been concentrating in this district of late. Four days ago the Connaught rangers had one of their patrols ambushed, one officer and 10 men being thoroughly trapped. All the horses were shot, six men and the officer were wounded, and the other four captured. I just got back to Aliwal hospital in time to assist.

My mother and father.

The following passage, written in June 1902, illustrates what British soldiers had to put up with:

> We are buried in snow, there is eight inches of it and it is still falling heavily. I wonder if you will realise what this means. You know we are in an exposed position over 5,000' in altitude and we live in tents. This morning we woke up to find everything covered with snow and the whole day the storm has continued. The discomfort is more than slight, the snow being nearly up to one's knees. I did a three-mile walk to visit a patient, otherwise have sat tight. I got so far in my letter when I was sent for to see three native boys who were dying on the roadside of cold. They are pretty bad. I have had them brought into a tent in camp.

After the peace at the end of 1902 my father returned to England in 1903, where he signed on as ship's doctor with P & O. The following year took him to India, South America, Australia and the Far East. It was also the year he met Ursula Foster, who was travelling to England from Australia to study at the Slade. Her charm, poise and graceful manner made an immediate impact on the young and handsome doctor. By coincidence, then, a day or so past Aden, as the ship steamed through a pall of humidity unstirred by any breeze, Ursula was overcome by a severe case of prickly heat. The story goes that Philip – opportunist and gambler that he was – transferred her to the isolation ward. I sometimes wonder whether the isolation ward idea was not a calculated arrangement between themselves. The fact remains that two or three years later they became engaged and married. Meanwhile my father had established his practice and built his home at Herschel just as he had promised himself that winter morning in 1899.

Eventually in 1907 my mother arrived from England. My father met her at the railhead at Aliwal North and the two of them rode the 40 miles to their new home. They now lived in an oasis in a strange but beautiful world. The view looking to the east towards the Wittebergen was always breathtaking, and in the distance, further to the north, was the Basutoland plateau with the Xinodo range just visible beyond Majuba and the high blue hills near Bensonvale.

This was Herschel, where Barbara, Joan and I were brought up and where for a period of 35 years my parents dedicated themselves to the task of making a happy home for us and a place where friends and acquaintances, great and small and of all races and creeds, were welcome at all times. In her spare time my mother continued with her painting and my father with almost missionary fervour devoted himself to his medical work and the well-being of the people of his district.

If you were a man you would have taken to my father immediately, if you were a woman you loved him. He was one of a large family of girls and boys, the children of the country parson at Costock, near Nottingham. The boys all became doctors or went into the Church. Good doctors they were and good churchmen too, but my father Philip and his elder brother Charles were the best of the bunch. Philip the adventurer and man of action went abroad. Charles appealed to me because he learned to fly and got his pilot's licence at the age of sixty, quite an achievement at that time, added to which he was Medical Officer for Health of Leicester City and an ardent believer in euthanasia. At the time of his death he was head of the Euthanasia Society in Britain. Maurice, his son, also a doctor, played regularly for the Barbarians rugger side but was never actually capped for England.

Soon after my arrival at Cambridge in 1930 I went to Leicester by train to make my number with Uncle Charles. He met me at the station and drove me to his home on the far side of the city. Just at about that time the first green yellow and red traffic lights had been installed in Leicester. My uncle announced that he disapproved of these new-fangled things and ignored them completely. It was a hair-raising journey. I was more than impressed by his courage, dash and skill at missing other vehicles.

I think my father was an exceptional doctor and surgeon by any standard and no doubt his Boer War experience stood him in good stead. Very early on in his career in South Africa he became quite famous and was well loved by the African community and the European farmers far and wide.

I remember an occasion when a man working a cliff face path had his foot crushed to pulp and pinned down by a rock weighing a ton or more. There was no way of releasing the foot, which was beyond repair anyway, so my father allowed himself to be lowered down the cliffside on a rope and then, entirely on his own, he amputated the foot and saved the man's life.

Once while riding with my father, when I was about nine, a woman was brought to him completely blinded by a spitting cobra. The best first aid treatment was then thought to be to wash out the eyes with milk, but there was no milk in the village. However as it happened a mother breast-feeding her baby was nearby and provided the necessary eyewash.

My mother Ursula was the daughter of Roger Foster, a senior administrator and magistrate in Melbourne, Australia and related to Charles Joseph La Trobe, Superintendent of Port Philip and Lieutenant Governor of Victoria. Roger is still remembered for the part he played in improving living conditions and establishing justice and a fair deal for the hundreds of Chinese brought into the country at that time to work for a pittance on the goldfields. Among the new immigrants he was affectionately known as "China Foster". It was Roger also who sentenced the notorious highwayman and murderer, Ned Kelly, to death. Ned has since become a legendary figure in Australia, a sort of Robin Hood. Sadly in his diary, which we still have, Roger tells nothing of the period leading up to Kelly's trial and execution: it has just a brief entry: "Sentenced Ned Kelly to death today."

I imagine that Roger Foster's daughters enjoyed the rather restricted life-style

John Millard OBE, as a young man, 1911.

of upper class young ladies during the Victorian era. Ursula was shy but beautiful, a good horsewoman and a talented artist. Her marriage to Philip and departure for Darkest Africa must have come as an awful shock to her parents. However, like so many Australian girls, she was full of character and tough as nails. Moreover, she was in love. Very soon she had her home looking beautiful and the garden a blaze of colour. At times she helped my father in the surgery and soon adapted to her new and totally strange environment.

My earliest memory is of Barbara and myself out on a walk with the ayah. The sky turned black and a huge downpour followed. Just then my father and his African assistant, Jacob, galloped up shouting orders above the racket of the storm. I remember being held on the front of my father's saddle as we galloped homewards through the hail, my sister riding with old Jacob as lightning slashed and thunder roared like a thousand lions. The life I now look back upon started on that day. I must have been about three and a half years old at that time.

The next milestone in our lives was the First World War when in 1915, after the birth of my sister Joan, my father sailed for German East Africa. The campaign there was going badly for the British. My father's letters complain that many of the mistakes made in the Boer War were being repeated. Poor leadership was exacerbated by over-confidence and lack of experience in bush warfare under tropical conditions.

By contrast, the Germans had Lt-Col von Lettow Vorbeck, a truly great guerilla leader, who with his elite, disciplined, and highly-trained force of African tribesmen officered by German settlers inflicted terrible losses on the British. Not until after the arrival of tough well-armed South African and Rhodesian troops under the command of Lt-Gen Jan C. Smuts, formerly a Boer leader fighting against the British, were the tables turned on von Lettow, who surrendered at Abercorn in Northern Rhodesia on 25th November 1918 – exactly a fortnight after the signing of the armistice.

Meanwhile, we at Herschel were living cut off from the rest of the world. It was during that period, when I was about five, that I came up against a serious problem, but because I was scared and ashamed I told no one. The problem was that I was seeing terrible things in the dark. I would wake up in my small bedroom and see shadowy shapes moving silently and very slowly. Something dark and lumpy crouching in a far corner would rise on invisible legs and became a huge, horrific beast that seemed to be half crab half toad. Its nightly appearances and perambulations went on for weeks until I became desperate.

I had a toy pistol which fired a dart-like projectile with a squashy rubber head and was supposed to stick to the target. My faith in this weapon was total. I looked upon it as my only real friend. One night I plucked up enough courage to shoot at one of the creeping horrors. It didn't even grunt, but it stopped moving. Next morning I found my dart stuck in my felt hat next to the china washbasin! The sight of it dissolved my terrible secret problem and with the realisation that I had rid myself of the monster all on my own came a new sense of self-confidence. Unknowingly, I had made a great stride forward in the process of growing up.

My father returned after the war ended and we all went to meet him in Durban. He was on the platform when our train pulled in. In her desperate excitement, my mother rushed to the window, forgetting that it was shut, and shattered the plate glass with her head. Miraculously, she was saved by her thick auburn hair, but the incident caused much laughter among the grown-ups. I remember being seriously worried, fearing that she would be arrested for damaging railway property!

How proud I was of my father as we walked hand in hand along the seafront. He looked so elegant in his uniform that I believed he was a field marshal or at least a general. I told my school friends and was believed. Then we went home to Herschel, together again for the first time after three long years.

One day, soon after his return, my father was pushing his motor cycle across

My father extracting a tooth by the wayside in those early days – such events were all in a day's work for a country doctor.

a shallow mountain stream and had got about half-way across when suddenly a wall of water from a cloudburst swept him and the cycle away like bundles of straw. Being a strong swimmer, he kept his head and was able to climb out about a mile downstream, but the cycle disappeared without trace.

Disappearing without trace was also a fate that my father schemed for Mr Smith, an Airedale. Mr Smith had become doddery and smelly to the extent that my father decided the best thing would be to take him for a long walk and give him a lethal injection.

The evening after the deed was done, we were told that Mr Smith had gone to his final hunting grounds, where he would be happy. Gloom descended on us children as we realised we had lost our oldest friend. Then, five days on, during breakfast on the verandah, who should stagger up the steps looking as if he had been out on the tiles for a month, grinning from ear to ear and feebly wagging his stumpy tail, but the great Mr Smith. To us this was a second coming and Mr Smith became a hero and a legend. However, having made his point, the old hound died naturally a month later, much to the relief of my father, who would never have had the heart to repeat the deed.

He did rather better the day he sent me off to catch a lizard and bring it to his surgery. An African had told him of having been bewitched. His enemy had

placed a lizard in his chest where it was incessantly running up and down, causing him great pain and discomfort. He thought he was about to die. Having a
profound understanding of the very real power of African superstitions, my
father used his stethoscope and said: "You are absolutely right. I can hear the
lizard and I will cure you."

The man was given a whiff of chloroform, a small incision was made in his
chest and neatly sewn up. When he regained consciousness, my father presented him with my lizard. The patient went away laughing and rejoicing.

My best friend up to the age of ten was Nzonzwa, the son of Ndolombo, a
peasant farmer who owned a few head of livestock and lived on the escarpment
near our home. Ndolombo and his two buxom wives treated me like one of
their sons, and I was always welcome at their kraal, a cluster of circular thatched
huts. Nzonzwa and I were always hungry, and I remember many a good meal
shared with his people, taken with our fingers from a black three-legged pot
simmering over a smoky cow-dung fire. Ndolombo was a Xhosa, but, like most
tribesmen along the Basutoland border, always wore a brightly coloured Basuto
blanket over his shoulders. Intelligent and kindly, he loved and respected my
parents.

Nzonzwa and I were inseparable. We were both crack shots with our cata-
pults and whenever Nzonzwa was able to off-load his cattle-herding duties onto
his younger brother, who was considered unreliable, we would sneak off with a
pinch of salt in a twist of paper and pockets full of specially selected round peb-
bles. Normally it was possible – for we became very cunning – to knock off a
fat pigeon or two, which we plucked, gutted, sprinkled with salt and then roasted over the coals in a secret cave. We were also skilled at snaring. The snares
made of hairs from a horse's tail were pegged down an inch off the ground over
some scattered grain on the edge of a field of stubble and were very effective.

* * * *

The carefree life I led after my father's return from the war ended in 1920, when
it was decided I was to go to St Andrew's Prep School and Barbara to the
Diocesan Girls' School, both in Grahamstown. Neither of us had lived in a big
town and our experience of mixing with European children was minimal. That,
coupled with the prospect of having to leave our pets and a way of life we understood, filled us with dread.

The journey took two days and two nights, commencing with a two-hour
drive in a Cape cart with our tin trunks and tuck-boxes lashed to the carrier
behind the seat and drawn by two trotting horses. At a little siding, we picked
up the train to Aliwal North, our nearest town, and the same evening joined the
southbound train to Rosmead in the heart of the desolate Great Karroo, where

we had to wait six hours. The only tree and the only shade were in the cemetery and that was where we always camped and rested until nightfall, before picking up the train from Johannesburg and Rhodesia to Grahamstown, arriving there on the morning of the third day.

At the prep I was shy, homesick and unsure of myself. I hated wearing an Eton collar and on Sundays a blue suit and flat "cheese-cutter" straw hat. I was backward in class and no good at cricket or rugby. I could draw though, and later won the school competition which gave me some confidence in myself. But it was my fight with Pasco Grenfell that did more for my morale than anything else.

I forget how the quarrel arose, but the senior six, who were the school's big shots, and old too at 11 or 12, decided that the matter should be settled in the locker-room. I had been taking lessons from a professional boxer so had some knowledge of how to use my fists, but so had Pasco, and he was bigger and a year older. I was scared, but managed to get in a haymaker to his nose early on. Pasco started bleeding profusely, which curbed his style and spirit so much that the senior six stopped the fight and declared me the winner. After that, Pasco and I made friends.

Ours was a happy home. Our parents had a wonderful understanding of young people and there are, I believe, few children in the world today who enjoyed their home and surroundings as much as we did during our childhood years.

In those faraway times there were none of the marvellous gadgets, vehicles and games of this modern age. As a youngster all you had was your horse, saddle, rifle, fishing rod, blankets, cooking utensils and your "Bushman's Friend" hunting knife. You were highly mobile and independent. You camped, fished, hunted, climbed and explored remote gorges and mountains. Nearby was the Orange River roaring down through a great kloof or canyon. There we would hobble our horses at a suitable spot and walk up-stream for a mile or two, find a big fallen tree or log, drag it to the water's edge and then climb aboard and sitting astride go hurtling downstream. At a given signal as you came opposite the horses everyone abandoned ship and swam for the shore. Nearby was an enormous cave, its reddish brown sandstone walls a gallery of prehistoric rock paintings, the work of Stone Age man going back from fairly recent times a thousand years or more. This was a favourite camp site, and if you dug around with your hunting knife in the ancient midden at the entrance to the cave you found ostrich eggshell beads, arrow-heads fashioned from flint-like stone, scrapers and other artefacts.

School holidays were usually spent at Herschel, which was always full of my friends and those of my sisters. Most days we were out on mounted expeditions to nearby hills and gorges, but there were paper-chases, treasure-hunts, surprise visits to farms across the district border, partridge shoots over pointer dogs and long walks.

My father was the best story-teller I have known. He would read a book or a short story, adapt it to our environment and then after dinner candles would be blown out, the paraffin lamps turned low, and we would sit on the floor in front of the fire and listen spellbound to his tales. Sometimes my mother, who had a sweet gentle voice, would go to the piano and sing to us.

Twice a week the post cart came in drawn by four trotting mules. The postman had a battered old army bugle on which he trumpeted as he approached down the hill towards the village, and then everyone ran to the post office to collect the mail. Nearby was an outspan area for ox-wagon transporters taking bales of wool and other produce from the highlands of Basutoland to the railhead at Lady Grey, and when there was an assembly of wagons here we would visit and chat up the African drivers and sit round their fires. If fruit was ripe at the time we took them apples, peaches and apricots, and they in turn would give us small presents of beads and other trinkets and teach us how to crack their great wagon whips.

Nearby was an outspan area for ox-wagon transporters taking bales of wool for the highlands to railhead.

I was a year below the average age when I went to St. Andrew's College, the senior school. By now I was growing fast and putting on weight and muscle. To my surprise, I became an above average athlete and this, probably more than anything else, helped me adjust to my new environment.

In those days it was considered rather sissy for teenage boys to associate too closely with girls, but I had a special relationship with Molly, my sister's school friend, because she seemed so different from the other girls. She could do anything I could, and often better, and I hated her when she did. One day she challenged me to a cross-country horse race to an outlying trading station, total distance there and back 10 miles. Her terms were bareback and the first home the winner. Yet again she gave me cause to hate her and, as if to humiliate me even more, she then bet my father five shillings that she could escape from the local prison. As district surgeon he had access to it, and the deal was on. While the convicts were out on the prison farm, Molly was locked up in the central courtyard. Time passed as the rest of us waited outside on our horses. Then, just as I was coming to the tempting conclusion that for once she had overplayed her hand, a barefooted sunburnt leg appeared over the high wall, followed by its owner, green gym dress tucked into knickers and hair askew. We cheered and clapped as she sat astride the wall above us and waved.

My special friend at that time was Gerald Leach, who subsequently, at Rhodes University, distinguished himself as an exceptional athlete. Sadly, Gerald was killed in action in the Western Desert in 1942. His father, tall, lean and weather-beaten, was a schoolboy's dream of a superstar. We saw him as a combination of explorer, cowboy, big game hunter and gun-fighter. As a young man he had been one of the engineers who built the bridge over the Zambezi in the then Southern Rhodesia. At this point the river plunges with a mighty roar 300 feet into the narrow gorge below, pounding forth a great cloud of spray visible 30 miles away. In his day this was an almost unexplored region, and even now the Zambezi valley is still rugged and remote.

During one of our holidays, Gerald's father arranged a trek by ox-wagon from Grahamstown to the coast. We loaded on the wagon everything we needed for three weeks in the wild. Kleinboi, our wagon owner and driver, brought with him his son as "voorloper" to lead the ox team. So professional was Kleinboi that with his 14-foot bamboo whip and its 30 foot kudu-hide lash, he could pick off a fly on the horns of the leading ox or bring down a guinea-fowl in full flight. Our ox-span numbered 16 and we travelled mostly by night. While outspanned in camp the oxen were driven off to graze. The meals of guinea-fowl, venison and vegetables were cooked in big three-legged cast iron pots over open fires. To make bread, our cook would dig a hole in the side of an anthill and fill it with glowing coals; the dough was inserted on a metal plate and the entrance closed. Then came those breakfasts after a long night's trek – maize meal porridge, bacon and eggs, hot crusty bread and butter and Boere rusks washed down with mugs of coffee. The smell of it!

Eventually, taking our time across the sparsely populated bushveld of the coastal plain, we reached the sea and made our final camp. Now there was

The Millard family in 1932: from left to right J.M., father, mother, Barbara and Joan.

swimming in the lagoon and fishing off the rocks for big, powerful steenbras and kappeljou.

But life was not always so benign and carefree. In 1923 when I was 12, the rains had been plentiful, the garden was lush, the wild flowers exceptionally brilliant and the veld green and serene under a cloudless sky. Suddenly, an imminent disaster was proclaimed. A neighbour, red-faced and sweating, galloped up on his horse and announced the approach of a large swarm of locusts. We all ran to high ground and there, far away to the north, stretching for miles across the horizon and into the sky, hung a reddish-brown cloud.

Already the distant sound of millions upon millions of beating wings was clearly audible, growing ever louder. Piles of rubbish and dry sticks covered with green grass and leaves had been made ready for firing, as smoke, together with the beating of tins and buckets, had sometimes been known to prevent a swarm from actually landing. But very soon every tree, bush and blade of grass was transformed into a heaving mass of the two inch-long invaders. They came in a never-ending cloud, which blotted out the sun like a cloudburst. Soon, too, the surface of the earth appeared to be moving under a crawling, hopping layer of locusts, weighing down the trees till branches cracked and fell to the ground.

My two sisters, Barbara and Joan.

Locusts hurled themselves like a violent hailstorm at the corrugated iron roof of our house. At times the rustling of wings and the crunch of mastication drowned speech. Clothing was covered by a crawling, clinging mass. All the while we and our workers beat on our tin cans and stoked the fires. The air was full of smoke and noise, but still the locusts came on like a tidal wave.

The dreadful day dragged on, but not until darkness fell was there silence. That night we lay on our beds utterly exhausted. At dawn we woke to a new world, trees stripped of leaves, the earth of vegetation, but still seemingly moving under a living brown carpet. Gradually then, as the sun rose above the horizon and dried the dew from the locusts' shining wings, the invading army took flight, heading south.

CHAPTER 2

CHARIOTS OF FIRE

I N 1929 my school days ended and an exciting new life lay ahead. I was due
to go up to St John's College, Cambridge, for the October term. I had never
been out of South Africa and for me the voyage from Cape Town to
Southampton was a glamorous and fascinating experience. I tried unsuccessfully to sit up all night to get a first glimpse of the white cliffs of Dover, which
everyone at home had talked about. When I woke, it was to a grey, dreary dawn.
The ship had already docked and it was pelting with rain. Everything was soak-
ing, including myself.

On the train between Liverpool Street Station and Cambridge, I shared a
compartment with a young Englishman, who failed to answer my greeting
when I got in. It took me half an hour to learn his name and that he was also
going up to John's. The information was extracted from him two words at a
time when he condescended to lower "The Times" for a second or two. To me
this was sheer impoliteness, but then I knew little about the British character.

At the college gate I was met by an imposing figure wearing a shining top hat
and tail coat – Mr Palmer, the head porter. I wasn't quite sure whether I should
call him "sir" or not. However, he knew how to handle things. One of his min-
ions was detailed to show me my rooms on the second floor in Chapel Court.
Early the next morning I was standing on one of the lawns admiring the grass.
The Dean, Canon Raven, who happened to be passing, confronted me, and said
in a tone of considerable severity: "Young man, please don't stamp around on
our lawns. You may not appreciate it, but that lawn has taken perhaps 400 years
to reach its present perfection, and all you do is to walk on it. Where do you
come from anyway?"

I explained that I was from the backveld of South Africa, where the grass was
usually brown and parched and that I was filled with wonder because I had
never seen anything like this before. I apologised. The Dean laughed and invited me for breakfast. The result was the creation between us of a very close bond
which lasted throughout my time at the university.

The general zest for exploration and adventure was never stronger in English universities than during the early thirties. In spite of the depression and the scarcity of funds, expeditions were being launched at regular intervals to Greenland, Spitzbergen, the Antarctic, Central Africa and the Blue Nile. Unconquered Everest was subjected to repeated attacks by British climbing teams. Cambridge was full of young adventurers, leadership and inspiration coming from such men as James Wordie, Launcelot Fleming and Frank Debenham, mainly with the Arctic or Antarctic as their background.

I was no scientist, but one did not need to be highly qualified or an intellectual to be accepted. Willingness to take chances and to give it a go was the key. The Polar Institute became our main meeting place, due partly to its carefully chosen and beautiful secretaries.

I got a freshman's rugger trial, ran regularly at Fenners and, on the strength of the fact that I had captained the team in South Africa which won the Empire Challenge Shield, was given a place in the university shooting eight. I was elected a member of the Hawk's Club and the Eagles. I was settling in.

The Cambridge University Artillery Battery provided good horses and free riding. Our fortnightly early morning training sessions took place in the wasteland at the end of the Barton Road. We had a splendid camp on Salisbury Plain and another with the 17th Field Brigade at Colchester. Full dress mess nights were always parties to be remembered, and on Salisbury Plain I was persuaded to bring my charger into the mess marquee. After dinner, tables were tipped onto their sides and I, followed by others on foot, jumped them until the place looked like a ploughed field.

There were many undergraduates from Canada, Australia, South Africa and New Zealand and we ran a very good Dominion Students' Rugby XV and an athletics team. The athletics team never did very well, as we seldom got our members from Oxford and other universities together to work out strategies. Our star turn was Jack Lovelock, the New Zealand world record holder in the mile at that time. Jack and I would sometimes run together. My function was to set the pace for the first lap or two and fade out. Jack did the serious running. I was right out of his class.

Much interest was being taken in the Dominions. The Commonwealth had not yet taken shape, so they were very much part of the British Empire. Nationalism was yet to surface and links with the Crown forged by the First World War were still strong. One Dominions fan was Lady MacDonald of the Isles, who devoted much time to being helpful to Dominions students. If you were lonely or unhappy, she was there as fairy godmother to wipe away your tears.

Her big annual social occasion was the Goldsmiths' and Silversmiths' Ball, and if you had handed in your name you were invited to attend. There were many hairy-chested rugger types who shamelessly cashed in on this splendid party with its lovely girls, superb food and champagne. In the course of my duty dance with her, the Lady asked me if I was happy. Had I got friends? Was there anything she could do for me? I confessed I was by no means lonely, but had only taken advantage of her kindness to attend the ball. My reply seemed to please, but surely there must be something I missed? I said I had one ambition, which, as a keen horseman, was to have just one day's fox hunting with a well-known pack.

A fortnight later I was overwhelmed by a totally unexpected result of my conversation with Lady MacDonald. I was invited to stay for a fortnight of the Christmas vacation by Maj Fred Carr* MFH of the Galway Blazers. I took off for Moss Bros, where I told an elderly and distinguished-looking gentleman I was an impecunious undergraduate from a faraway land who needed advice as to the right sort of rig-out. He assured me he would dress me in a manner I would be proud of and would personally see to it that I was not financially ruined. By the time he had finished with me and I had seen myself in his mirror all booted, spurred and cravatted, I was impressed and he was delighted. Not only that, but the cost was minimal.

A third class ticket brought me to Holyhead. The steerage passage to Kingstown (County Dublin) was a memorable experience. Men, women, children, dogs, parrots, other livestock and baggage were bundled into a below-decks cabin, where you stood, sat or lay on the floor for the duration; an awful journey on a rough crossing.

At Ballyglunin station, I was met by the head groom, and driven in a pony trap to Newtown, an old Irish estate astride the Clare-Galway river. It took the Carr family and myself only half an hour to strike up a friendship destined to last a lifetime. So much so that I was adopted into the family with Newtown becoming a second home.

There were thrilling hunts over the rough stonewalled countryside. The fields were usually small, not more than 25 or 30 horsemen, and everyone rode hard and fast. Here is a description of one of those chases as recorded in my diary:

28th December 1932. Meet at Newtown. Major Carr on First Flight, Barbara, the daughter of the house, a superb horsewoman at the time, on Hackler, self on Polly and Geraghty the groom on Hacket. Drew the cover out towards the bog, and put up two foxes, one a vixen. Hounds ran very fast over the bog and then crossed the river. We got through near Kelly's cottage and then had to negotiate some very boggy country, but there was firm ground ahead and soon we were in full cry. Walls not too bad, but going rather heavy and difficult for a mile or so. Fox went to ground in a belt of timber, and Bowes-Daley, who was hunting the pack today, then worked up the face of Knock Roe, drawing the covers en-route – a few big

* Major Carr was too old for World War II so he gave the RAF a Spitfire fighter aircraft as his own personal contribution to the war effort.

The Galway Blazers in 1933: my introduction to fox-hunting.

walls then a bank or two. Suddenly there was a holla away, and Bowes threw in his hounds at the spot where the fox had crossed the boreen. Away we went with every hound speaking. Barbara, Harry the whip, Molly O'Rorke and me taking a line of country parallel to hounds. There were a few low walls, then a bank. Polly refused for some reason at one wall and I was nearly down, but she flew it at the second attempt, and I took a short cut over two walls and came up again with Barbara and the whip. Then followed a series of exceedingly big walls, two of which I shall always remember. At one Harry's horse refused and Barbara and I rode together at a huge solid rampart. To my horror Polly took the highest spot but fairly flew it, never touching a stone. The next one was equally high, but on we went and over, though Polly's take-off was short. All this time hounds were going full tilt and it was every man for himself as we worked our way down the long slope towards the Ballyglunin road. Then slap through a farmyard, chickens and geese flying in all directions. We had to jump out of the road over a biggish wall and were heading for the bog again when Major Carr came to grief. First Flight charged a wall, mis-timed his stride, and the whole outfit, including the wall, went down with a mighty crash. I stopped to help both horse and rider to their feet and on we went together. By this time, the hunt had got well ahead, but we soon made up lost ground. The fox cut straight across the bog and up the hill on the far side. The horses were now fairly blown and the pace was slackening, but my mare was going fine and flying her walls in great style. We killed the fox in the open about a mile from the crest of the hill. It was a great hunt with a five mile point and not a single check – about eight miles as the hounds ran, all in 33 minutes.

At the end of a hunting day everyone, including the priest, the farmers, trades-men and the "gentry", would all gravitate to the nearest country house for tea with scones, cakes, turkey and ham. After that Irish whisky would appear, and as darkness fell, we would drift off home. Then it was hot baths, more whisky, dinner and finally, round the fire, talk on the day's events, and tales of other great hunts and of times gone by.

Back to Cambridge: my 21st birthday. We celebrated it rowdily in my rooms, now in New Court at the top of the spiral staircase. Near midnight we had a visitation from the university police – the proctor, fully dressed up in gown and other regalia, accompanied by his two "bulldogs" in top hats and tails. They grouped themselves on the ground floor directly below the staircase and loudly summoned me. The target these gentlemen made was too good to miss. While I was on my way down, the lads up top grabbed the large kettle off the gas ring and poured a stream of warm water down on the proctor (a distinguished professor from another college) and his bulldogs.

By the time I got to the bottom of the stairs the trio was drenched, alleging they had been urinated upon. My name taken, I had to report to the Dean next morning. Canon Raven looked at me just as severely as he had on the day he had caught me on the grass. He said: "I was afraid it would be you. What have you to say?"

After I explained what had happened, a sly look of amusement crossed his features. He said: "Of course I believe you, but dammit, I have to do something about it. You just can't go round peeing or pouring hot water on proctors. At the very least I must go through the motions of punishing you. You are gated for three weeks."

The Dean then said, "I am under the impression that you are playing at Richmond tomorrow?" I replied that I was but would not be there now. He asked whether I could be back by midnight tomorrow and I replied that this would be no problem as I could get the 1050 pm train from Liverpool Street. "Then your gating starts at midnight tomorrow," said the Dean.

I thanked him for his leniency. As I made for the door, he called me back. "Are you certain you did not pee on the proctor?"

"Absolutely certain," I replied.

"Oh," said the Dean, "what a pity. Never took to the fellow myself!"

Towards the end of that term, Andy Blumenthal, also a South African, and I decided to go to Scotland. We were very hard up. The cheapest way to travel was to work one's passage on a tramp. Trade union and Board of Trade controls were lax and for the price of a bottle of whisky a skipper could be persuaded to take you on as a stoker or deck-hand. The procedure was to go, dressed in cloth caps, seamen's sweaters and old slacks, to Charlie Brown's, a seamen's pub in the London docks famous for its good food, cheap booze and pretty girls. There we located the skipper of a package due to sail with the dawn tide to Aberdeen. He accepted our whisky and told us to be on board before 0200.

There was only one small cabin with four berths. Already installed was a non-descript middle-aged man, and a young fellow of about 23 holding a tiny baby. There was no food, but Bloom and I had brought a small primus, tea, sugar,

On the tramp steamer that took us to Scotland: an epic journey.

condensed milk, a loaf of bread, and a tin of jam. As we cleared the Thames estuary a storm hit us with almost hurricane velocity and soon our little tub was being tossed around like a pea in a bucket. Huge waves crashed down on the deck and empty whisky casks rolled about above our cabin. The whole ship reeked of stale whisky, coal smoke and soot. Water seeped in everywhere. Wind howled through the rigging. The clatter and creaking of the hull and the sound of the screw flogging around every time the stern rose clear of the waves were deafening. I am a good sailor, but the others were soon horribly and pathetically seasick. The cabin became a stinking shambles and the baby screamed incessantly. I did what I could for the three men, wrapped the baby in one of the greasy blankets and tied the little bundle to my bunk with string. Dawn saw no let-up in the storm. If anything, it increased in intensity as we crawled northwards.

There remained no one but me to assume responsibility for the baby, who might well have died of exposure and dehydration had I not been there. She soon became something of a pet, and although she continued to scream she did seem to cheer up when I was around to feed her. This involved warming up a mixture of water and sweet condensed milk, which I then poured into a saucer. She sucked the milk off the tip of my finger until she filled up. Whenever she needed to evacuate I simply held her up over the floor, which by that time was past worrying about.

At last, early in the morning of the third day, a sudden calm blissfully descended. I rushed up on deck. The grey granite of Aberdeen was just visible beyond the grey, cobbled quayside and an equally grey curtain of rain. My companions came to life. Having said goodbye to the skipper, we assembled on the quayside. At that moment, just as I was hitching my pack on my back, the owner of the baby thrust her into my arms, shouting, "You have been so kind to this baby, you can have it." With that he tore off. My reaction was immediate. I dumped the little mite on the cobbles and gave chase, bringing the man down with a flying rugger tackle. He was bruised and shaken, so I was able to frog-march him back. By this time he was weeping and ready to confess. On the day we left London he had been released from jail, at the gates of which he had been confronted by a girl. She had handed him the baby, saying: "This is your child. You keep it." She then sped off in a taxi. He did not deny that the child was his and I felt he deserved a bit of help.

At a nearby seamen's mission, which was still deserted as it was early in the day, a charlady advised us to visit the convent. The Mother Superior gave the impression that she had handled this sort of situation before. She believed the story and accepted the child. I sometimes wonder what happened to "my" baby. What sort of life did she lead and where as an elderly lady is she on this day?

Looking back over the years I remember my father saying to me (it was about the time I left home for university), "First, never lend money to someone you don't know. Secondly, never offer to look after a stranger's suitcase. Thirdly, never under any circumstances agree to hold someone's baby." Number three came to mind that rainy morning on the Aberdeen dockside just in time, but it was a very close-run thing!

Bloom and I hitch-hiked until we reached Drumnadrochit. Our destination was a shooting lodge belonging to a friend of Bloom's. It was away up in the hills and superbly situated. The caretaker-cum-gamekeeper, gave us a good welcome. He had a family of seven bonny bairns, whose sole sustenance, so far as we could tell, came from a vast bowl of porridge in the morning and another in the evening. The eldest daughter fed us like kings.

Like many gamekeepers, Alexander Morrison had once been a professional poacher. He showed us how to make and use an otterboard and how to knock off a stag. The fishing on Loch Ness was good and we killed sufficient sea trout and the occasional salmon to satisfy our needs. I forget how we travelled on our return journey, but it was not by sea. Bloom's mind was made up: he would have no part in another voyage on a tramp steamer!

* * * *

My university friends were some of the best that I ever made. In particular I remember Raymond Bark-Jones who captained the university rugger XV. So, too, do I recall with great fondness Idwal Reese, also a rugger blue, Noel Symington, the great skier, James Keckwick with whom I climbed, and John Buchanan, who was incredibly tough and strong. Guy Lorimer was different, a quiet, gentle person who succeeded in giving me some knowledge of and

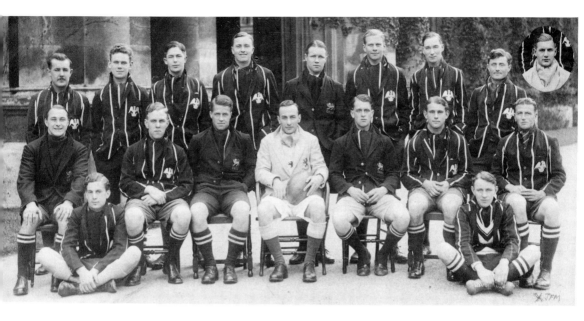

My university friends were some of the best I ever made. Many played rugby and this scratch team, all from St John's College, had many successes. One face brings back Twickenham, the inter-varsity match, a collapsed scrum, and a sudden silence in which a voice (the owner of which I think later became a bishop) from beneath the pile of bodies said "kick the bastard, he's still breathing." It was heard in the nearby stands and, in keeping with the Twickenham spirit of those days, greeted with laughter and a roar of applause.

appreciation for classical music: we often went to evensong at King's College Chapel together.

John Buchanan's parents lived near Glasgow, but owned an ancient farm-house on the Isle of Arran. Old Man Buchanan was a great character, albeit something of a tyrant. There were three golden rules on the farm. One: all the lads slept in one boat-house and all the lassies slept in the other. Two: no one was entitled to breakfast until he or she had been in the burn for an early morning dip. The lads' pool was upstream and the lassies' further down, unfortunately round a bend in the glen. Three: everyone, but everyone, had to be present at the Kirk on Sundays. The days, very happy days, were spent walking, climbing and playing golf. There was highland dancing and other fun and games in the evenings.

Finally and never to be forgotten there was my lovely auburn-haired Jocelyn Waller, with her tiny freckles and gay and gorgeous smile. Everything about Jocelyn was lovely. We went to May Week Balls, walked in the Gog Magog Hills and enjoyed many other splendid things together and I loved her very much.

Cambridge 1932: Raymond Bark-Jones, Lois Biddle (who subsequently married Raymond), Jocelyn Waller and J.M.

There were many other new experiences and adventures during those university years: skiing in Austria, salmon fishing on the Eden, rock-climbing in Scotland, Corsica and elsewhere. A memorable expedition was to some early prehistoric exposures in France with Louis Leakey, a Fellow of my college, and the famous Abbé Breuil, followed by a spell in Paris living with the Abbé and attending some of his lectures at the Sorbonne. It was during this expedition that I stumbled upon a Roman centurion's grave, and I can recall how amazed I was by my companions' complete lack of interest in such ultra modern remains – I was learning fast!

On another occasion Louis invited me to accompany him to the British Association for the Advancement of Science meeting that was held that year in Leicester. Louis was delivering an address to the Association and Mary, his future wife, came with us. I doubt whether any of us dreamed at that time, least of all Mary herself for she was a dedicated but modest girl, that one day she would be regarded as one of the world's most distinguished prehistorians.

Three of us undergraduates clubbed together and bought an outdated racing car. It was very flashy with a shining outside exhaust pipe and a heavy leather strap over the bonnet. There was just room for two in the front seat, but it could

My Baby Austin that cost £12.

carry more distributed over its frame. Finally, overloaded as usual, we took a level-crossing at high speed and the car broke in half. We were a bit bruised, but no one was seriously hurt. As none of the four wheels touched the ground after this event, we left the car in a nearby thicket: a sad end to an aristocratic old lady that had once raced at Brooklands.

I had another car in my last year – a Baby Austin about the size of a bath, and it cost me twelve pounds. It used to fill up with rain water, so we drilled a few holes in the floor. My rugger friends, mainly John Buchanan, Chris Love and Paddy MacDonald had a bad habit of lifting it up with the help of a few others, and hanging it eight feet up by the front bumper on the spiked iron railings near the front of the college. But it was a great vehicle and nothing seemed to stop it running.

During my second year, Louis Leakey took me under his wing and we began seeing a good deal of each other. My own interest in the Stone Age cultures of Africa dated back to my school days when we used to ride off during our holidays and spend long days digging and collecting artefacts in caves and rock shelters near Herschel. My father had encouraged this interest and I had further incitement from the curator of the Albany Museum in Grahamstown, who commissioned me while still at school to describe all the sites known to me and make a map of them. It was that map and the notes that first brought Louis and me together. As a person I liked Louis Leakey. As a Don he went out of his way to take an interest in me personally and share his enthusiasms. Yet after leaving Cambridge our paths diverged and, though we both lived in East Africa within reach of one another, we never re-established the close rapport we had enjoyed – he as mentor and I as pupil.

For my part, the more I learned of this science the more absorbed I became in it. I had been reading for the Law tripos because I had set my heart on the Colonial Service, but now I came to realise that unless I intended to enter its legal branch the subject would be useful, but far from essential. Although I had wasted a whole year, I could make up for it with Leakey's help by acquiring training in prehistory. This proved to be the case, for my knowledge of the subject (thanks to Louis, the Abbé Breuil and my contacts with other eminent prehistorians) considerably influenced the course of my life. Thus it came to be that I changed over to read for an ordinary degree, and with less pressure on my time was able to dedicate myself to my chosen subject.

My Cambridge days were drawing towards an end. As it happened just then a certain Major Bagnold reported evidence of Stone Age Man in the Libyan Desert. Here was a challenge, and the possibility of getting together a small expedition to investigate Bagnold's discovery appealed to me. I began working on the idea, but funds for a venture such as this were not easy to come by.

I consulted Louis Leakey. Louis told me that whereas research into the Stone Age cultures in Kenya and Tanganyika had made great strides in recent years, the Lake Rudolf basin in the Great Rift Valley remained largely unexplored, and he would welcome information on this region as an extension to the work already carried out further south in preference to the Libyan Desert.

Soon after this, a mutual friend, Vivian Fuchs, who was organising an expedition to Lake Rudolf invited me to join it. I accepted with alacrity, which put paid to my plans for the Libyan Desert. At the time of this Lake Rudolf expedition, Vivian Fuchs (now Sir Vivian Fuchs F.R.S.)[*] had previous experience of Africa having been with Leakey at Olduvai and with Worthington on the

---

[*] As time went on 'Bunny', for that was his name to all of us who knew him well, gravitated to the Arctic and Antarctic, mainly Antarctica, where he became involved in the Falkland Islands Dependencies and projects connected with British interests generally in that region. Among the many journeys of exploration made by Fuchs was an epic 1000 mile reconnaissance with dogs and sledges and a single South African companion. It was during this expedition that the possibility of crossing the Antarctic continent by way of the South Pole began to take shape in his mind. James Wordie (Sir James, Master of St John's College Cambridge) who had at one time been Chief of Shackleton's Scientific Staff, and many other great men of that time, gave Fuchs the encouragement and support he needed for this tremendous 2000 mile trek. In 1958, for crossing the vast frozen wastes of the Antarctic by an unexplored route, Fuchs was knighted and earned his place alongside Shackleton, Amundsen and Scott, as the greatest explorer since them. In 1959 Fuchs was appointed Director of the British Antarctic Survey, a position he held until his retirement in 1973.

Cambridge African Lakes Expedition. Very early on in his career his ability as a geologist in the field became evident and those of us who accompanied him to Rudolf in 1934 soon recognised in him a born leader of men with exceptional general scientific talent.

The time inevitably came for my departure from Cambridge. My friends decided that my going down was an occasion which called for a very special party and insisted on seeing me off from Southampton. We set off from Cambridge in two full car loads and had a hilarious lunch in the first class saloon of the Winchester Castle mail boat. In a sense this was a sad occasion, the end of a chapter in fact. And for most of us present on that day, a new life lay ahead full of great expectations. Jocelyn came with us to see me on my way. I would miss her and knew this all too well. On the other hand, neither of us, I think, really expected that our relationship would extend beyond Cambridge. And so it turned out. Finally we said our goodbyes and went our various ways. My university days were over.

CHAPTER 3

THE LAKE RUDOLF EXPEDITION

T HE main objective of the Lake Rudolf Rift Valley expedition, which was funded by the Royal Society, the Percy Sladen Trustees, the Royal Geographical Society, the geographical and geological sections of the British Association, and the Geological Society, was to conduct a geological survey of the Lake Rudolf basin.

Lake Rudolf, or Turkana as it is now known, is some 300 km from north to south and up to 60 km from east to west. Huge as it may be, it was even bigger only a few thousand years ago. At its greatest it was 450 km long and was connected to Lake Baringo in the south and to the Nile by way of a river that flowed from its north-west corner. This great lake also had connections to the Rift Valley lakes in southern Ethiopia, which explains their essentially Nilotic fish faunas. Massive subterranean upheavals and volcanic activity isolated it, cutting it off from the Nile, the Ethiopian lakes and Baringo in the south. Now Turkana has no surface outlet and only one perennial contributor, the River Omo, which flows into its north end from Ethiopia.

Lake Turkana was the last of Africa's great lakes to be "discovered" by Europeans. By the late 1880s many of the Dark Continent's mysteries had been revealed to them and Lake Victoria had been identified as the source of the Nile. Rumours were emerging, however, of two other lakes in the unknown territory south of Abyssinia. They reached the adventurous and well-connected young naval officer, Lt (later Admiral) Ludwig von Höhnel, who with the help of Crown Prince Rudolf of Austria, persuaded a wealthy Hungarian sportsman, Count Samuel Teleki, to change his original plans for a hunting expedition to Lake Tanganyika and explore what was to become north-western Kenya in search of these lakes.

Landing at Pangani north of Dar-es-Salaam, they travelled northwards for 5 months in some style. They finally approached the lake basin and von Höhnel wrote:

… we hurried to the top of the ridge, the scene gradually developing, until a new world spread out before us. For a long time we gazed in speechless delight, spellbound by the beauty of … the great lake which seemed to melt on the horizon into the deep blue of the sky.

Teleki and von Höhnel named it Lake Rudolf in honour of Austria's Crown Prince. They then explored up the eastern shore observing that there were three islands roughly on the lake's midline from north to south. The most northerly – North Island – 60 km from the Omo delta. Mid way down the lake was another – Central Island. The largest, in the south, was nearly 10 km long and five wide. They named it Höhnel Island, though over time this has been changed to South Island. In as far as they could see and from what they learned from local people, the islands were uninhabited.

The discovery of Lake Rudolf unleashed a veritable flood of expeditions to visit it. In 1895 and again in 1900 it was explored by the American Arthur Donaldson Smith. In 1895/96 the elephant hunter Arthur Neumann travelled up the east shore and hunted elephants at the north end of the lake and on the lower Omo River. In 1896 Vittorio Bottego and his companions went down the west shore as far as the mouth of the Turkwel. In 1897 the Cavendish expedition covered both east and west shores and in the same year the pioneer settler, Lord Delamere walked its southern shore. In 1899 there was the Welby expedition that arrived at Lake Rudolf then went on to reach the Sobat and Nile - the first white men to cross this country. The Harrison hunting party visited the lake in 1900 and in 1901 a military survey party under Major Herbert Austin arrived from Khartoum to link survey work radiating out from Khartoum with that commenced on the East African coast. In the same year the Austrian Count Wickenburg also visited it. In 1902 there was the De Bozas expedition and in 1903 the party demarcating the Abyssinian/British East African boundary arrived. This work was repeated again by another party in 1908. The last of the first wave of explorers – Stigand – went up the lake's east shore in 1909. While all these expeditions collected valuable scientific data, none of them spent much time studying the lake and its environs. Most did not have the resources to stay long.

The explorers were followed by the British administrators. As the area was unsettled and greatly disturbed by raiders from Ethiopia, the majority of the early British officials were military men – officers of the King's African Rifles. No serious research of any kind was undertaken until, in 1930/31, the Cambridge expedition to the East African lakes under Barton Worthington reached Ferguson's Gulf mid way up Turkana's west shore and described some of the fishes. Bunny Fuchs was a junior member of that expedition and the brief experience both whetted his desire to return and make a much more thorough exploration, and made him the obvious choice to lead the 1934 expedition. At the time von Höhnel was still alive and Bunny corresponded with him in Vienna. Naturally he took a keen interest in our expedition which was the first planned to stay in the area collecting scientific data methodically over a period of months.

Officially, the expedition's goal was to carry out geological and survey work in the Lake Rudolf basin. The idea was, however, that while in the area, the expedition should try to achieve as much as possible in other fields of interest as well. The expedition surveyors were: R. C. 'Jumbo' Wakefield – Director Surveys in the Sudan Political Service together with William 'Snaffles' Martin of Yale University and St John's College, Oxford. Dr Bill Dyson a well known mountaineer, was our medical officer and anthropologist, and Dr Donald MacInnes our palaeontologist. My function was to provide information on the Stone Age cultures and prehistory of the region. Finally, for a period, while we were covering the western shoreline of Lake Rudolf, we were joined by David Buxton of the Desert Locust Research Organisation.

I landed in Nairobi on 25th January 1934, having travelled by sea to the Cape and on by air from Johannesburg on one of the early Imperial Airways flights. For me, this was a never to be forgotten magic carpet experience, which at that time took two days. There were only four passengers including myself.

I was met on arrival in Nairobi by Bunny Fuchs and other members of the expedition. A few days were devoted to purchasing vehicles, laying in stores, recruiting staff, buying kit, registering firearms, liaising with the museum and generally preparing for an absence of several months. Finally early in February we set out for the far north in our Bedford truck and two Chevrolet box-body cars, and established our first camp on the shores of Lake Naivasha.

By 10th February we had reached the point where a large notice-board said : Turkana Province Forbidden Territory, and then we dropped thousands of feet down into the arid, burning Turkana desert, where every mile was a battle with sand rivers, shifting dunes and rocky lava escarpments. But that was what we had expected and were prepared for.

Hardly an inch of rain had fallen during the past two years. Water levels in the wells were running low; some had dried up completely and camel grazing had never been worse. Shade temperatures were always somewhere between 100°F and 105°F and on some days went up to nearly 110°F .

It took three days to reach Lodwar, a true outpost of the Empire. The Union Jack fluttered above a low mud building on a lava ridge overlooking the broad sandy bed of the dried-up Turkwell river. This was the District Commissioner's residence and office, and, apart from a handful of other mud buildings, there was not much else.

That evening we were invited to supper. We sat out in the open with a view of the desert. It was a beautiful, still, starlit night, and one had the feeling of

The Rudolf Expedition halted by the wayside to examine one of the termite mounds, characteristic of this arid land.

being at the extreme outer perimeter of the world. In due course, a completely naked Turkana appeared, stood stiffly to attention and in a loud raucous voice announced: "She sells seashells on the seashore." I asked the DC what the hell was going on, and he replied, "Oh that. Well, you see, I have told him that she sells seashells on the seashore means dinner is served, and so, gentlemen, let's see what my man has to offer!"

Fuchs had planned to make a continuous journey round the lake, but the Ethiopian government, refused him permission to enter Abyssinian territory so we were obliged to omit the north end, which lies just over the Ethiopian border, and to conduct the work in two parts: first we would tackle the west side and later, the east. We immediately began work by looking for mammalian fossils in the Losodok Hills.

Searching for evidence of prehistoric man in the Rift Valley was best done in areas where wind and water erosion had cut through or exposed the beaches laid down over the ages by fluctuations in the level of the lake due to climatic change. Such beaches, often miles from the present levels of lakes, are likely sites for finding the tools and implements of those who lived there in the distant past, buried beneath layers of silt, rubble, and wind-blown sand. Also associated with these sites are the fossils of the fauna related to that particular habitat.

It was not until late Acheulian times that early man began using caves and rock shelters, but in a region as low-lying as Rudolf it is probable that the lake shore was his normal habitat. Here, food was plentiful and his stone hand axes, cleavers, scrapers and other artefacts can be found in large numbers. Most of

The Expedition members clockwise from 12 o'clock: Jumbo Wakefield, Snaffles Martin, Bunny Fuchs, Donald MacInnes, Joyce Fuchs (who joined us temporarily) and Bill Dyson. J.M. took the photo and is present as a shadow to the left.

them are rejects, but occasionally a perfect specimen can be picked up. Although in general the results of this work were disappointing, I found several prehistoric axe-heads of the late Acheulian era which were the first pre-Neolithic tools to be discovered in the region.

One of the major tasks on the west side of the lake was to map the area accurately, because there were numerous discrepancies between the different maps available at that time. This was achieved, but not without difficulty. In addition, the triangulation which was complete over a greater portion of southern and central Kenya, had not extended that far north, so our surveyors intended to link the area with the known fixed points in the Sudan and along the Ethiopian border. With this in view, Fuchs decided to move north before devoting time to the other parts of the lake. Jumbo Wakefield and Martin were fully equipped for this task. Thus we moved to Koitherin via Todenyang.

At Todenyang I joined a camel patrol of the King's African Rifles marching in a northwesterly direction, which gave me an opportunity to inspect the ancient raised beaches below the Lapurr mountain range. At the same time, the surveyors were busy laying out the base-line required for their calculations from the summit of Mt Lapurr, and then set off with pack donkeys carrying every drop of water needed for several days.

Our journey to Koitherin took us through a land empty of human habitation, with views to the west over the seemingly endless Lotagipi swamp. This flood plain may be all that is left of the river that once linked Rudolf with the Nile system. Far to the north and northeast was the great barrier of the Ethiopian highlands.

Koitherin is a remote, very little known and often disputed area where the boundaries of Ethiopia, Sudan and Kenya meet. It was from the summit of Koitherin Mountain that our surveyors hoped to pick up Tid, a distant tooth-like point on the Sudan/Ethiopian border. After the surveyors had done their work, we turned south to base ourselves at Ferguson's Gulf to explore the central portion of the west shore. The lake water in the area tasted particularly vile, like dirty bath water. Drinking water was brought in by camels, but we also built

I found prehistoric hand axes, the first pre-Neolithic artefacts to be discovered in the region.

Bunny Fuchs, our leader, who later went on to Antarctic fame and a knighthood.

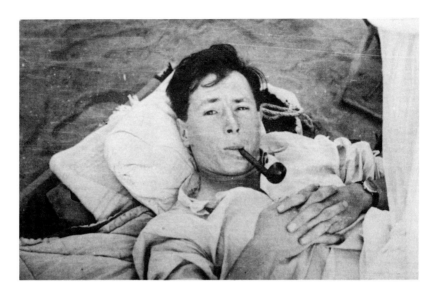

Donald MacInnes: our palaeontologist.

a distilling plant to provide a few extra gallons. One of the objectives during this period was to cross over to Central Island, which lies about 16 km offshore opposite Ferguson's Gulf. (The crossing had been made only once before, by Dr Worthington during the 1930 Cambridge expedition.) To achieve this, we had brought with us a Hudson collapsible boat, considered an exceptionally stable craft for its size. A wooden boat with an outboard motor, it had been approved by the British Air Ministry for use in connection with flying boats, and was therefore thought to be suitable on a lake such as Rudolf. With his wife, who had come to join him for a short time before making a solitary ascent of the Mountains of the Moon in Uganda, Fuchs made the first crossing.

Some days later Bill Dyson and I went over, intending to spend three days on a survey. We set off in a dead calm, but then a sudden storm threw us off course and we were able to keep afloat only by frantic bailing. By nightfall we were still battling on and it was only hours later that we made our landfall on the island. Having dragged the boat up a small beach, we fell asleep, completely exhausted. During the night we were woken several times by the sound of shuffling footsteps, but with the screeching wind sending the waves crashing against the bare lava cliffs about us, it was impossible to identify their source. It was not until dawn that we discovered we had slept in a narrow defile. Tracks in the soft sand revealed that all night long there had been a steady procession of crocodiles moving to and from the main lake to a crater lake on the island. They had passed our sleeping forms, merely deviating a few feet to avoid treading on us. As we both knew that crocodiles will attack on dry land just as readily as in water, we beat a hasty retreat with the hairs standing up on the back of our necks.

There was no shade, so we tipped the boat up and straddled it across two large boulders. It was astoundingly hot. Meanwhile, the storm of the day before became a dust storm, turning the lake into a heaving mass of white waves. There was no hope of returning to the mainland. Three days later we were getting short of food and had drunk all our fresh water, but even the lake water is potable when you are really thirsty, and tilapia – a type of bream – could be taken from the lake. We also found a colony of spoonbills and their eggs, scrambled, were a pleasant change from fish.

That evening we were fishing from the boat near the shore on the sheltered side of the island when a crocodile, the biggest either of us had ever seen, attacked us. The little four horse-power engine did not suffice for a getaway. Our only weapon was a .22 rifle. Although a rifle of this calibre was entirely inadequate against such an adversary, it soon became obvious that even at the risk of angering the brute we would have to open up with it. The first five shots seemed to make no difference; he didn't dive and the boat's every manoeuvre was relentlessly pursued by his mud-brown, snapping snout. Then one of the tiny bullets must have hit a sensitive spot, for he turned tail and dived. We made a dash for a sandy bay, beached and scrambled up the lava cliff. To our relief, the monster stayed away.

On the sixth day there was a comparative calm and we decided to return to camp. But our troubles were not yet over, for the wind got up again and forced us to spend the night on a sandbank only about a mile from the Ferguson's Gulf shoreline.

* * * *

During the break between the time the expedition ended its work on the west of the lake and set off for the east shore, Bill Dyson and I decided to have a go at the summit of Mount Kenya, which had then been climbed only by Sir Halford Mackinder towards the end of the last century, and by Eric Shipton and Wyn Harris, both of Everest fame, in 1929. In 1933 Dutton spent several weeks on the mountain, but failed to find a route up the final 1,000-foot rock-face. We heard he had built a small corrugated iron hut on the edge of the Lewis Glacier and decided to make for this.

On 1st June 1934, Bill and I set off on foot from our base near Naivasha. We carried boots, warm clothes, sleeping bags, ice axes, ground-sheets and 150 feet of climbing rope. Each of our packs weighed about 50 pounds. We followed an ancient, little known footpath over the Aberdare range heading for Nyeri on the far side. The highest point of this great mountain barrier is 13,120 ft, while the path we followed must have been between 10,000 and 11,000 ft. That day we marched for 10 hours through forest and high altitude moorland covered in bracken and giant heather and camped on the edge of the moorland above the forest and bamboo belts. It was cold. Elephant were trumpeting in the distance and we were hungry and tired.

We woke to a clear dawn with a white frost crackling underfoot. Soon the sun rose and we went on. What a beautiful land this was with rushing streams every few miles and wild flowers everywhere. We skirted round several herds of buffalo and met elephant. Best of all, we saw two bongo, one of the finest and rarest species of antelope, at the edge of a stand of bamboo. They allowed us to approach to within 30 yards, their bright chestnut hides glistening in the sunlight. Soon the snow and glacier-faced peak of Kenya itself rose majestically in the distance above the morning mists, seemingly beckoning us.

That night we reached the administrative headquarters of Nyeri district on the eastern slope of the Aberdares. Having a beer at the Outspan Hotel, where a fire was blazing, we were beginning to think of spending the night in this snug place instead of camping in the forest, when the owner of the hotel insisted we should stay as his guests.

A lot of young people came in later and a good old-fashioned party went on until 0200. One of the men very apologetically said: "I hope you guys won't mind, but you see at this hour we usually throw the dice to see who sleeps with who, and unfortunately you are the odd men out!" I was shocked. Although this happened at the tail-end of the famous Happy Valley era, it was the only occasion I came face to face with an example of those wild ways.

Next day we thumbed a ride on a lorry to Nanyuki and walked out to the farm of Raymond Hook, who, everyone said, knew the mountain well. Raymond was a well-known eccentric farming an enormous tract at the edge of the forest below Mt Kenya. In his spare time he trapped wild animals for zoos. His methods were rough but effective. He, his Afrikaner assistant and African farm-hands mounted on Somali ponies would ride down any animal – lesser kudu, wart-hog, cheetah and even leopard. When the animal turned at bay, they would dismount and, holding a heavy tarpaulin in front of them, literally fall on their prey and pin it down, while several African outriders tied up its legs. It was then bundled into a pick-up and taken back to the farmstead.

Raymond provided us with three pack ponies and a couple of syces. He gave us a rifle to get ourselves some meat. Next day, after buying provisions, we set off, following elephant and rhino trails. The forest teemed with elephant, buffalo and rhino. After the horses had been stampeded several times, we took turns banging a tin mug against our tea kettle to give warning of our approach. That night the horses were stampeded yet again by a bull elephant who came pounding down the game trail on which we were camped. It took over an hour

We managed to get the horses up to 15,500 ft.

in the pitch darkness to find them.

We managed to get the horses up to about 15,500 ft, then sent them back with the syces. From the little tin hut on the edge of the "skating rink" next to the Lewis Glacier (16,000 ft), the great bastion towering above us looked impregnable and filled me with awe. Bill Dyson, the professional, scanned the, 1000-foot face with binoculars and indicated several possible routes, the sight of which chilled my blood. A wind got up during the night, battering and rattling the loose corrugated iron of the hut and when we woke it was snowing heavily and blowing a half gale.

This was the beginning of a storm which seriously hampered our search for a route up the face, now sheathed in ice and snow. In the morning of the third

From the Lewis glacier the great bastion towering above us looked impregnable.

day we decided to try walking round the base of the summit peaks in a clock-wise direction.

This expedition turned into a real challenge of ice work and rock climbing. The weather throughout was miserable and when darkness fell we were still far from our base. Freezing cold and dead tired as we were by then, the journey home became a battle of will against the elements. Stronger than me, Bill was supportive, coaxing me on hour after hour. When finally we crept into our sleeping bags it was very late and we had been on the move for nearly 16 hours.

By next morning the weather had cleared to some extent, but as we were becoming increasingly affected by mountain sickness and dehydration, we decided that, if we were to make the summit at all, this would have to be the day for it. After crossing the Lewis Glacier, we roped up and attempted a frontal attack on the north west face. About 300 feet on we found a short length of Mackinder's rope. That told us we had hit his route, which had also been followed by Shipton and Wyn Harris. I had never climbed with so expert and experienced a rock climber as Bill, and this gave me great confidence. All the same, I was going badly and the ice holds were becoming increasingly difficult as we gained height. The tremendous strain of the previous day's climb, coupled with mountain sickness was also beginning to tell on me, but Bill was in his element and I was actually holding him back.

We had negotiated a chimney sheathed in ice. Bill was far ahead and out of sight when a foothold gave under me. Bill had passed the rope behind a rock buttress and established a secure belay, so I only fell a few inches, butting my kneecap: nothing serious, but copious bleeding. After a minor battle I joined Bill, who then went on and up, taking most of the rope. It was at this point that he shouted back that our main difficulties were over and that he was coming down for a talk.

It was now mid-afternoon and cloud had settled on the mountain. It was snowing and getting late, so although we were only 200 feet from the Batian summit Bill decided to turn back. We were familiar with the route now and would make the ascent on the morrow.

Another gale blew that night and at first light we saw that the whole face, and in particular our route, was plastered in snow and ice. The gale had not abated, we were nearly out of food and could not wait for things to change. It was a bitter disappointment. We cleaned out the hut, shouldered our packs and set off downwards through the mist.

I have recently read Shipton's account of his climb with Wyn Harris and it is interesting to note that two of the greatest mountaineers of that time twice turned back before finally making their ascent in 1929. Note too that they followed much the same route as we did. Shipton says that on their climb they took 16 porters and their expedition set them back £45. Bill and I spent a total of £5 on our sortie.

* * * *

We re-joined the other members of the expedition to begin our exploration of the eastern shore of the lake at Marsabit. We then crossed the Koroli desert to the Sirima water hole at the southeastern corner of the lake, where we were joined by our camels.

Martin and Dyson set off with their camels and equipment for Mt Kulal (7,500 ft) where they were to begin the survey programme for the eastern shore. They had continual trouble with the camels, the weather was unfavourable throughout, and water and rations ran short. When Bunny and I found them nine days later, they had eaten the last of their food and had just started on the long journey northwards along the lake shore.

Meanwhile, Fuchs and I had the job of moving our gear and supplies down the perilous lava escarpment east of the lake. The collapsible boat proved impossible to move on camels which made desperately slow progress, so it had to be manhandled all the way by relays of four men, and finally I then sailed it to our new base camp at Loiengalani while Fuchs marched with the pack camels.

Loiengalani was an uninhabited oasis in the midst of a wasteland of lava and sand. Here at last we were able to relax in the shade of the doum palms and big acacia trees and bathe in the crystal clear waters of the little stream bubbling forth from a spring overgrown by rushes and coarse green grass only to disappear underground again after a short stretch. At its source the water was hot, too hot to wash in.

This oasis had been used by travellers, raiders, and hunters since Neolithic times and was mentioned by von Höhnel in the course of his 1887-9 expedition with Count Teleki. It was near here that Teleki and von Höhnel found a pile of over 100 camel skeletons, but of these we found no trace.

Several miles to the north, on some small islands and sand spits, lived the El Molo, a dirt-poor community of lake-dwellers, who numbered only 84, though in von Höhnel's time they were counted in hundreds. They suffered from an almost universal deformity which took the form of a forward and sometimes outward bowing of the shin bones. They lived almost entirely on fish, crocodiles and turtles, and the deformity was no doubt due to some dietary deficiency. Dyson spent time with these people, taking anthropological measurements and studying their general physical characteristics.

Fuchs had been planning to visit the large unexplored volcanic island known to us as Höhnel Island, but defined in maps as South Island. We were under no illusions as to the difficulty of this project. In a letter to Fuchs dated March 1 1934, Admiral von Höhnel had written that he was

> looking forward with great interest to the results of your investigations ... above all, I hope that you will be in a position to pay a visit to the great island in the south of the lake.

The southern end of the lake is flanked by vast lava escarpments. Thus it lies in a mighty trough, swept by winds which can reach gale force within minutes. However, during the weeks we spent beside the lake we had made a careful study of the winds, finding that they followed a definite daily pattern and, provided the 12 mile crossing was made during certain hours, fairly constant conditions might be expected. On 25th July Fuchs and Martin made a successful crossing in an hour and three quarters. They landed in a sheltered cove and camped in the lee of some sloping rocks.

Fuchs remained on the island for three days during which time he and

Martin climbed to the top, whereupon they got their first surprise. Fuchs writes :

> There below us was a herd of thirteen domestic goats grazing on some scanty tufts of grass. When we attempted to approach them they were as wild as the wildest antelope.

Fuchs returned to the mainland and thence to the Teleki volcano region, leaving Martin to his survey, and on 29th July Dyson joined Martin with sufficient supplies for at least ten days.

Just at this time I received a message by runner, from the Dominions Office in London via Marsabit, offering me an appointment as a District Officer in the Basutoland Administrative Service. Fuchs advised me to return to Marsabit and if necessary to Nairobi and arrange for an extension of time to enable me to complete my work with the expedition.

I set off immediately with two baggage camels and a guide from our base at Loiengalani and made the long journey to Marsabit on foot, travelling mainly by night, in six days, and then continued in a Somali trader's truck to Nairobi where the desperate news of the non-return of Dyson and Martin reached me.

Fuchs had arrived back at camp from his trip to the south on August 4, a day before Dyson and Martin were expected back. In his subsequent report to the Royal Geographical Society, he wrote:

> In making our plans we had arranged that if Dyson and Martin were in need of assistance they should light three fires, the reason for three being that at any time it might become necessary for the two to separate and to camp at different points.

My camels with which I trekked from Lake Rudolf to Marsabit.

So when, on August 9, there was still no sign of his companions, Fuchs went down to the lake shore camp to try to get in touch with them. He subsequently wrote:

> On that evening and also on those of the 10th and 11th August, I could get no reply from the island.

He realised that in case something had gone wrong it was important to avoid unnecessary delay in organising rescue for them, so on August 12 he left for Marsabit to arrange an aeroplane to stand by in Nairobi awaiting a final instruction. At the same time he would be able to arrange some more food, but before leaving the lake shore camp, he wrote a note :

> Dear Snaffles and Bill,
> This is in case you should come over after we have left. I have gone to Marsabit for food and an aeroplane to find out what's happened to you. ... Since ... you are nearly two weeks overdue by your estimate and five days by mine ... I ... conclude ... that something must have gone wrong. Your last fire was seen on 5th in the North Bay... I m getting a bit worried, and so I am off to borrow the Shell plane if I can.
>   Should you return STAY HERE; you'll never find Sirima on your own. If we have food enough I'll leave you a couple of men ... Immediately you arrive, please send the Kanga over to Sirima so that I can stop the aeroplane stunt. You see, I shall return to Sirima in three days with food. Hoping it's all a false alarm.
> Yours, Bunny
> 12th August, 1934

When Fuchs got to Marsabit he called Nairobi and arranged for a plane to stand by. In the meantime he returned to the lake with a police patrol, to find that the missing men had not returned. He therefore retraced his steps to Marsabit and sent a cable to Nairobi asking for the plane to pick him up at Marsabit and proceed to the lake. The aircraft, piloted by Sir Piers Mosteyn, arrived on August 18 carrying myself and MacInnes, who had returned to help, and flew on to the lake. Fuchs later wrote :

> We first flew over the base camp to make sure that the missing men had not returned the previous day, then straight across to the island ... but there was nothing to be seen.

Downhearted, we returned to Marsabit to find a wireless message had been received, stating that a pith helmet – probably that of Dyson – had been found on the western shore of the lake during a massive land search by several hundred soldiers of the KAR who had been rapidly moved to the area. It had been found 11 miles south of Ferguson's Gulf some 120 km to the north. Accordingly a message was immediately sent for a plane to search that area, including Central Island.

Our military escort: necessary for protection against armed bands of raiders from across the Abyssinian border.

On August 23, I wrote in my diary :

> Back at our base camp on Marsabit mountain Bunny Fuchs, Donald and I, with all hope gone.

The aeroplane search had proved fruitless, my trek up the east shore of the lake with camels had revealed nothing, and since the discovery of the doctor's topee just south of Ferguson's Gulf, the KAR had found no trace. There seemed nothing for it but to head for home. We were actually tuning up our engines and ready to leave when a messenger came running from the boma with a note from the wireless operator. It read as follows:

> Wireless message from Todenyang Fort on West shore of lake reports fires, possibly signal fires, in uninhabited country on north east shore of lake. Suggest expedition accompanied by KAR equip immediately and investigate.

The message also gave a compass bearing. It was unlikely that Dyson and Martin could have fetched up so very far from where they had been lost, but we clutched at this straw of hope and immediately set about preparing to investigate. We decided to take the big Albion, our Bedford truck, and the old red Chev box-body. In addition to the 6 men, a KAR sergeant and Lt. Holmes, their provisions and equipment, our rations and equipment and spares for the motors, we had to take on roughly 150 gallons of water, 140 gallons of petrol, 2,000 rounds of ammunition, two goats as meat, and our rifles and a machine gun. The armament was advisable because heavily armed and aggressive Ethiopian raiders were common in the north.[*]

Within the hour we were off and drove through the moonlit night thankful for the coolness it afforded. At our first stop we camped at Kalacha water hole among a clump of doum palms. That night I could not sleep and lay for hours listening to the rustle of the palm fronds, the breathing of the men and the far-off sound of camel bells. Visible in the moonlight, away to the west and coming ever nearer, floated a white dust cloud, like the smoke of a steamer out to sea. Under it was a herd of camels coming in from some distant pasture for their fortnightly drink. An hour or two later, as they drew nearer, the soft clonk of their wooden bells blended with the singing of the herdsmen. By morning they were gone.

Very reluctantly, then, we left the cool shady palms and once more struck out into the blazing heat. The country's deadly monotony was now alleviated by ever-changing mirages and the occasional rocky hill or outcrop of black lava. In the distance to the north-east were the Huri Hills. On our left, barren and forbidding, was Arusi, a hump of lava and ashes rising some 2,200 feet above the Chalbi.

Then we crossed the rich agate fields near North Horr and the going got rougher with mile after mile of heavy sand, dongas (gullies) and boulders. Often we were forced to lay paving stones across the dongas in order to get over – all in appalling heat. There were no other landmarks, and it was uncanny how our guides kept us on course. On every side was the desert, stretching to the horizon, the salt-caked surface gleaming like a vast ocean – not a tree, not a rock, not a tuft of grass to be seen. With the heat rising from the salt-caked surface and wrapping us like a hot blanket, lips and cheeks became parched and blistered and we were half blinded by the sun's glare and flying sand. Far ahead, dancing drunkenly in a sparkling lake, I saw a grotesque monster, a tiny body supported by absurdly long legs. As we drew closer, the monster, now huge, then a mere speck, continued its crazy journey. At last the mirage disappeared and an animal, a lone oryx, took shape, walking on some errand known only to himself. He paused to gaze at us as we drove by, before plodding on, at every step a tiny puff of dust rising from each hoof. Finally he was lost to sight in the empty desert.

But now there was a scorching following wind and every few miles we had to

---

* The lake has never been other than a dangerous area and still is. In 1965 a tourist lodge had been established at Loiengalani. The lodge manager, Guy Poole, learned that Somali shifta poachers were operating on nearby Mount Kulal and informed the police. The gang learned of this and raided the lodge. Fortunately, other than for Poole, an Italian Catholic Father and an Italian friend, the lodge was empty. The gang tied Poole and the Father to chairs before shooting them dead. They made the visiting Italian drive them away in the lodge Land Rover until it ran out of petrol. His body was never found, but unquestionably he was later murdered.

replenish the radiator tanks. The deathly silence ensuing after the engines were switched off was unnerving. So accustomed was one to hearing at least the chirp of a bird, the distant barking of a dog, the sigh of wind in a thorn bush, or even the scraping of a beetle crawling over a stone; but here there was only a silence you could almost touch. We steered for a low, flat-topped hill which marked the position of North Horr. Here we met two Borans who said a large band of raiders had been seen to the west near Mt Longondoti. Suspecting them to be scouts for a still larger force the two were on their way to warn their people.

At Hurran Hurra the well was dry, so we decided to press on to Galas water point. Finding a route across this unmapped terrain was proving even more difficult than we had anticipated. Only one of our guides had ever been farther north than Galas and all our attention concentrated on him as the going got rougher and rougher. Here there had been good rain and there was grass, the many trees were in leaf and herds of zebra, topi, oryx and Grant's gazelle roamed. Birds too were plentiful: wild-fowl in great numbers, vultures, and marabou storks feeding on the mud-fish in the rain pools that were starting to dry out.

Our progress was slow, and repeatedly we had to send someone ahead to pick out a route. Wherever there was such a hold-up the soldiers got out and made for the nearest pool. One would strip and go in to corner the fish, the rest would stand round ready to grab them as they floundered about in the shallows. [*]

About noon one of the men on the leading vehicle shouted he could see people on the lake shore a mile or so away. We trained our glasses on them, hoping they might be Martin and Dyson, but they were a group of men with canoes, who ignored our signals and made hasty preparations to embark. There was no doubt they were the raiders we had been told about earlier and, leaving a section to guard the lorries, the troops set off to take them by force. Our men opened fire at long range hoping to induce surrender, but in no time they had already pushed out their canoes to head full speed northwards.

We were now nearing our destination and the thoughts of everyone were on the two lost men. There was little hope left of finding them, but still just enough to spur us on. As the sun set we were exhausted and tempted to camp, but decided to push on while we could. However, a few moments later the leading truck buried its nose in a sand dune and the rest of us piled up all round it, hopelessly stuck.

After supper I climbed a dune and sat watching flights of geese and flamingos across the path of the moon. It was a perfect night, the wind had dropped

---

[*] Von Höhnel describes how his men caught fish in this selfsame manner in Allia Bay in 1888 when he and Count Teleki were battling their way northwards in search of a second great lake, which they finally discovered and named Stefanie.

and there was no sound save the cries of wildfowl and the swish of the waves as they broke on the shore.

Thinking back over our long search, I was coming to the conclusion that unless our men were prisoners of a raiding band they would not be in the area, because they both knew all too well the danger of wandering unarmed in this region. If they had drifted so far north, they would have turned southwards, hugging the shore as far as Mt Longondoti, where they might have found El Molo to guide them on. Before sunrise we manhandled the lorries out of their sandy graves and were off again.

We came across a dead crocodile wedged in the fork of a thorn tree, all around which were the tracks of a large bull elephant. Here a dramatic story was clearly written in the sand and mud between the tree and the lake shore. The crocodile had been bold enough to fasten its jaws on the elephant's trunk while he was drinking. The elephant had responded by dragging the crocodile inland, where he had battered it to death against the tree and the hard-baked earth and then parked the corpse in the tree fork above him.

But that day our eyes were not for the game. We scanned the shore and the northern horizon for fire, smoke, or any other sign of life, but there was nothing save the ever-present mirage which mocked us with every passing yard. At last we reached the spot indicated by the Turkana signallers. Scattered among a few low rocks were the remains of fires, but it was nothing more than a typical Shangilla (raiders from Ethiopia) encampment. Footprints, sleeping places and camp rubbish were still there and the fire ash had not yet been scattered by the wind. It was this scene that turned our last rays of hope, like the mirages, into sand. A more utterly desolate spot would be hard to find. The rocks afforded neither shade nor shelter from the flying sand. The tent pegs would not hold and big stones had to be used. In the afternoon we sent out a patrol to a low hill which commanded a view of the lake shore and the Ethiopian lowlands. They found further encampments, but no trace of life.

Next morning we broke camp and started set off southwards on the journey back to Marsabit. It was a slow business and the shifting sand had blotted out our tracks. We frequently got stuck. It must have been about noon when one of the men on the leading lorry shouted that he could see people on the lake shore a mile or two away. It turned out to be a party of men with canoes.

Ours were the first vehicles ever to have penetrated as far north as Allia Bay, and it had been a long, hard journey. We were short of sleep, dirty, and bone tired, and so for two or three days we rested at Marsabit.

Here I left the group to take up my appointment in Basutoland, and Fuchs and MacInnes set off with all haste for Lake Victoria. Fuchs thought they might find some trace of what had happened on South Island itself and had therefore arranged with Kenya and Uganda Railways and Harbours to borrow a steel lifeboat and transport it up to the western shore at Ferguson's Gulf, a rough journey of at least 500 km. Landing the boat at Ferguson's Gulf, they sailed southwards for eight days. One night the boat sank at the mouth of the Kerio watercourse, but they raised it, repaired it with old debbies (tins) and waited for the winds to die down. With supplies running out, Fuchs wrote :

> Finally we were compelled to make a one-day dash for the island, all went well till we had covered 15 miles of the 20 mile crossing, when a strong wind began to blow directly off the island. Half an hour after darkness fell, the outboard engine was swamped for a third time and we were compelled to turn before the wind when only 2 miles from the island.

Afraid of being wrecked in the darkness on the rocky shore, they hoisted a sail and set a northerly course up the centre of the lake and in the small hours of the morning spotted the fires lit by the rest of the party on the western shore. They had failed to reach the island, had been lucky to survive and finally admitted defeat: Martin and Dyson had been lost. To this day, the fate of the two men remains a mystery. It seems probable that they were wrecked and drowned in a storm and this is certainly Fuchs' conclusion. I think, however, it more likely that they were attacked by a monster crocodile as we so nearly were off Central Island.

In the six months they had spent in the field together, Dyson and Martin had endeared themselves to the other expedition members. Dyson had succeeded in doing some valuable anthropological work and had collected some fine zoological specimens while Martin, working partly with Wakefield, had mapped large sections of the region. Their tragic death brought a premature end to the expedition.

We who survived will never forget these two men. Indeed, even now, so many years later, Bill Dyson's voice rings clearly in my ears. Martin was a gentle and quiet man with a never-to-be-forgotten smile, and I can still

Snaffles Martin: a gentle and quiet man with a never-to-be forgotten smile.

remember his expression and tone of voice. I wrote a letter to his mother and, as an afterthought, enclosed a few of the thick whippy hairs from the tail of an elephant, saying they were supposed to bring good fortune and happiness. She replied and also sent me a beautiful old gold bracelet. One of the elephant hairs had been expertly inlaid into its outer perimeter. In her letter Mrs Martin said she wished me to have it and someday to give it to the girl I married. Many years later I did just that.

* * * *

In later years I returned to Lake Rudolf, as it always is to me, on a number of occasions. Yet the visit I made on the 5th March 1988 was special as it was exactly 100 years to the day that Count Samuel Teleki and his young companion, Lt Ludwig von Höhnel, were the first white men to set eyes on it. Four parties met on the remote and desiccated south shore under the shadow of Nabuyatom, a perfectly formed volcano cone. There was a group of Hungarians led by Gyula Gabris, senior lecturer in physical geography at the University of Sciences in Budapest and which included highly qualified scientists and technical personnel.

Another was brought by Fiona Alexander, a renowned aviator who loves Kenya's wild northern Rift Valley, and had walked across with camels from North Horr. It had left there on the on the 28th of February and included His Excellency Mr John Johnson C.M.G., the British High Commissioner to Kenya and Dr Hugh Lamprey, a distinguished ecologist with many years experience of this northern frontier region.

The third party, a small section of British army officers and other ranks had based themselves at Tum under the western face of Nyiro mountain, and then walked with pack donkeys over the great barrier range to the south of the lake, then down via Teleki's volcano to our camp on the shore. This was the route nearest to Teleki's, albeit a bit further to the east and of which von Höhnel said in his journal it was a veritable hell!

Finally, in our own party there was Baroness Marie Theres Waldblott, whose father, Count E. Wickenburg had in 1901 journeyed with horses and pack camels from Djibouti in the Horn of Africa through Abyssinia and then southwards by way of the Ethiopian Rift lakes to Rudolf, and then to Lamu on the coast of Kenya. Also with us was my daughter Caroline and the photographer, David Coulson, who has explored some of the least known parts of the Namib and Kalahari deserts. We had hoped that Bunny Fuchs would join us, but at the last moment he was unable to do so, to our great disappointment.

We had all gathered to pay tribute to Teleki and von Höhnel. When they first cast eyes on the lake, aeroplanes had yet to fly. Now, as we stood on its shores, jets high overhead completed the trip to Europe in less than what had then been a day's march. Fifty four years earlier we had lost Snaffles Martin and Bill Dyson. In 1988 the camel party coming across from North Horr had likewise

nearly come to grief through extreme heat and all but failed to reach our rendezvous. Had they not been found by my daughter, Caroline, they would have
been in very deep trouble. For all that the lake can now be reached with extreme
ease, compared with what we had to put up with, not to mention Teleki's and
von Höhnel's journey, it is still a mysterious, beautiful and very dangerous place.

CHAPTER 4

BASUTOLAND, SOUTH AFRICA

I T   W A S while I was still on Fuchs' expedition that news of my appointment to the Basutoland Civil Administration reached me. To save money I booked myself steerage on a British India boat sailing from Mombasa to Durban. It was rough and ready, but the food was adequate and my bunk comfortable.

In the process of settling down to a quiet voyage I met the young and beautiful Mary. She was in the expensive, sharp end of the boat and I was in the blunt end. There was a heavy rail to keep the hoi polloi away from the elite, but it did not prevent Mary and me from talking over it. The result was that I convinced myself that I deserved a better deal. The purser was sympathetic and took my £10 extra payment for a berth among the toffs. But as I turned to go, he said: "Funny you should wish to move, as that lovely piece, Mary, came here half an hour ago and for some extraordinary reason changed over to steerage."

By the time we shifted Mary's kit back to her original cabin and I had moved my own bags, most of the night had gone.

Several days later we docked at Durban. The people meeting Mary included a burly and athletic looking man, who, judging from his behaviour, must have been more than a little familiar with her. I was also quick to realise that he knew his Mary well and had made a rapid and accurate assessment of the situation. Suddenly he left her side and moved in my direction. He drew me aside, lowered his mouth to within an inch of my ear and rasped: "Fuck off!" I took one more quick look at him as he towered over me, arms adangle, and took his advice. So ended a beautiful romance!

My home-coming was a joyous occasion and there was much to tell and discuss. My university days and the Lake Rudolf expedition were behind me and I was now about to launch forth on my own. A week later I travelled to Maseru and took up my appointment in the Basutoland Administrative Service.

Most of the bachelors lived in the officers' mess. A bottle of good brandy cost 4/= and daily messing 6/=, and we lived well. I was earning £15 a month plus horse and uniform allowance, so there was enough money to buy a pony and a 12-bore shotgun.

I set off with six pack horses.

My fellow officers and the younger married couples all kept horses and played polo, tennis, golf, or rugby, so off-duty there was plenty to do.

I had just settled in when I was told to take over as Assistant District Officer (ADO) at Qachas Nek (then usually called the Nek) on the eastern border, which marched with East Griqualand. There was no direct road to it, but the bridle paths over the mountains were well kept. I set off with six pack horses, my own pony and an escort of three Basutoland Mounted Police. We trekked at between 9,000 and 10,000 ft above sea level. Snow drifts lay in the gullies and the nights were frosty.

At the Maletsunyane Falls, a mountain torrent plunges 600 feet into the gorge. We camped on the lip of the cliff with a view down on the thread of white water far below. Vultures circled beneath us and baboons barked across the valleys. We were now roughly at the centre point of Basutoland, and most of the high landmarks were visible in the cold crystal-clear atmosphere. Fuel was scarce, so each evening I shared the camp-fire with my Basuto mounties and told them about the big game of East Africa and the deserts of northern Kenya. I shared my tent with a large and very intelligent Alsatian dog belonging to a friend away on leave. On the second day he wore through his pads on the sharp gravel. Having unsuccessfully loaded him on one of the packs, I bought a sheep-skin from a mountain shepherd and made boots for him. These were a success, but by the end of four hours he had worn them out. I watched him limp ahead and lie down on the path with his paws raised, a clear signal to renew his footwear.

On the fifth day we reached the headwaters of the Orange River. Melting

The Basutoland high country where horses were the sole means of transport.

snow and recent rain had brought about a spate, so we had to ferry the gear across in a rickety row-boat. The horses swam over and by noon we were in the saddle again. That night we reached the Nek and I was given a warm welcome by Peter Strong, the DC, who spoke Sesuto like a native. It was he who was to teach me the elements of my job as a junior District Officer (DO) and about the region and its inhabitants.

My horse, Champagne, had been a Government Mounted Police charger but, as he had been outlawed as unmanageable, I was able to buy him for a fiver. There was nothing really wrong with Champagne other than his exceptionally high spirits, which fitted in well with mine. Every morning I would throw a

Sir William Clark, KCSI, KCMG

bridle on Champagne and the two of us would set off for a swim. I took no saddle and would run beside him for a while before swinging up on his back. Two miles from the house there was a waterfall, which poured into a deep pool. Both horse and I would be in a muck-sweat by the time we reached the pool, and Champagne enjoyed the exhilaration of the icy water as much as I did.

All too soon, Jack Gage,[*] whose temporary replacement as ADO I was, returned from leave in Ireland. He had married very young, but things had gone wrong and his wife had now refused to return to Basutoland. That afternoon, having sized me up, he said: "Look, there's a super girl called Sandra, just qualified as a doctor. I met her on the boat. I love her, and somehow, sometime, I'm going to marry her. She is in my car about two miles down the escarpment and I want you to bring her in secretly, as all hell will be let loose at headquarters if this gets round, and I must have time to think things over."

I was more than impressed with what I found in the car and a friendship

---

[*] Jack Gage had been an Irish rugger international, and when he came to South Africa in the early thirties he was immediately picked up by the Springbok Selectors, and is still remembered in S.A. as one of the greatest wing threequarters of all time.

General (later Field Marshall) Smuts was a great walker, a
distinguished naturalist and a wonderful companion.

which lasted as long as Sandra's life ensued. I tucked her into the boot with a
stick wedged in the hinge for air and then drove through the border post back
to the house I shared with Jack. After the two of them had made plans for their
future and he and I had gone through the motions of handing over our duties,
we finally shifted Sandra back across the border on her way to Johannesburg.

On the whole I was pleased when eventually Jack resigned from service life
and married Sandra, as in many ways they were well suited and there would be
better opportunities for Sandra outside the service than in it.

* * * *

At this point a telegram arrived:

> Inform Millard that he has been appointed Private Secretary and ADC to His
> Excellency Sir William Clark, KCSI, KCMG, High Commissioner for the UK in
> the Union of South Africa and High Commissioner for Basutoland, Swaziland
> and Bechuanaland. He should report back immediately to the Resident
> Commissioner in Maseru where he will receive further instructions.

Although this new appointment considerably boosted my morale, it left me feeling uneasy and inadequate. But after thinking it over I came to the conclusion that the dice were falling right for me. I returned over the mountains to Maseru, sold my horse, said goodbye to Basutoland, and headed for the Cape.

I think I was probably the nearest thing to useless as a private secretary by Sir William Clark's standards. One day I made an error of judgement so gross that I felt obliged to apologise for it. All he said was: "Thank you for your apology, which I appreciate, but remember one thing, young man: a private secretary is never wrong."

After that we became good friends and he more of a father to me than a distinguished master.

Life in the Cape at the time was a kaleidoscope of activity. Lord Clarendon was Governor General of South Africa, Admiral Evans VC of the "Brooke" was the Admiral commanding the Cape Station, and in Parliament were such legendary figures as Smuts, Deneys Reitz, de Villiers Graaf, Leif Egeland and many others. Sir John Carew Pole, a particular friend, was Controller to Clarendon, and on the High Commissioner's staff were men such as Percy Lieching, and Geoffrey Wallinger who rose to great heights in the Foreign Service. I was fortunate in getting to know Smuts and Deneys Reitz well as they were close

General Smuts, Diana Clark, J.M. and Geoffrey Wallinger (later Ambassador to Paris). We did most of our long hikes southward along the plateau of the Table Mountain massif.

friends of the High Commissioner, and was able to get from these two ex-Boer leaders firsthand accounts from the Boer angle of a campaign which has always intrigued me. Reitz himself gave me a copy of his book "Commando" which I still have, and also "Trekking On" which covers the period after the Vereeniging Peace. General Smuts, even at that time, 1936, was a great walker and mountaineer, and for some reason we got on well together which is surprising as I was a young, and no doubt, brash young man. Among his many talents Smuts was a distinguished naturalist, and a wonderful companion to be with on all occasions. His favourite expedition was southwards along the plateau of the Table Mountain massif, or in the arid broken country down towards Cape Point. It was in these areas we did most of our long hikes.

I remember also when Smuts visited my father at our Herschel home. My father's African interpreter and assistant was an old fellow called Jacob, who, at the time of the Boer War had been a member of a small African Field Force recruited by the British and duly armed. The force was used on occasions to harass the remnants of the Boer Commandos who were still at large towards the end of the war, mainly in the Free State and along the Orange River itself. At about that time Smuts made his last desperate raid into the Cape Province in the hope of rallying the war-weary Afrikaners to arms in a final bid to save defeat. Jacob told us that he, and a detachment of the African Field Force, had actually had a go at Smuts and his commando as they fought their way southwards across the Orange River. (They crossed the river at a point about eight miles from where we then lived at Herschel.) Smuts insisted on meeting his old enemy and the two laughed and joked together.

On that same occasion my father asked Smuts why, when he was so hard pressed, had he bothered to repair fences as he and his small commando penetrated deep into the farming region of the North Eastern Cape Province. Smuts replied - "Well, you see we were mostly farmers or country people at heart, and fully aware of the problems caused to neighbouring farms, when, due to a broken fence stock is able to stray from one farm to another and it was only natural that we should feel bound to repair fences while on the march."

While I was with Sir William we used to visit Smuts at his hide-out, a small farm off the Johannesburg/Pretoria road. These were fascinating occasions I shall always remember. Sir William, previously British High Commissioner in Canada, was held in high esteem, and his office in Parliament Street became the Mecca of the diplomatic corps and many of the senior personalities in the South African government. All of us on his staff worked hard. Being rather slow off the mark, I had to push hard to keep pace. However, I was assisted by an experienced lady secretary who knew everyone and everything, so I managed somehow.

Outside office hours life was also hectic. Young unmarried private secretaries, flag lieutenants, and ADCs were the prey of hostesses, who spoilt them thoroughly. There were barbecues, picnics, parties, tennis and race meetings. One was lent polo ponies and hacks and I joined the Cape hunt, enjoyed diplomatic privileges and duty free booze and petrol. I acquired a car and was entitled to special number plates. All this was in total contrast to what I had experienced during my months in the wastelands of northern Kenya.

On Saturday nights there was dancing, usually preceded by dinner at Kelvin Grove Country Club, formal occasions at which tails or dinner jackets were mandatory. There were official occasions when I had to accompany Sir William, myself dressed up in fancy white Dominions' Office uniform plus sword and David Livingstone type hat, or in morning dress, and feeling most uncomfortable. These were not my favourite outings.

Every four months we visited one of the High Commission territories. It was my function to plan the itinerary and tie up details with the government concerned. Sometimes we travelled by car, but usually by special train or in a fully-equipped coach of our own provided by the South African government, complete with chef and staff. On these occasions I often moved forward to the locomotive and helped with the stoking, or perched myself on the cow-catcher. Great gatherings of Africans assembled and local Europeans and officials paraded in their Sunday best. Speeches were made, and gifts of lion skins, karosses and carvings presented.

The South African government operated from two official capitals, Cape Town and Pretoria. At the start of each winter we moved to Pretoria. I usually went ahead to open up the High Commission house and office and get everything ready.

Life on the Transvaal highveld was more relaxed than at the Cape. I was able to get first class polo at the Roberts Heights military base. There were friends in the SAAF who took me up in their open-cockpit Hartebeeste fighters and we looped, spun, and slow-rolled in the clear sky. It was the delight of these flying forays that convinced me of the need to learn to fly myself, a dream which was later to become a reality.

My closest companion was Theo de Klerk, a young motor car salesman with whom for a while I shared digs at the Cape. Theo, an Afrikaner, passionately loved his country, its people, and history. He was liked and respected by all regardless of colour, class or creed, and in that he was unusual. He and I were from dissimilar backgrounds, but as I got to know him, I came to realise he was a man and a friend I could trust unequivocally. Occasionally one could detect in him an animosity towards Britain (which probably had its roots in the history of his tribe going back to 1795 when the British flag was first raised over Cape Town Castle, and memories of Slagters Nek, the Great Trek of 1838, and the Boer War), but this attitude never impinged on our close relationship.

We stripped down an open V8 Ford tourer and replaced the back seat with a wooden cradle to hold a 44-gallon drum of petrol. This baobab was on the Chobi river in Bechuanaland.

On one occasion Theo and I decided to hunt so-called dangerous game in the wilds of the Kalahari. We lacked experience, but hankered after adventure and a challenge. We had been told that in the Mababi Depression, vaguely marked on the map of the Bechuanaland Protectorate, there were many lions, buffalo and elephants.

We stripped down an open V-8 Ford tourer and replaced the back seat with a wooden cradle to hold a 44-gallon drum of petrol. We took no tent, just a tarpaulin.

Sharing the driving and travelling non-stop we soon covered the 2,000 miles to Kasani, a police post at the northeastern corner of Bechuanaland. Here we engaged a bushman tracker, whom we christened Kaalgat ("Bare Bottom"). Communication with him was only possible by way of sign language.

By the evening of the third day, as we were heading west along the south bank of the Chobi, a tributary of the Zambezi, we came upon the small wattle and daub home of Mrs van Staden, which we made our base. Her husband had been killed by a lion three months earlier while extracting commercial timber from the riverine forest, and we were the first whites she had seen since his death.

Next day we set out for the Mababi Depression and Okavango swamps. At Kachikau village all the dwellings and cattle pens were completely surrounded by high timber stockades. The headman and his elders begged us to help them deal with the lions which were decimating their cattle.

Already an hour before sunset, cattle were being herded into the stockades, fires were kindled and drums beaten. It was as if preparations for a siege were being made and there was an atmosphere of panic. We backed our vehicle against one of the stockades and folded down the windshield and canvas hood. At the onset of dusk the grunting of lions reached us from three directions. Then, for a period, dead silence. It became pitch dark. Suddenly we were aware of lions on all sides. Theo nudged me, indicating a point a yard from his elbow. I switched on the headlights, and at that moment all hell broke out. The cattle in the stockade started milling around and bellowing, part of the stockade collapsed, and a stampede ensued. The surrounding area instantly became a battlefield of rising dust, shouts, gunfire, drums, lions roaring and snarling and cattle dying. There were at least 25 lions and over 100 cattle. Theo and I blazed away, but dust and general chaos precluded accurate shooting. Cattle ran for their lives and the lions followed them. Then, suddenly, all was quiet again. Six dead cattle lay within 50 yards of our car. We were thoroughly shaken, and, had we felt able to admit it, happy to run for home.

Next morning we followed the blood spoor of a lion we had wounded and finished it off, and then decided to return to Mrs van Staden to calm down.

During our absence there had also been a drama at the homestead. Quietly and nonchalantly, old Mrs van Staden said during the previous night a pride had broken into her goat stockade. Holding a hurricane lamp she had shot dead one of the lions with her husband's .303 rifle. The rest made off, but when she returned to her house she found three lions standing on their hind legs to tear down the biltong from the rafters of the verandah. She shot and wounded one of them and they retreated into the darkness. Before leaving next morning and with Kaalgat's help we tracked down that lion. Theo finished him off with his 9.3 Mauser while I gave covering fire with SSG from my 12-bore.

At last, then, we reached the Depression and based ourselves at a pan which Kaalgat called Tsotsorogo. Theo and I were little better than a pair of muddlers.

Theo de Klerk and J.M. lost for 16 hours in the Kwaai area of Bechuanaland. The picture was taken with my automatic camera. We were tracked down and rescued by our Bushman guide Kaalgat.

The first thing we did was to get lost without water. Kaalgat had been left in the camp to guard our food against hyenas, and it was only 16 hours later that he succeeded in tracking us down. By then we were desperate. No doubt he saved our lives.

On the way back I saw a dead zebra under an acacia. I strolled up to the carcass, curious to determine how it had died. One barrel of my shotgun was loaded with No 5 shot and the other with lethal ball. I was pushing my way through the tall elephant grass when only five paces from the zebra, a gigantic lioness emerged from its rib-cage and came straight for me. I shut both eyes and pulled both triggers. Off balance, I was knocked flat on my back by the recoil! But the lioness had dropped dead at my feet with half her skull blown off – lucky!

That afternoon in camp, a fully-grown impala doe ran towards us and collapsed at our feet. On her heels followed a pack of wild hunting dogs, which surrounded us on all sides. For a while they sat or stood gazing at us until for no apparent reason they faded away. An hour later the impala got shakily to her feet and walked to the edge of the firelight. There she turned as if to say goodbye before disappearing silently into the shadows.

A fully grown impala doe collapsed at our feet … a pack of hunting dogs on her heels.

Capt Struben RN lived in "Needeberg", one of those old Cape houses full of beautiful things, including his daughter, Lavinia, who was exceptional in many ways. She was a superb horsewoman, had sophistication and poise and, at 21, was just as much at ease in a room full of men as with an assembly of women. In male company she could always cap a story with a better and more risque one and would see to it that she always became the centre-piece. Lavinia was the queen bee of the younger generation in the Cape.

Lavinia and I saw a good deal of each other and were usually bracketed together at parties. In spite of this, her arrogance and intolerance irritated me so that we sometimes quarrelled. She had a sixth sense, an uncanny under-standing of men and a man's rather than a woman's outlook, which appealed to me, and we got on well together.

One day Lavinia was to give a dinner party at "Needeberg". Being short of a man, she asked me to bring a friend. I decided on Theo, and he behaved splen-didly. Some of his anecdotes might have been toned down a bit, but it was he who dominated the gathering, and for once Lavinia was slightly eclipsed. After everyone else had left and I was about to follow suit Lavinia suggested that as it was so late I should stay the night, but first she had a bone to pick with me. And then she began to rant. What the bloody hell did I think I was doing bringing a man of this sort to her party? Was I trying to make a fool of her, lower the tone?

I lost my temper and told her Theo was worth 10 of her sort, that she was a spoilt and conceited brat and as far as I was concerned she could jump into the fish-pond. I stomped off to my car and disappeared down the drive, leaving a cloud of dust.

A week later Theo came to see me. "Look old boet," he said, "would you mind very much if I invited Lavinia to dine with me? I thought she was a fantastic girl and I would like to thank her for that party and get to know her better."

I said of course I had no objection, but that if he really wanted to get close to Lavinia he must be able to ride. "Right," said Theo, "we'll buy a horse and you'll teach me."

Jos Duncan, who ran a string of thoroughbreds at his racing stables near Muzenberg, had a beautiful three year-old. But although Gay Prince was as fast as the wind, he refused to win races. As such, he would make a splendid hack and we could have him for £50. Riding lessons began the very next day.

Ten days later Theo plucked up the courage to invite Lavinia to ride with him. She accepted, they rode, and in due course they married.[*]

During my second year with him, Sir William had a fact-finding visit from Sir Ralph Furse, who was Director of Recruitment in the Colonial Office. Sir Ralph wished to tour the three High Commission territories and I arranged his itinerary. On his way back he offered me an appointment in the Colonial Service.

He explained that he was considering taking the recruitment of administrative personnel for both services under his wing, but before he did so, he wanted a couple of guinea-pigs from the Dominions Service to try out on the Colonial Office. Brian Marwick from Swaziland would go to Nigeria and I to Tanganyika. But first we were to spend two or three terms at Oxford or Cambridge at the expense of HMG on what was known as the Devonshire Course.

For Brian and myself this was promotion and we accepted.

Returning to my old college at Cambridge was like coming home. Many of my friends were still around. I was given good rooms, but was no longer subject to the normal rules and regulations. Most of the subjects covered (such as

---

[*] Theo became one of South Africa's top racehorse trainers and reached his thousandth winner as far back as 1972. Lavinia and he remained happy, but there was a terrible tragedy. Together with Francis Brett Young, the writer, I was godfather to their son, Stephen. At Oxford he did brilliantly well and among other things was a boxing blue. He was having a minor operation to his damaged nose when, under anaesthetic, he died.

elementary survey, anthropology, accountancy, tropical hygiene and simple engineering) I had already had experience of in the field. Instead I concentrated on the law and learning Swahili.

After taking an exam we had to appear before a selection board of senior civil servants. I was pleasantly surprised when the chairman, who had my file before him, greeted me cheerfully, congratulated me on my appointment and wished me the best of luck.

I was just disappearing down the passage when a messenger called me back. On re-entering the room I found that the atmosphere had chilled somewhat. I went back to the lonely chair at the end of the table and prepared for the worst. The chairman apologised for recalling me but said his attention had been drawn to the fact that I had made a complete nonsense of the accountancy paper. How, with all my experience, could I explain this?

I replied that, as the board must be aware, a good district officer was one of the hardest-pressed men on earth and if he had any sense he would, at an early stage, delegate the cash and accounting to his most reliable clerk. He would, of course, keep a close check on this person, but frankly a district officer worth his salt had more important things to do than to get bogged down with the petty cash.

This evoked a chuckle and nothing more was said about accountancy.

* * * *

In 1936 I was posted as a junior District Officer to Mbeya, a high, healthy and fertile station in southwestern Tanganyika. The district covered an area of infinite variety and interest. There were high mountains, great escarpments, dusty plains, as well as rivers, lakes and forests. I moved into a comfortably furnished house with a tiled roof and colourful garden. The ladies on the station fixed up my curtains. Wilkins, the DC, had the reputation of being a great trout fisherman and hunter, and a good administrator. He gave me time to settle in and then had me in on a formal talk. He listened sympathetically as I told him about myself, leaving me feeling that I had given a good impression.

Then, tersely, he said: "Well, clearly you don't know much, and I have decided that you should go off immediately into the district for two months. On the table over there is a pile of old German maps, the only maps we have of this part of Tanganyika. I would like you to take them with you and bring them up to date, filling in new tracks, roads, water-holes, villages and headmen's names. You should make yourself known to all chiefs and headmen en route. Tentage and other camp equipment can be had from the District Office store, food you can buy in the village. You must take two tribal police or messengers and 25 porters, not less, as you must be comfortable and keep fit. Furthermore, you will keep your porters in meat and pay them 50 cents daily and you will handle all problems you may encounter to the best of your ability. You may have to cope with raiding elephants, and while in the Usangu area deal with man-eating lions who are causing havoc. Please bear in mind that this district is 22,000 square miles, so you have much to do, a long way to go, and not much time. Report back to me after two months and I will require full details of your route, your impressions, and your views on how we should handle any of the more difficult problems you are bound to encounter and unable to cope with on the spot. I presume you have firearms?"

I confirmed that I had a .425 and a .318 Westley Richards rifle, and Wilkins was satisfied. Going off as a greenhorn I inevitably encountered many frustrations. I made embarrassing mistakes. I was terrified when I shot my first rogue elephant and even more so when I held my first big baraza (meeting) of African chiefs and tribesmen. But I came back with hairs on my chest and a love for the country, the people, the wildlife and the work itself that remained with me for the rest of my career. Back on the station I wrote up my report and brought the old German maps up to date.

One day Wilkins said we both deserved a break. So off we went to the Mperoto Mountains 30 miles east of Mbeya. The setting was perfect: bracken-covered hills and crater mounds towering over the valley, and the river roaring down from the moorlands. The days were warm and sunny, but at night during most of the year there was frost. There were deep, long pools, waterfalls and rapids, and the fish were thickset and fierce fighters. The brown trout averaged three pounds, but five and six-pounders were not uncommon.

My bull-terrier, Bullet, always took a great interest in my encounters with fish. I was working a big pool directly above a waterfall when a fish took my fly. I tightened up, the reel screamed, and away he went full tilt for the far side of the pool. But from the opposite bank, a third pair of eyes had been watching. Suddenly an otter slid into the water and in a flash attached himself to my fish. Instantly, Bullet zoomed down from the rock overlooking the pool and fastened onto the otter. For a few hectic seconds spray, foam, and fur flew in every direction as I struggled with three pounds of trout, 20 pounds of otter and 30 pounds of terrier. Then the whole caboodle disappeared over the waterfall and my line came back minus cast and flies. What happened below the waterfall is a story only Bullet can tell, but when he rejoined me grinning from ear to ear I knew he was saying he had a great old punch-up.

During my time at Mbeya, I established a hatchery near the source of the Kiwira stream, where the average water temperature was 44°F, and from this camp stocked a number of virgin streams in the district and on the Ukinga plateau. They all did well for a while, but the war intervened. However, I did have a letter from a forest officer during the war saying he had taken a three-pound fish on the Ukinga plateau 18 months after my stocking. Such rapid growth must be well nigh a record.

The elderly Provincial Commissioner and his very young and pretty new wife, decided to join me at one of my bush camps. Having discussed the evening meal with the cook, I decided to go off to shoot a brace of guinea-fowl or francolin. Young wife asked to go with me.

After walking about a mile, we ran into a flock of guinea-fowl. I told young wife to stay put under a thorn tree and dashed off after the running birds. Suddenly, from behind me rose screams of panic and anguish. Imagining the girl was being attacked by a rhino I went racing back. She was frantically tearing off her clothes and dancing round like a madwoman. By the time I reached her there was nothing more to take off except the safari ants.

She made me promise not to say a word to her husband. I replied that I might look it, but was not so stupid as to say a word to anyone. As a young and innocent bachelor struggling to make his way, I could not possibly jeopardise my future by telling the most senior officer in the province of the incident.

* * * *

Shortly before I arrived there had been a gold rush to the Lupa river basin in the low-lying, broken country reaching down towards Lake Rukwa to the north west. Although it was classified as the Lupa Controlled Area, it was part of Mbeya district, but administered separately by a DC. One day, the DC became seriously ill and I was told to take over.

The headquarters at Chunya, a one-street trading centre near the headwaters of the Lupa River, looked like a wild west set. There were no proper houses; the DC, the Inspector of Mines, the police chief and the doctor lived in tents or wattle and daub thatched huts. The district office, the revenue office and the court-house were similar makeshift affairs, but fairly cool and airy. The kitchen was an open hearth under a thorn tree, and water was brought by prisoners each morning. The pit latrine in the nearest thicket blended in nicely with the surrounding bushveld. Lions and other predators were common and there were all sorts of insects and snakes. Malaria was rife.

The only substantial building in Chunya was the Goldfields Hotel. It was here that one drank, danced, got married and paid homage to your God if a priest, predicant, or parson happened to venture into the area. The hotel was run by Ken and May Menzies, who were the hub of the goldfields. Ken was also a licensed gold buyer and did most of his business over the bar. Tough, bearded diggers, after weeks and months on their lonely claims, would stride in and place a quinine bottle full of dust and nuggets on the bar saying, "Right, Ken old cock, weigh that will you?" Scales would be produced and then Ken would say: "Okay Bob, that's worth £270, so you can have £240 credit." Ken always set aside £30 so that the digger had something to get going on again when he had burned up his credit. Digger Bob would reply, "Right Ken, you old robber, now pass me down that Dimple Haig." You always poured your own drinks.

Most of the trouble-makers on the Lupa in those days were the Afrikaners. There were daily fights over water rights, claim jumping, and labour issues and there had been several rather nasty incidents. In short, the key to peace throughout the field of some 2,500 square miles was control of the Afrikaners.

The small nuggets common in the Lupa were known as rice gold, but most of the gold was found in the form of dust washed in pans during the rainy season, or dry-blown when the creeks ran low. Dry-blowing is a process whereby trays of gold-bearing rubble are subjected to a flow of air produced by a fan which in turn is driven from a small Lister or Petter engine, or even by a belt over the back wheel of a jacked-up model T Ford. In theory the dirt and light rubble is blasted away by the blower, while the heavy gold dust and nuggets settle on the floor of the tray and it was a method which worked quite well. Likely-looking quartz was also crushed and blown or panned. Larger nuggets, usually intermixed with the quartz, were sometimes found, but this was not common as the gold-bearing reefs on the Lupa had mostly decomposed over the ages and the gold had been washed into the creeks and depressions.

After supper on my first day at Lupa, I reluctantly walked up to the Hotel. It was something I had to do sooner or later. Everyone already knew that the new DC had arrived. Word always gets around faster in remote areas than near headquarters. As I pushed open the swing door into the bar I wished I was a wild west sheriff with a star on my chest and a six-shooter at my hip. Instead I was very nervous, knowing only too well that much depended on my ability to create the right impression at this first encounter with my parishioners.

Silence descended as I entered. Twenty or so ruffians turned round to face me. I raised my arm in greeting, but got no response. As I was about to continue on my way to the bar, one of the men spat on the floor. "Got nog'n ander verdomde Rooinek," he said. (My God, yet another goddam Englishman.) I ordered a drink. Still dead silence. In the end I turned to the group nearest to me and asked: "Wie van julle kerels wil 'n sopie met my hê?" (Which of you fellows will have a drink with me?). They rose to their feet as one man. I was mobbed, slapped on the back, hand-shaken and carried round the room.

This happened during the great depression, so the lure of gold was irresistible, particularly to old-timers. One old man, who had panned gold in the Klondike, had a watch chain of small, rough nuggets draped across his barrel of a chest. Like him, all the miners were a tough, hard lot. Greeks, South Africans, Germans, Poles, Indians, Africans, and a few Englishmen, including several remittance men. Jim, an Etonian, would turn up every three months or so to collect his Fortnum and Mason hamper from the post office and spend a day or two in one of my tents, where he kept a clean shirt and slacks. The hamper would be opened with great ceremony and we would wine and dine like gentry, but not before Jim's parents, who had laid on the feast from afar, had been toasted. Clearly Daddy knew his claret, for he always sent the best.

Among them too was Whisky Wolff, soon to be found sitting in the doorway of his shack, at a table on which were arranged a hurricane lamp, a bottle of brandy, a .303 and a clip of five cartridges. Each of the five had a name on it in black marking ink. One of the names was Millard. Whisky had noised it abroad that he intended to dispose of any of those rats such as me and challenged any of them to come within range. We bided our time and in due course Whisky slumped over his table and was admitted into the makeshift hospital, where he died of DTs. I kept the cartridge with my name on it in his memory.

Diggers with spare cash would often order from the shops in Mbeya special delicacies unavailable at Chunya. Porters would be sent over the mountain to return with loads of tinned fruit, cigarettes, yeast, Worcester sauce, lime juice and jam. Occasionally, too, a crate of whisky would be ordered, but by the time it arrived it usually contained nothing but a dozen scraps of paper bearing messages such as: "Dear Tom, Have borrowed a bottle, will return same next week." Or: "You owe me this one from last month."

Any reef or good-sized nugget found provided an excuse for a party. One digger came to the hotel with a nugget of almost solid gold about the size and shape of a tennis ball. By the time I got there celebrations were in full swing. Someone suggested we should pick sides for a scrum and see which side could heel out and place the nugget against the wall. This game continued well into the night and by the time I left the scene of battle, several players had passed out and were lying in various corners of the bar.

Next morning the long-faced nugget-owner arrived at my office. Someone, sometime, when everyone had passed out or gone to sleep on the floor, had sawed the nugget in two with a hacksaw and gone off with half of it. We never traced the missing half.

I moved round the district a good deal, usually accompanied by the Inspector of Mines and soon got to like the community. On the whole they were a pretty tough hard nosed mob, but decent folk at heart, and I made many good friends.

Among them were characters such as Ropesole Jones, Ipogolo Thomas, Smelly Thomas, Papadopoulos the Greek, who was known as "Popitupalass", and another Greek, Rasbistos, who answered to the name "Rabbitsarse". Then there was Charlie Goss, one of the most famous elephant hunters of all time, and a great poacher of ivory and a big dear lady, I forget her proper name, who was always referred to as the "Covered Wagon". Not to be forgotten was Lupa

Lill. Lill was an unusual and likeable character, and I was all for Lill; moreover she was a real asset in an area such as this.

I remember one night Charlie Goss and MacHugh were doing some serious talking and drinking at the far end of Ken Menzies' bar. MacHugh always removed his dentures when he got down to booze-ups and normally put them in an ashtray. Somehow the top set fell to the floor, whereupon Charlie roared, "Bejasus, look at that bloody great cockroach" and promptly crushed the denture to powder under his boot. No offence was taken and when I departed about midnight they were still hob-nobbing and happily drinking in their special corner.

With a view to taking diggers' minds off water rights, claim jumping, labour issues and the like, I found a flat piece of ground, laid out a rugger pitch and set about getting together a Lupa Goldfields rugby XV. Soon our practice games attracted big crowds and finally I took my side to Dar-es-Salaam. We won all our matches against Dar-es-Salaam, the Navy and the Army, and there was great rejoicing and celebrations.

It was during my time on the Lupa that my mother died. It is impossible for me to describe how much this saddened me. We were a very closely knit and happy family and for some time I was unable to reconcile myself to the fact that she was no longer with us. My mother was in so many ways an exceptional woman, totally unselfish, brave, resourceful and talented. Above all she was a mother who was at the same time a friend and companion to us, her children.

Many famous people came to our simple Herschel home, and many of the most humble. Whoever they were, great or small, old or young, they cherished throughout their lives the experience of having known my parents. Over the years this has been brought home to me time and again by people who knew and remembered them.

* * * *

Back in Mbeya, my function became covering the Mbozi coffee-farming area, a German stronghold. I was to spend much of my time on safari getting to know the Germans to report on their political leanings. That was important, because about this time there was growing awareness of the build-up of Nazism, and many were convinced that war with Germany was becoming inevitable. We in Tanganyika were probably the worst affected, as most of the settlers were Germans, many of whom were known to be associated with the Nazi movement. Agents were being infiltrated as farm assistants, commercial representatives and tourists. The Lutheran missions, whose main sphere of influence was in the southwest, were not overlooked by the Party in Germany, and moderate or pro-British leaders in the missions and in every walk of life were being replaced by firebrands direct from Germany.

A sinister situation was developing: some of the poison generated in the beer halls and back streets of Berlin and Munich was finding its way in no uncertain manner to the remote corners of this former German colony. There was a German club at Mbozi, and sometimes I would drop in for a beer. One evening a brawl broke out between two rival factions. Bottles flew and the club-house was reduced to a shambles. The arrogance and bloody-mindedness of these people, shocked me, but from my corner in the bar I was filled with schadenfreude as members of Hitler's master race tore each other and their club apart!

Meanwhile, tension was building up and time was running out. I had already enlisted in the KAR reserve of officers. We were heavily involved in the so-called "Z Plans" for the arrest, internment and disposal of German nationals in the event of war. Assessments had to be made of fuel supplies, transport, food reserves, firearms and ammunition. Code messages flew back and forth and there was feverish activity. The Africans: how would they react? Where did their loyalties lie? How far would the Germans go? What was their secret plan? It was only 21 years earlier that German influence had been strong in this part of Tanganyika. The famous Lt-Col Paul Emil von Lettow Vorbeck was still a legendary figure to many of the southwestern tribes. A likely hot spot was Njombe district southeast of Mbeya. I was instructed to go there with all speed to assist the DC. Almost immediately, he told me he was off on safari. Nothing I said seemed to impress upon him the importance of his remaining at district headquarters at a time like this. Away he went, and I was left in charge of a district about which I knew nothing other than that it was lousy with Hitlerites. The date was 26th August 1939. On 2nd September 1939, I set up a road-block on the bridge over the trout stream below my office on the pretext of examining licences and checking the movement of food and arms. My real objective was to keep tabs on the Germans beginning to filter through Njombe, heading south for neutral Portuguese East Africa.

Within the hour a car approached at high speed, crashed through the barrier and went careening up the road past the district office. The two African policemen at the bridge blew whistles and fired shots in the air. For my part, I jumped into my box-body Ford V8. After a hectic, brake-screeching, horn-blowing gallop of about five miles, I succeeded in riding the Germans into a ditch.

There were five of them, a tough looking bunch who could well have passed as members of von Lettow Vorbeck's 1915 Schutztruppe. They were more than a little upset at being picked up and quite clearly had every intention of having a go at me. They were talking in German and crowding in on me. However, first they wanted to know if war had been declared.

I feigned surprise at such an absurd question and said I intended to charge them for crashing the road-block. At that they cooled off and agreed to go back with me on condition that their case was heard immediately.

Meanwhile, news of the chase had spread all round the station and by the time we pulled up at the boma, a crowd had assembled, including the entire police force. This was just what I wanted. Without further ado the barrier-crashers were relieved of their vehicle and marched to the courtroom, where they were charged, remanded, and their case put down for hearing when I had more time. Furious and loudly protesting, they were taken away by policemen. We found two rifles and two Luger pistols lashed to the chassis of their car.

That night 10 special constables arrived from Lupa and the next day came a signal containing the fateful code word which meant we were at war. From that moment life became even more hectic. Our first target was the head of the Berlin Lutheran mission at Makambako, 30 miles away. He was a new arrival and bad news in every respect. Within minutes, accompanied by five special constables and five African police, I went roaring off.

At the mission complex we were informed by a local that our man was at home. The house was surrounded and I marched in alone, to be faced immediately by the man himself. I told him war had been declared and that I had come to take him, his radio and his firearms away.

The Reverend went paper white and stared at me for a long moment. Then he walked over to his radio - quite a sophisticated piece of equipment - lifted it above his head and crashed it to the floor. He then attempted to rush to the gun-rack at the far end of the room, but by then I had stuck a pistol into his ribs, and sounded several blasts on my whistle. This brought my security men in at a run. The rest was easy. We collected two others on the "baddies" list and went on from there to make a few more arrests. Thus ended my first day of the Second World War.

During the days and nights that followed we were constantly on the move bringing in wanted Nazis and collecting firearms, radios and fuel dumps. I believe some sort of rebellion had been planned, but so convinced were the Germans that Britain would not declare war on account of Poland that we caught them unprepared and off balance. One resolute German, Hunger, took off for Portuguese territory on horseback. The only way to go after him was also to be mounted, for he was reported to be travelling light and fast. I took a very good horse from a nearby mission. I had the advantage over Hunger, as the Africans along his route soon found out that the Bwana Shauri (District Officer) was on the job, so I was able to get detailed information. By the evening of the second day I was hard on his heels. Early on the morning of the third, Hunger and I met face to face on a mountain path. I don't know who got the bigger fright, but the poor man was worn out and his horse a wreck. He handed over his rifle and meekly rode back with me.

On 9th September, there was an urgent signal from the Rungwe District DC: "Party of five or six Germans hijacked motor-boat from Mwayo at north end of Lake Nyasa stop party believed heading south for Mozambique border stop urgently request attempt be made to intercept them."

Lake Nyasa lies within the Rift at an altitude of about 3,000 feet. The Livingstone Mountains forming the eastern wall rise almost vertically from the lake shore to 9,000 feet. It was this range we would have to cross in order to intercept the Germans.

I took two African police constables and two game scouts armed with .404 elephant control rifles. One of the scouts, Athumani, had been with me on most of my sorties during the first days of the Njombe round-up and was tough and reliable. Saidi, the other, knew every path in the district.

It was a cold night. The stars shone so brilliantly in a blue-black sky that we had no problem in following the narrow path through the forest and moorland above the lake. Towards sunset the following day we reached the lake - a clear 24 hours earlier than my original estimate.

Saidi was allotted the first watch, while the rest of us set about collecting firewood. Almost immediately Saidi came running to announce the approach of a boat from the north. It was about half a mile away, on a course which would take it to within 80 yards of our position.

We agreed that I should challenge the boat, but unless we were fired upon everyone should hold their fire pending further instructions.

As the boat chugged up I stepped out. A large figure hoisted itself upon the roof of the small cabin and shouted: "I'm the Admiral of the Lake Nyasa Navy. Who the bloody hell are you?"

It was Latham Leslie-Moore, the Agricultural Officer from Tukuyu at the north end of the lake, bent on the same quest as ourselves! He had been at sea for four days without sighting the enemy. Latham was holding a bottle of whisky when my men emerged and he took several gulps as he realised how close he had been to getting a broadside.

Clearly the Germans had made a clean getaway, so, after a day's rest, the "Admiral", enveloped in diesel smoke, set course for home, and we returned to Njombe.

CHAPTER 5

NAIROBI TO ADDIS

T HE build-up to the war with Germany and the exciting period immediately following the outbreak of hostilities were over and there was a danger that I would get bogged down in a backwater for the duration. I was becoming restless and frustrated. Somehow I needed to get away, and soon, in order to play an active part in the great struggle ahead. This historic turn of the tide was something in which I felt I must be completely involved. My friend, Robin Johnston, felt exactly as I did and we met to talk things over and make plans.

Just at this time we were experiencing that strange and uncertain period at the beginning of the war which came to be known as the "phony war." Hitler was involved in eliminating Poland and a new battle technique had developed which was a combination of tremendous striking power coupled with rapid movement and complete air superiority. This was the "blitzkrieg", a highly effective and deadly form of warfare, and Hitler's ultimate intentions were crystal clear: namely the defeat of the western powers – France, Belgium, Holland and then, unless the island people capitulated, the complete destruction of Britain. France, crouching behind what she considered her impregnable Maginot Line, was complacent and unprepared for a German onslaught of the blitzkrieg variety. Her army was badly trained and led, morale was at a low ebb and she was demoralised and deeply divided. Indeed there was much that was wrong with the French during this critical period, and our great leaders of the time, in particular Field Marshal Viscount Alanbrook, Churchill, Lord Gort and the commanders of the hastily formed II Corps were all too aware of this.

In short it was high time that Robin Johnston, who had flown Tiger Moths in the Cambridge Air Squadron, and John Millard, who had a vague idea of how to fire an 18-pounder field gun having been with the Cambridge Battery, stepped into the breach and came to the rescue of the great Empire they represented. This was splendid high sounding stuff which to us fully justified the action we were about to take!

Armed with Robin's letter of resignation and a similar one from myself, I visited the PC (Provincial Commissioner) in Mbeya, explained the reason for my visit and asked him to release us. He replied that it was not within his powers to do so.

I said, "What if we resign?" He merely smiled and nodded.

"What would you do if you had my background and if you were my age?"

"Resign," said he!

I handed him the letters, we laughed, shook hands and said goodbye. I walked across to the post office and sent a brief telegram to Robin:

> Have Tendered Our Resignations Stop Meet Me Sparrowfart Monday Morning At Chamala Stop Sell Your Car Keep Mine Stop Bring Shotgun and Fishing Rod Ends

The Asian postmaster said he could not understand this word "sparrowfart". I whispered: "Code, means very early." The postmaster whispered back: "Top secret?" I nodded and winked. He winked back and nodded. He was obviously very chuffed that I had taken him into my confidence over what must be such an important and secret issue!

And so as dawn broke that fine Monday morning, we met at Chamala on the great north road below the Ukinga escarpment, and so too, began a great new chapter in each of our lives. The possibility that either or both of us might not survive never entered our heads. This was the life. This was what we had been longing for, and here we were on our way.

Somewhere near Malangali an old headman I knew stopped the car and begged us to deal with a herd of raiding elephants. His crops were being devastated and nothing he and his people did seemed to help. The herd was there now and by evening he, a poor man, would be ruined and his people would face starvation.

At this moment a young friend and his wife came up on a motor bike and asked to go with us and be in on the hunt. We agreed but insisted that they took up a safe position on a nearby kopje from which they could watch while the "professionals" dealt with this little problem. We had our rifles with us, taking them to Nairobi for storage.

What happened next is best left unsaid. It was clear that these elephants had been continually and ruthlessly harassed by the villagers and were in an unfriendly mood. The next hour was spent running for our lives being severely rumbled by about fifty extremely angry elephants in very hairy country. Anyway, I seem to remember that we knocked off one of the raiders and the rest eventually made off for pastures new. We ourselves, bedraggled and thoroughly shaken by the ordeal, joined our young friends for the picnic lunch and then gladly went on our way. The war and all it had to offer in the way of hazards was peanuts by comparison with what we had just experienced! The old headman was pleased, and even congratulated us on our performance. We must be great and famous hunters. Little did he know!

We had our bed rolls and food, so each evening we slept where we found ourselves on the eight hundred mile journey to Nairobi. We deviated at Makuyuni
to visit the Ngorongoro crater. At that time the crater was undeveloped, there
were no buildings other than what was known as Governor's Camp, a comfortable log cabin situated on the rim of the crater with tremendous views across to
the west and north. We slept on the forest edge, and the next day, using game
trails, we found our way down to the floor of the crater where we spent the day
walking among the vast herds of animals, wildebeest, zebra, buffalo – you name
them – and they merely moved off a matter of a few yards on either side to let
us through. We steered clear of the big buffalo concentrations and had to retreat
rapidly on several occasions from rhino and elephant. Lion were plentiful, but
in the heat of the day they were mostly lying in the shade and hardly raised their
heads as we walked by.

We arrived in Nairobi one morning at about 11.00 am to be met by what
appeared to be the entire Asian and African population running for the outskirts of the city. We stopped a portly gentleman pounding, or perhaps I should
say staggering up the hill towards the secretariat and the Nairobi Club.

"Air raid," he croaked and plunged on.

We paused to have a look, and there, about 4,000 feet up, a lonely Puss Moth
was quietly circling and clearly just checking out its engine, but someone had
started the headlong rush for bush. Panic is always infectious.

Robin and I had about £100 between us, big money in those days, so we
decided that before going off to deal with the enemy, we would have a "money's
no object week". We took splendid rooms at the New Stanley Hotel and hit it
up for the whole week. We pub-crawled, we took out any pretty girls we could
find, played golf, went to night clubs and parties, and pushed the boat out in a
very big way. The great pub song of the day went something like this:

> I don't want to join the army.
> I don't want to go to war.
> I'd rather be in Dar,
> Where all the FANYS are
> And live upon the earnings of an unskilled typist.
>
> I don't want to join the army
> And I don't want to go to war
> And I don't want to marry,
> So I'm going on safari,
> And taking all the FANYS along with me, gorblimey ... etc.

The rest of this ditty is unprintable!

Life was one long party, the town was full of friends mostly already in
uniform and our £100 disappeared rapidly. Came the day when we ran out of

brasso and decided that this was "it" at last. Robin drove me to Command Headquarters to sign on for the duration and he, in turn, would do likewise at Air Force Command. Unfortunately, having said our farewells, Robin then reversed into a telegraph pole which carried the entire communications system to Command HQ. There was an awful crash. Sentries started shouting and all hell was let loose. Clearly we had to make ourselves scarce which we did at high speed. Then with our tails between our legs and empty pockets we cadged a bed and food from friends that night and next day walked to HQ to be on the safe side!*

A Kenya Regiment training course was about to commence. I was given a movement order, a rail warrant to Eldoret and a number tag – 10144 C of E. The C of E was so that they would know what prayer book to use when they buried me!

I found a number of old friends at Eldoret. Some were administrative officers who like myself had resigned, and there were others from several departments in the Service who had been specially released: bank managers, farmers, doctors, company directors, and miners from the Lupa, we were all there and the training under specially seconded non-commissioned officers from various famous regiments was first class.

Half-way through the course it was discovered that headquarters had overlooked the fact that, J. F. Millard No 10144 Lieutenant, Kings African Rifles Reserve of Officers, was actually an officer and gentleman, and should have been on the officers' training course at Nakuru and not with the Kenya Regiment as a private soldier at Eldoret. The Brigadier gave me the option of transferring immediately or put up one pip and live in the officers' quarters, but train with the men. I chose the latter and never regretted it. As for the training programme, I took the rough with the smooth, the only difference was that I was referred to rather sarcastically I thought, as "Sir" by the training staff!

Settler families in the Eldoret district went out of their way to entertain officers and men from the camp. We were under canvas on the racecourse and our off-duty outings to the farms and homes of the local people made a welcome change from the very tough routine in the course. Special friends of mine were the Mervyn Ridleys who had a lovely home at Kapsiliat overlooking the Rift

---

* And so it was that at this point Robin and I parted company and did not meet again till 1944, but kept in touch with occasional letters. Robin was with a Hurricane squadron (73) for the Alam Halfa and El Alamein battles and in at the final defeat of Rommel's Afrika Korps. During this time he was credited with seven enemy aircraft confirmed and seven probables. Later on in the war as Wing Commander his Wing accounted for 53 enemy aircraft and destroyed 97 railway engines and countless barges and other enemy war material. For his outstanding ability as a fighter pilot and leader, Robin was awarded a D.F.C. and Bar in 1942 and the D.S.O. in 1944.

Valley, and my visits there were memorable occasions with trout fishing, polo at Moiben and tremendous rides through the high, heavily forested terrain within the farm boundaries.

Finally the time came for me to appear before the military secretary at Army headquarters for posting. The assistant military secretary on duty was the famous, or perhaps more correctly, the infamous Josslyn Hay 22nd Earl of Erroll, who, soon after my official visit to him was bumped off, giving rise to the best whodunit murder story and the best juicy scandal that Kenya has ever enjoyed: Happy Valley, disgraceful behaviour by the blue-blooded aristocracy, splendid bedroom stuff, and similar goings on.

I found Erroll quite charming and we got on well. He asked what I really wanted to do. I said I was ready for anything but that I rather fancied myself as an officer in an armoured reconnaissance unit. No vacancies, Erroll said, but noted from my file that I had been with the Cambridge battery and obviously knew all about gunnery. I explained that my knowledge of this branch of the service was limited to say the least but that if there was any possibility of a posting to a gunner unit that would be just fine. Erroll mumbled something about the 22nd Mountain Battery fairly recently arrived from Quetta, adding, "Smashing show, very pukka sahibs, professionals, screw guns, Kipling and all that sort of thing, you know."

I couldn't quite twig what all this was about, but the long and short of it was that I found myself at the artillery base on the road to Lake Naivasha.

Just at this time the war with Mussolini's enormous Abyssinian based Colonial Army was hotting up. We of the East African forces were hopelessly outnumbered and outgunned, but South African, Rhodesian and West African units were beginning to trickle in.

Meanwhile the 22nd Battery was well north of the Tana River and had already been in action at Moyale.

For my part I was kept busy at the base, and to the best of my ability I adjusted to the new routine, and in my spare time tried to learn as much as I could about the Battery and to get to know the rank and file of the unit who were still at base. But I was getting impatient and was longing to join up with the Battery in the field. Twice movement orders came through for me but were cancelled. Then, one Sunday (I was duty officer that day), I received a signal requiring Lt Millard to proceed immediately to his unit. I handed over my duties to a fellow officer and in less than a couple of hours was heading for Nairobi railway station to get the first possible train north to the railhead at Thika. There would be road convoys to Garissa and beyond, and with any luck in two or three days I would be on the job at last. There was a strong rumour that the Battery was in action at Afmadu in Jubaland.

By the time I reached the station I was walking on air. At long last, after months of training and periods of extreme boredom I was home and dry, and the war was just up the road. So, imagine my feelings when there on the Railway Transport Officer's blackboard were the fateful words in large letters, "Lt. Millard posting cancelled."

A loaded goods-train with steam up and pointing in the right direction was lying on the double track further down from the main station. I decided that this was no time for fooling around, and my mind was made up. I back-ped-alled out of the station, rang a friend who agreed to pick up my car and then, lumping my bedroll I wandered unobtrusively down the line to chat up the driver of the goods train. Yes, he was scheduled to go to Thika and was merely standing by for clearance. I found a half empty goods wagon and piled in with my kit. Ten minutes later we were clattering northwards. Sometime that night we reached Thika and I thumbed a ride on an army three tonner to Garissa and beyond to an assembly area in the dreary inhospitable scrub-land north of the Tana river.

Fortunately, at Garissa itself, I had time to pick up three days rations from a depot on the river. Rations in those days were pretty basic and my allocation was three tins of peaches, three tins of bully, one of butter, some tea, sugar, a tin of jam, a few pounds of biscuits, four inches by four inches, hard, dry and stale. I had a canvas water bag with my kit and had also taken the precaution to fill it.

Years later for the D-day landings on the Normandy beaches there was hot soup whenever we wanted it, eggs, bacon, marmalade and toast for breakfast and self-heating tins of cocoa. By then things had changed somewhat!

I must have spent a full day and a night on the roadside. The heat was intense and there was no shade whatsoever. However, the next morning I stopped a camouflaged staff car; this was Col. Fisher of the Gold Coast Regiment and he was heading for Afmadu where he said there was a bit of a punch-up going on.

"Yes, the 22nd Mountain Battery was there and in action" and he would give me a lift. I must have dozed off and woke up with a bump. The car had stopped and Col. Fisher said: "Wake up old mate. This is the end of the road, it's 3 a.m. and that bloody awful noise over there must be Bulgy's cannons, so just follow the flashes and the bangs. Good hunting."

It was a pitch black night, overhead droned a solitary Italian Caproni bomber. Flares were dropped some way off and there were a few heavy thumps. Somewhere a Bren gun opened up and further to the west the sound of light automatic and rifle fire. This was the first time in my life that I had heard a shot fired in anger and the atmosphere of this place and the scene generally made an unforgettable impression upon me.

There were voices speaking quietly in Urdu and I became aware of men about me sleeping and resting on blankets and ground sheets. Everyone except me seemed to be completely relaxed. I asked to see the Battery Commander and was guided to the gun position to meet Capt Leach known to everyone as Bulgy.

Bulgy became one of my greatest friends and ours is a friendship which has run for fifty years and is stronger now than ever, but that night he was not over pleased to see me. So far as he was concerned I was a civilian soldier, untrained, and lacking in experience and probably a complete passenger.

Had I not received his signal cancelling my posting?

No answer.

"Is that your bedroll?"

"It is sir."

"Is that a shot-gun and a fishing rod in it?"

"It is sir."

The look on his face amused me. The fact that I had chosen to go to war with a sporting gun in my bedroll clearly put me into a slightly different category. The great man actually smiled and told me to go off and get myself a whisky under that bush over there. With the first streak of light the Battery "stood to" and so dawned my first day of actual warfare in World War II.

Italian resistance at Afmadu began to crack up after a few days, and in the end our shelling, coupled with bombing by South African fighter bombers and pressure from our ground troops was too much for the Italians and they began to move back towards the Juba River where a very substantial enemy force under General de Simeone was grouped, mainly on the east bank of the river. A few prisoners were taken at Afmadu and a certain amount of equipment and ammunition but the main force got clear and made for the Juba.

Water for our own use was becoming a real problem. For some time we had relied upon the deep wells at Belas Gugani. The water at this oasis was crystal clear, sweet and cold, and was much enjoyed by one and all till the level fell and we discovered a very ripe corpse in the bottom of the main well! The Juba river has its source in the highlands of Abyssinia, runs fast, cool and wide, and we looked forward in no uncertain manner to reaching the river. It would be a real luxury to wash off the dust and again drink one's fill.

As was to be expected the bridge at Gilib had been destroyed and we were faced by a formidable force consisting of six brigades of regular troops with armoured cars and artillery and six groups of irregulars. The Italians were covering all likely crossing points and were established in strength at Gilib and Jumbo.

Our Gold Coast Brigade opened the offensive and had a rough time with many killed and wounded in the first action, but they did succeed in taking Bulo Erillo, and the South African Brigade under Brigadier Pienaar, after some heavy fighting, crossed the river in canvas boats and established themselves in strength on the far bank. As for the 22nd Mountain Battery, we were in action most days eliminating well dug-in machine gun positions and searching out enemy strong points and concentrations.

Our Marmon Harrington armoured car, which I usually drove, was used to locate targets in the thick bush and to direct fire from the Battery which was positioned well back from the river itself. On one occasion we in the armoured car were cut off and surrounded by enemy riflemen. Fortunately one of our infantry patrols was within wireless contact and came to our rescue, but for a short while our situation was a bit tricky. For me this was a new experience, because it was the first time I had been the specific target of enemy fire, and frankly, I was more than pleased when we got back home. Home in the shape of a hot, dusty, flyblown gun position was never sweeter!

The crossing of the Juba and the advance towards Kismayu and Mogadishu was achieved by a hair-raising left hook through most awful dense bush. Somehow the pathfinders seemed to lose direction and for three days we crawled forward, bashing and hacking a route through the riverine jungle. The dust, heat and general discomfort of that expedition is something I shall not forget. I shall always remember too the relief when at last one day, just before dawn, we emerged suddenly from the wall of scrub and forest to open desert and a star spangled sky.

We had by-passed most of the enemy positions and intercepted a large enemy column retreating northwards. There was a great old haul of prisoners-of-war, vehicles, guns, equipment and ammunition. Soon, we of the East African Brigade, were joined by the South Africans and the Nigerians and we swept on to Brava, Merca, and Mogadishu on the coast. During the advance enemy strong points and rear-guard positions were bombarded from the sea by H.M.S. Shropshire. Now at last we had the initiative and the Italian army ahead of us was very definitely on the run. 380,000 gallons of petrol were abandoned by the Italians in Mogadishu and this enabled us, after a short rest by the seaside, to continue the chase. We were now in full cry via Jijjiga, Harar, the Awash river, and on to Addis Ababa the capital of Abyssinia.

Somewhere in Italian Somaliland, just north of Merca it must have been, Bulgy, my Battery Commander, received a signal from General Mitchell the Senior Political Officer with the advancing army. The signal required Lt. Millard to report to him for political duties in the newly occupied Italian colony. Bulgy called me in, showed me the signal and asked:

"What do you wish to do about this?"

I replied that I had joined up to fight and if required to do so right up to the bitter end and had no wish whatsoever to get bogged down administering a vast tract of ex-Italian real estate for the rest of the war. Bulgy then asked:

"Have we seen this signal?"

I said "Of course not."

"Then why the hell are you hanging round here, we march in 20 minutes. Move!"

There were hold-ups, rear-guard encounters and a few set piece battles en route, then at last on a cold grey evening, the long wooded ridge of the Ntoto appeared on the horizon and, straggling beneath it lay Addis Ababa. The small column roared into the city. We had covered over 1,500 miles since leaving Kenya's northern border. The date was 6th April 1941.

* * * *

Addis Ababa city had not been bombed, nor was there any street fighting. Most of the Italian troops had moved out to take up defensive positions on the main roads leading south to the lakes area, north to Dese, and southwest to Jima. They had abandoned quantities of material and most of their mules and horses.

The 22nd Mountain Battery was quartered at the military aerodrome, which was in a mess. On and around the main runway lay 32 wrecked aircraft, shot up and bombed by the SAAF. Meanwhile shops reopened and good food became available in restaurants and hotels. The market, the city's hub, also reopened and brothels (one of them a smart joint) were back in business almost before we arrived.

Three days later I was seconded to the senior political officer's staff at the British legation. My new CO, Brig Maurice Lush, was an energetic leader with whom I got on well from the start. His team consisted mainly of DCs and political officers from the Sudan. Our job was to restore the city's infrastructure in the areas of power, lighting, telephones, sewerage and water, and to re-establish law and order, recruit policemen, draft, print and post proclamations, release political prisoners and make contact with prominent Ethiopians. There was plenty to do.

Soon after settling into my quarters in the British legation, which had been without a minister since the occupation of Ethiopia by the Italians in 1935, Brig Lush authorised me to collect for myself a couple of horses from the classy cavalry chargers abandoned by the Italians. I was also instructed to select the best horses I could find, and fill the 12 loose boxes in the legation stables. It was on this sortie that I found Addis, a half-Arab half country-bred grey, the best horse I have ever had, and a bay polo pony.

The Italian civilians appeared to be pleased to see us, but the Ethiopians initially, before they fully realised they were free of their Fascist oppressors, were subdued and rather uncooperative. Before long, however, they found out that

Map 1: Showing the British invasion routes of Italian-held Abyssinia. The 4th and 5th Indian Divisions came from the Sudan in the north. The 11th and 12th African Divisions came from Kenya in the south. J. M. was initially with the 11th African Division.

the Emperor had re-entered Ethiopia from the Sudan and was battling towards
the capital. Then there was an upsurge of nationalism, and dumps of Italian
small arms were located and looted, and in the countryside around Addis
Ababa, the tribesmen, now armed but leaderless and without direction, were
soon on the rampage. Old scores were settled and collaborators massacred. The
task of sorting out the mayhem fell on my shoulders. I spent several rather dangerous days intervening in factional fighting, convening peace meetings, banging heads together and spreading the gospel of peace and calm pending the
arrival of the Lion of Judah.

On 26th April 1941, I became involved in the patriot war against the Italians.
What follows is not an account of the Ethiopian campaign, but just that very
small part of it in which I was personally involved. I kept a diary which was
written during the long evenings on the march when, in the absence of anyone of my own sort to talk to, I would jot down the events of the day and my
future plans. My light was usually a candle perched on a pack saddle, or just the
camp fire.

Long before Italy came into the war, a plan had been worked out to use patri-
otic guerillas in Ethiopia and in the event, they proved to be one of our most
deadly weapons. In 1941, the Ethiopians after five years of merciless persecution
and suppression following the war with Italy, seemed cowed and subdued. Their
leaders had been massacred by the Italians. The fighting men were disarmed
after they had been bombed, shelled, gassed and broken. Many scattered into
the hills and forests, where they settled down to shoulder the yoke of defeat
rather than lose all in a futile struggle against enormous odds.

A few resolute men and women refused to accept defeat and continued to
fight, raid, ambush and snipe. They were hunted like wild beasts throughout
the land, but still continued to resist.

The tribesmen of the mountainous northwestern border area never surrendered and when Italy joined the Axis, the patriot leaders in the provinces of
Gojam, Welega and Begemder were invited by the British to rebel. They were
offered arms and ammunition and the promise of freedom. The move was made
by 101 Mission under Col Sandford.[*] With his small band of British officers and

---

* The Abyssinians called him Fiki Mariam (Love of Mary) Brig. Sandford's contribution in the
campaign against the Italians in Abyssinia was outstanding. His knowledge of the country and
its people and the support he gave to the regular forces and those involved in the Patriot upris-
ings behind the enemy lines will never be forgotten. Dan Sandford was born in 1892, educated at St Paul's School and at the Royal Military Academy at Woolwich. He was in the
Sudan Administration for a period, and then served with distinction as a gunner in World War
I, receiving a D.S.O. and the French Legion d' Honeur. After that he farmed in Abyssinia and
was for a while British Consul in Addis Ababa. In 1935 when the Italians invaded Abyssinia,
Col. Sandford moved back to England but returned again in 1940 to head the so-called 101
mission. From his base on the Sudan Abyssinian border he built up a large patriot army and

NCOs he smuggled weapons and ammunition across the remote Italian held border between Sudan and Ethiopia.

Early in February 1941, East, West and South African columns, began advancing at a speed unheard of in the history of war across the deserts of northern Kenya and up through Italian Somaliland to Addis Ababa. Simultaneously, the northern forces under Gen Sir William Platt were blasting their way through the Italian northern and eastern defences, forcing the enemy to fall back on the Gondar and Amba Alagi areas. By the time of our arrival in Addis Ababa, 101 Mission had not yet reached the capital, but news of an impending British invasion and the return of the Emperor was already known to all, and many patriots armed themselves from hidden caches and rode off to join other groups of fighters.

Ethiopian refugees who had fled as a result of the 1935 Italian invasion had been grouped along the Kenya border as a partly-trained irregular force led by British officers. These irregulars began to infiltrate into Ethiopia at the same time as the regular offensive began.

We, the vanguard of the advancing columns from the south, had outstripped the carefully planned scheme to stir up resistance from within and our small force now in the heart of Ethiopia was faced with a partly mauled, yet very substantial Italian army.

* * * *

Appreciating this, the Italians endeavoured to split up our regular formations by deploying their strength in a number of carefully selected defensive positions. To counter the manoeuvre we used Ethiopian patriots, but it soon became apparent that they were not up to the job. The Ethiopians in and around Addis Ababa being the most influenced by the Italians could not be fully relied on to cooperate, while those in the countryside lacked organisation and arms. So, guerilla leaders, as we were called, were selected and sent to contact patriot formations and create centres of resistance behind the enemy lines.

---

then, accompanied by the Emperor Haile Selassie, battled his way through to the capital arriving there soon after it had been liberated by the Allied columns from the south. Eventually Sandford, now a Brigadier, became military adviser to the Emperor and assumed, inter alia, responsibility for the organisation and distribution of formations, officered mostly by British personnel operating with Abyssinian Patriots in enemy occupied territory. It was Sandford who gave me his wholehearted support when I raised a Patriot force to deal with the enemy strongholds at Endeber, Muggo and Hosaena on the Guraghi plateau and later commissioned me to deal with the Wajarat/Azebo Galla uprising in Tigre province. Dan Sandford died aged 89 in 1970.

A selection of my Patriots who were members of Millard's Scouts or Milcol.

One of my Patriot leaders in the uniform of an Italian Colonel who had been killed in one of our battles.

The enemy was playing the same game, arming and bribing large numbers of irregulars and recruiting spies and fifth columnists. Clashes between patriots and pro-Italian guerillas were not infrequent. Many of those on the Italian payroll gradually joined us, but in the early days true patriots were few and far between.

We guerilla leaders were given a free hand and our methods varied considerably. I preferred to work on my own. I took no wireless, travelled light, and kept well away from our regular army formations. However, others operated in close contact with our troops, scouting and covering the flanks of the advancing columns and harassing enemy patrols and outlying positions. Thus the patriots made life for the Italians very stressful.

However far they were from roads, however deep their defences, the Italians could never feel safe. The patriots showed no mercy. The Italians knew this and whenever we cut off their formations they would fight like tigers.

Our casualties were often heavy, because the patriots were undisciplined and inadequately trained. But they were born fighters, capable of effectively using every scrap of cover and moving silently and swiftly across any type of country.

I had 2 2 patriot leaders, who usually lived with me when not actually fighting, and this enabled me to keep in constant touch with them. Each had his own band of followers, who, although reluctant to take orders from me, carried out the orders of their leaders promptly and to the letter.

Initially I carried no money. Coin is bulky and heavy and I was anxious to employ only true patriots. At one time my force was about 3,0 0 0 strong, but that was while booty was plentiful. Later, as the sources of loot dried up, a proper pay system was introduced. By then, my strength was about 1,3 0 0, in addition to a host of camp followers, who would swoop in like vultures after every

victory. It was these uncontrollable scavengers who gave most patriot formations a bad name wherever they came into contact with regular troops. And yet,
the fighters themselves were also to blame, for in the heat of battle it was impossible to prevent them from behaving likewise.

We were fighting mostly in the highlands, sometimes at an altitude of 10,000
ft or more. The cold was intense and continual rain and mist added to the general discomfort. Food was a problem, as the peasants invariably moved with
their flocks away from our axis of advance, leaving nothing behind.

The Ethiopian patriot's hard life was reflected in his appearance. He wore a
tunic and jodhpurs, his feet bare or in sandals, and his bearded face crowned by
a mop of fuzzy black hair. Sometimes, as a gesture to dressiness, he would sport
a topee perched precariously on the crown of his head or crammed down as far
as the ears. He always wore a decorated leather bandoleer with a pistol or sword
attached and carried a small haversack for the parched corn and dried meat he
could subsist on for days. His rifle never left his hand and it was caressed and
cherished as no woman ever was. His frame and everything on it might be caked
with dirt, but his Mauser and its cartridges were kept spotlessly clean. Many of
the fighters were mounted on horses or mules. An important personage would
ride accompanied by a medley of slaves and retainers trotting along beside their
lord, ready to hold his mount should he wish to get down, to prepare his camp
and a meal at the end of a march and to protect him at night. Gun bearers aged
13 or 14 were common; they often took part in battle with visible enthusiasm.

Tactics were entirely guerilla, usually simply hit-and-run. Speed and mobili-
ty were their primary characteristics. When the enemy was in a fixed position,
we would move up under cover of darkness and, provided it was not raining too
hard and not too cold, the attack would go through at daybreak. But sometimes
they would fight even under the most terrible weather conditions. One could
not predict how they would react to any given situation. Most effective was the
headlong rush with bombamanoes. These little Italian grenades went off on
impact with a colossal flash and bang. The patriots would hurl them while running at top speed, compelling the enemy to keep his head down while the position was overrun. There was no organised system of sentries or protection by
night, yet reports about enemy patrols or movements never took long to reach
me. In any semi-permanent position, watchmen were placed on high points and
in outlying villages. The force was usually distributed among a number of villages, and the peasants found it paid to cooperate.

What follows is made up with extracts and paraphrases from the diary I wrote
on the spot during the weeks and months spent with my patriot force on the
Italian held Guraghi Plateau.

26th April 1941: The 3rd Nigerians pushing westwards down the Addis Ababa-
Jima road on the tail of the retreating Italians have bumped into the enemy, very

Patriot assembly after an attack when, joyful and disorganised, all recount their version of events. Note the Italian prisoners bottom right and the simple expedient of removing their trousers to discourage escape.

nicely installed astride the road on the far side of the Omo River. The escarpment beyond the blown road-bridge is a formidable natural barrier in itself and this is held in depth by the enemy as far back as Abalti village on the high ground overlooking the bridge. My immediate task is to investigate reports of inter-tribal fighting and considerable unrest among the locals. Furthermore, it seems that the Italian Resident, an unknown number of troops and a small community of civilians and missionaries have been surrounded and cut off by Ethiopian riflemen at Indibir, 30 miles west of the Nigerian position. An Italian major succeeded in escaping from the fort at Indibir and has given himself up; he has begged us to accept the Italian surrender and rescue the garrison who are in danger of massacre. To get to Indibir, I follow a track which takes me through our positions, then across the Webe river and 25 miles on due west. The Nigerians have given me two sections of Bren gunners to give me a sporting chance in the enemy held area beyond the Webe.

Same Night: The crossing of the river in the dim light of a stormy dusk was no easy matter. The Webe runs swift, yellow and broad, and today it was swollen by rain and in parts almost waist deep. However, somehow we managed to get the vehicles across without mishap. Rumour had it that the track ahead was mined, so for my own peace of mind I travelled where possible across country, no easy task in the fading light. During the night, just as we were at last nearing the summit of the escarpment, an ugly storm which had been brewing all afternoon burst upon us. We churned onwards for a while with no lights, our progress assisted every so often by dazzling flashes of lightning, which showed up the rocks, glistening wet, through a curtain of cold lashing rain, and the track, now a torrent, zigzagging seemingly forever upwards. Now as I write by torchlight, we are well and truly bogged and we crouch under the vehicles with tarpaulins pegged down for shelter from the lashing rain. Fortunately, we are still covered by our positions on the far side of the gorge, and in the event of an attack we can, at a pinch, fight our way back to the river.

* * * *

27th April: Daybreak and bitterly cold, but the rain over and every prospect of a perfect morning, the valleys below filled with swirling mist and the hills clean washed and clear-cut against the dawn sky. Horses have been raised in a nearby village and one of Garusa's representatives has gone forward with the local headman to contact the tribal leaders ahead, and to tell them to hold everything until my arrival.

About noon we came in sight of Indibir town and the mud brick fort, the Italian flag still floating above it, occupying a central position on high ground, and beyond that, in a warm sheltered valley, the town and a large mission complex.

The tribal leaders met me as previously arranged in some dead ground about 2,000 yards from the village. I explained that it was my intention to take the surrender from the garrison and that later in the day the Italians would be evacuated. I requested that they should withdraw their armed men at least three miles while negotiations were in progress and promised that I myself would stay on afterwards. We would then discuss the distribution of the captured weapons, ammunition and military materials taken over and the future of the armed Ethiopians in the neighbourhood – more especially themselves and their men who were directly concerned with the surrender of Indibir. They agreed to cooperate and galloped off to square their men.

Meanwhile, my tame Italian major was sent forward with an escort to inform the garrison that I was on my way and to hold their fire. The Italian army personnel and the civilians who had been pinned down inside the fort were in pretty poor shape and were so anxious to get away that all arms and ammunition except the automatic weapons on the four corners of the fort had been collected and listed ready to hand over. The Italian flag was hauled down and the West African Bren gunners manned the corner positions on the fort. At this very moment, over the hill came Col Marshall with the transport lorries and covering force. They made a spectacular sweep round the parade ground and drew up in line in front of the fort. The Italian civilians were bundled into 30 empty lorries and half an hour later they were on their way.

28th April: The meeting today with the chiefs and noblemen from the surrounding country went well. I sat at a table in the big square in the centre of the mission buildings and they would ride up on their horses and mules, dismount at the gate and walk forward slowly. When they were within 15 paces they would bow low and then advance with hand outstretched.

It seems that the main reason for the inter-tribal fighting and unrest has been lack of leadership and organisation. Partly this and partly the fact that they are out of touch with any area or centre where resistance by patriots is being fostered and supervised: the result is that numerous small parties of armed men, or Shifta as these bandits are called, are at large, filling in their time raiding, robbing and settling old feuds and generally creating a situation which verges on a reign of terror. They begged me to do something about it and assured me that, given the lead and definite orders by the British, all concerned in the recent troubles would be prepared to bury the hatchet and combine against the common enemy.

I realise that for the present I am a political officer and, as such, I am also painfully aware of the fact that maybe I should not meddle unduly in military affairs. On the other hand, this is what I have been dreaming of since the war started, the opportunity of striking out on my own with an irregular fighting force, free to roam and fight, unhampered by the red tape and restrictions, and responsible to myself alone for my mistakes. Well, right or wrong, I have decided to put this bunch to the test and have told them to noise it abroad far and wide that any armed man who is prepared to fight Italians and prove himself a true patriot should join me here tomorrow morning. I am informed that a substantial Italian force is holding a fortified position astride the road on Muggo Mountain ahead of us.

29th April – Geto Village: Early this morning the tribesmen began to assemble at Indibir. By noon a huge, ruffianly-looking mob were concentrated in the neighbourhood of my headquarters. Fitewerari Mekonen, who had accompanied me from Ras Garusa Duki's base at Walso, acted as my adjutant and, assisted by him and my interpreter, Engide Work Gebre Mariam, we selected likely looking types and equipped them with rifles and ammunition from the captured Italian stock. A small force was left to man the Indibir fort and to guard my base and then at about 1600 hours we galloped out of Indibir in high spirits, about 500 mounted riflemen, myself in the lead. As we went splashing full tilt through the stream below the town I wished that I had a hunting horn to blow: instead I yelled "tally-ho, tally-ho," but was not understood.

It is a most lovely ride from Indibir. The path climbs steadily through scattered cedar and podocarpus forest, views to the east over the valley of the upper Omo were beautiful and, as we climbed, I was able to get glimpses of high windswept moors ahead, ugly country to fight in if the Italians have artillery. Frequently it was necessary to dismount and lead the animals, and gradually our little force began to tail out into a broken straggling line two or three miles in

length. Every so often individuals or small parties of tribesmen would gallop up
on mules or flashy ponies, and beg to be permitted to join us. Many of these
were armed only with great curved swords and circular shields beautifully
embossed with copper or bronze. I hadn't the heart to turn them away; at least
they added colour to our cavalcade, and later they might win their weapons.
Darkness was upon us and it was cold when we reached Geto village, our destination for the night, and I accepted the invitation of a local headman, Basha
Gobana Jabi, to feed and sleep in his house. The men were absorbed in the surrounding villages, beasts were killed, the meat to be eaten raw as is the custom
when fighting.

Gobana's wife produced a magnificent meal of chicken roasted in butter and
spice, followed by sweet thick coffee, and now I am sitting over a fire of glowing cow dung, while old Katungi, who shares the hut with me and Engide Work
Gabre Mariam, lays out my valise for the night. Rushes have been spread on the
floor and over them a large red and blue rug. It is cold at this altitude and I am
glad to be indoors in spite of the fug and the smoke which makes my eyes run.

30th April: Late afternoon, and rain drumming down ceaselessly. My tent is
tucked away among a clump of bamboos. Some of the Guraghe warriors are
bivouacking nearby, while others take shelter in a deserted village. We are right
up close under Muggo Hill, but this little valley is hidden, and provided we lie
low we are fairly safe for the time being. As we were about to set off, a local
horseman galloped up waving his rifle above his head and shouting that a strong
Italian patrol, on foot but with machine-guns, was just ahead.

I gave Mekonen all our light machine-guns and a good deal of the precious
ammunition and he galloped off with about 100 of our best men. I moved forward and took up a position with the remaining riflemen to cover him.
Somehow or other the Italian patrol got wind of our approach and although we
did all in our power to cut them off, they succeeded in making the safety of the
perimeter defences of Muggo without apparent loss to themselves. However,
this is a moral victory for us and our tails are up.

Later in the day, we assembled in the valley where we are now. I called for
volunteers to accompany me on a reconnaissance of the enemy position. A
grand man, Fitewerari Rashid, with a great reputation for horsemanship and
bravery, came forward and, together with Engide Work, a horse-holder and a
few others, we set off. It was drizzling, and banks of cloud were driving at
ground level across the plain. As we closed in, all except the Fitewerari, Engide
Work and the horse-holder dropped out. Finally, Rashid stopped in a grove of
trees and insisted that I should disguise myself as an Ethiopian. We must have
looked like a harmless party of travellers as we rode forward, myself decked in
Rashid's coloured turban and Engide Work's cloak, doubled up against the driving rain, heads down.

In this way we reached the lee of the little hill on the edge of the enemy defences. Then, leaving the horses, we crawled forward to a deserted hut on the skyline. I pulled out my compass, field glasses and notebook, and very cautiously we edged forward to a gap in the turf wall. From this point the whole length of Muggo was laid out before us like a sand-table model, and it was simple enough to sketch a fairly accurate panorama of the layout, as the gun positions, tank traps, machine-gun nests and road demolitions were very close and clearly visible despite the rain.

The Italians were worried. Work parties were hastily repairing the wire. Ammunition was being rushed to the guns, and everywhere there was ant-like activity. Any moment we expected our position to be spotted, so I sketched on with the utmost speed. Then, half crawling, half running, we dashed back to the horses through a blinding flurry of rain and galloped back to our hide. A runner has just left for the Nigerians with my report and the panorama sketch.

6th May: Much has happened since my last diary entry. My action seems to have aroused a good deal of interest in the capital. I was immediately withdrawn from political duties and my orders now are to organise and equip a patriot force strong enough to cope with the enemy on the Guraghe plateau and the access road via Hosaena to the Omo River. It is considered desirable that the Italians should not realise that there is a British officer behind the revolt and for this reason I am to operate alone; but arms, ammunition and money are at my disposal. Brig Sandford is my contact in Addis Ababa and I could not wish for a finer commander. He has lived in Ethiopia for many years (before the 1935 Italian invasion) and knows the people and the personalities. My patriot force is to be known as Millard's Scouts (subsequently Milcol) and I am to be given full recognition by departments in Addis and by formations in the field.

This is good news, but already my problems are starting, for many of the men I originally armed have deserted with their weapons. However, those who remain can be relied upon, and I have brought with me about 500,000 rounds of ammunition, 500 rifles, several light machine-guns, and one anti-tank weapon.

I have written to Brig Sandford asking him for further reinforcements in the form of Amhara patriots. Sandford's reaction was immediate and a copy of his letter to G. Branch of Eleven Division is included below.

> Headquarters, 11 Division, G Branch.
> 1. I have had a talk with Capt. Millard and I agree with him that (additionally to the ammunition sent out to Shaka Bakala yesterday) he should take out tomorrow 100,000 S.A.A. and 10,000 Alpini Ammunition as a reserve under his own thumb at Endeber.
>
> 2. He has no M.T. of his own and it seems to me essential he should have at least

one lorry to keep with him for supply and other purposes.

3.   He should receive a reinforcement from Shaka Bakala of 500 men within 2 days; and I am hoping by the 20th inst. to stiffen the irregular force under his control by another 1000 men at least.

4.   The food question out there seems acute. I am studying this and will consult with Emperor. Meanwhile I suggest Capt. Millard be issued with $10,000 as a temporary measure for purchase of supplies.

5.   Could it be arranged that – until the position is straighter – Capt. Millard should be loaned a couple of sections of Nigerians to guard his S.A.A. and cash at Endeber.

14.5.41   (signed) D.A. Sandford
                 Brigadier

7th May: Evening: In my life I do not remember having felt so desperately lonely. It has been a bad day. My total strength at the moment is only about 800 rifles and this morning most of them turned up. Splitting them up into three groups, I took one lot, Mekonen another and Fitewerari Rashid the third. My intention was put the Muggo defences to the test, and at the same time, give my lads a chance of burning up some of their ammunition.

Fitewerari Rashid was the first to open up and for a while he appeared to be doing well. Then all of a sudden the cloud lifted and the enemy were able to get going with mortars and artillery. Fortunately the ground was broken and we all lay up praying for the cloud to settle once more. At about 1400 we were able to move forward again and had quite a nice little action in which Rashid again got in and wiped up a machine-gun. Towards sunset we withdrew through rain and cloud, tired out and taking things rather casually, a mistake for which we paid heavily, as just before dusk the sky cleared and we were caught out on the open plain at point-blank range from the Muggo batteries.

There was absolutely no cover and there was nothing for it but to work our way back through heavy shellfire to a valley below my camp. I was cold, wet through and thoroughly frightened. We have had a number of casualties, but Mekonen has not yet come in to report. Just at the moment the whole thing seems utterly futile. I realise that our job is to pin down and harass the enemy, but this shelling gets one down and we have no means of retaliating. I have begged Division to arrange for aircraft to bomb the Muggo garrison, and was promised that this would be done forthwith, but it is five days since I left Addis Ababa and there has been no sign of a bomber yet.

In my party this morning were two girls, one about 18 and the other a good deal older. These girl patriots are not uncommon and many of them are very stout fellows indeed. The elder of the two today was doing some pretty shooting and was quite unperturbed when we began to cop it.

8th May: The day started badly, as we found that some of the riflemen had deserted as a result of yesterday's shelling, and I spent the morning disarming doubtful gentry and making a register of picked men. Later we unpacked the brand new Boyes rifle. It is most valuable for knocking out lorries, light tanks, machine-gun nests and the like.

9th May: Evening: a most glorious sunset, marred only by the shelling from the Muggo batteries. Nine deserters in today. The Italians had told them that the Emperor was dead and that the British had been driven out of Ethiopia. From them I was able to get what I consider is probably the most accurate information yet regarding the Italian strength – 1,200 European soldiers, 600 native troops (mixed Eritreans and Ethiopians), 28 guns, four of them big fellows, probably about 105mm, and about 60 machine-guns; also eight lorries and two tanks.

10th May: Evening: I am just about all in after a hell of a day. Last night wasn't too good to start with. It was cold, the floor was hard as iron, and fleas the size of rabbits fairly mobbed me. Added to this, my patriots took several prisoners in a raid and were celebrating in the approved manner by popping off their muskets all through the night.

This morning, after endless discussions with my leaders, I eventually set off on a reconnaissance. I succeeded in getting up to within 500 yards of an enemy battery and was about to open fire with a machine-gun and the Boyes rifle, when I noticed the whole hillside behind me was black with people, mostly camp followers who had come up to see the fun. Through my glasses I could see the enemy gun detachments taking post and obviously preparing to fire over open sights at point-blank range. I had a hectic 60 seconds dispersing the mob amid bursting shrapnel and taking cover myself. Back to my village for a bite of food and then a long ride on to my new base at Kabaku village.

News came through overnight that just after my departure the Italians attacked my small garrison with a considerable force. The camp was completely overrun and then set on fire. All my kit is lost. We had two killed and seven wounded, against approximately 12 Italians killed. So that is that, and here I am without food or dry clothing, no razor, no toothbrush, nothing. Outside it is raining and my little tent is on the lost property list. Gone is my camera, my shot-gun, and all my reading matter, not to mention clothing other than that in which I stand. Most of the ammunition was salved, which is something, but about 30 shells for the anti-tank rifle, the big case and all its equipment has gone. I have absolutely no rations left, so will have to live on milk and meat till some rations come through. I am almost completely done in and sit huddled over the fireplace of a large hut, drying my damp clothes, while Katungi boils some milk for my supper.

11th May: Night: camp was moved on the advice of my leaders, who are convinced that the Italians are determined to get me. Indeed, they follow all my movements with uncanny accuracy, which no doubt indicates that we have informers in our ranks. Today's big excitement was the arrival of a bomber, obviously looking for Muggo, which by the worst of bad luck was under cloud at the time. I rushed out and wagged an Ethiopian flag at them, but they missed my camp.

I am at Kabaku village now overlooking the plateau, with here and there a small silver-grey tarn and duck and geese flighting against a lead-coloured sky. There is something very like the west of Ireland about this locality. The grass is a brilliant green and, wherever there is a village, the country for a mile or two around is broken up by Irish-type turf walls and banks. The grass is close-cropped by horses and cattle, and one expects any moment to come on a little whitewashed cottage, the inevitable geese and pigs, and blue smoke rising from the chimney. Instead, there are the neat Guraghe rondavels, exceedingly well thatched over bamboo walls. It is always cold at this altitude, so there are no windows. Smoke from the hearth finds its way out as best it can, and as a rule it is difficult to see across the room. Cow dung and dry bamboo are the main fuels. Nowadays I sleep like a babe in the company of smoke, cows, mules, horses, goats and human bodies. How I long for a toothbrush and a shave.

15th May: As I write I am in a rondavel in the legation compound, which serves as my base on my rare visits to the capital. I got in late this evening and return tomorrow loaded up with small arms ammunition, several light machine-guns, basic medical supplies, 15,000 Maria Theresa dollars, 24 pack saddles and, very important, 200 specially ordered tin hats as a morale booster for the elite among my Schutztruppe.

16th May: Took my pony "Addis" out early this a.m. for a work-out on the legation polo ground and ended up reining back and doing figures of eight. I became aware of someone watching who, as I came in, said in a rather imperious voice, "Make that horse passage."

I replied that the horse had done enough and that I was taking him back to the stables. Then he said, still rather arrogantly, "Do you know who I am?" (we were not in uniform). I replied that I thought he might be General Mitchell. There was a longish silence, himself looking rather red in the face, and then he relented and redeemed himself in my estimation by saying, "Let's have dinner together tonight."

But this was clearly not my day, for later on, while at the ordnance depot collecting my pack saddles and precious tin hats, a lieutenant-colonel marched in. I saluted smartly, but he ignored me, walked over to my pile of hats and said he wanted tin hats and was taking these. I protested, and he told me to shut up and ordered that they be loaded into his truck. I asked the NCO on duty who this extraordinary fellow was, and he replied, "Wot 'im sir? That's Wingate, a very discourteous something something officer, no gentleman, as one might say."

Next I went to the SAAF headquarters to explain to the CO that the hill they had been bombing on my behalf was not Muggo. He apologised and said he himself would carry out the next strike and would I come with him and direct him to the target. This seemed to be an excellent plan, and he immediately gave orders that a Glen Martin fighter-bomber should be refuelled and armed. I was eased into the observer position in the armour-plated, bullet-proof glass nose of the aircraft, and within half an hour we were slap over target. We made one or two runs down the length of the hill, while one of the air crew took photographs and bailed out propaganda pamphlets encouraging the colonial troops to desert. Then, through the intercom I heard: "Hold tight, skipper, here we go." We hurtled downwards. I could hear the guns hammering away on either side of me and see the tracer coming up as if to strike and then seemingly to glide away behind us. The terrific speed, the clatter of the guns and the roar of the engines were exhilarating. I was really quite sorry, in spite of being scared stiff, when finally we climbed away and headed for Addis Ababa.

22nd May: On the march again, this time at the head of a new and reorganised force, stiffened by 800 wild men from near Addis Ababa. They arrived yesterday at my Indibir base in 30 truckloads. After the endless business of issuing ammunition and organising them into fighting groups under their various leaders, we eventually got away at about 1630.

News came through by runner just before we left that the Muggo garrison had been evacuated. Four big guns (probably about 105mm) were taken by my men, also much ammunition, but the bulk of the force got away under the cover of darkness and rain. In view of this I have been travelling with all speed. We made camp last night at 2300 after a hell of a trip through mist and drizzle in pitch blackness. The riding mules were magnificent, but the packs fell behind and I slept rolled up in my greatcoat on the floor of an Ethiopian hut.

23rd May: Woke feeling blowzy, flea-bitten and covered in lice. Pack mules not yet arrived, so breakfasted on hot milk and roast chicken. Much trouble over looting, and I had to more or less read the riot act. One of the new leaders from Addis Ababa started to argue the toss and a big crowd collected round us to see who would win. Rightly or wrongly I felt that at this moment my leadership and the whole future of the rebellion was at stake. In the end I drew my revolver and made it clear that either he called his men in and got on with the march, or else I was going shoot him. I had put myself in a stupid and nasty position and this was quite the most dangerous situation I have ever been in. However, after a long, ghastly pause in dead silence from all quarters, he cracked, called in his thugs and we resumed the march. News followed me that there was a British officer camped nearby, so I returned to find 2/Lt Duncan, who had just arrived with a party of patriots and trained irregulars from the direction of Gogetti.

24th May: News came through before I left for Muggo that the Italians had been cut off by a party of my patriots and that now most of the Muggo force were boxed up in Hosaena, only five hours ride away. I told Duncan to collect his lads and follow me down. The news got hotter as we approached Hosaena. The Italians were short of food and water and were concentrated in the two big forts on the summit of Hosaena Hill. Towards evening I began moving our force up in groups of about 200 at a time with instructions that they should worm their way close in and attack at dawn, Duncan's force, some 500 strong on the left flank, and my bunch of now about 1,800 on the right. I myself, accompanied by Duncan, a guide and a small selected party of my men, went in after dark from the front. Except for occasional vivid flashes of lightning the night was again as black as ink with great masses of dark cloud banking up in the east and a terrific storm brewing. It was unpleasant work creeping up in the darkness over unknown country with no knowledge whatsoever of the enemy strong points and defences. Before long we were drenched and a bitterly cold wind had our teeth chattering. Then at last daybreak, and still raining, but Hosaena Hill clear of cloud. A heaven-sent bank of mist settled on the summit of the hill, and simultaneously the patriots attacked. There was a crackle of rifle fire from the right flank, followed by a roar of automatics as if every machine-gun in Africa had opened up. I found a suitable OP and Duncan was kept busy covering our left flank with his own and one of my machine-guns. I soon found that I was attracting the personal attention of a sniper, who was making some rather bad shooting from about 300 yards. He eventually got one shot between the legs of my light machine-gun and a few inches from my chin, so I decided to move and actually got a better OP.

All day long the battle raged with attacks and counter-attacks. About 1400 we drove the Italians from the lower fort and knocked them about badly as they battled their way up to the main fort on the hilltop.

At 1700 I moved back to a prearranged spot to receive reports. The day had gone well, our casualties had been heavy, but the men were full of fight and ready for more. I warned the leaders to hold the positions they had gained and to expect the Italians to make a break for it and scatter during the night.

I sent Duncan back to where we had left the pack mules for food and ammunition while I tried to snatch some sleep, but at 0200 the noise of a terrific running fight woke me. The Italians, as I had anticipated, were fighting their way out. Part of the fort was in flames, an ammunition dump was blazing, and there was a free-for-all bomb-throwing party on the go. A small force was still in the fort with machine-guns going full blast, but they too stopped suddenly and I could hear the action which followed fading away into the night. A few minutes later a horseman arrived with the inevitable news that the Italians were out, and being rounded up by the patriots, which was unlikely as they would all be far too busy looting and destroying.

Soon after daybreak I rode in to take over. What I found was worse than I had believed possible. It made me utterly sick. The dead had been castrated by the patriots, who were milling about in hundreds, accompanied by the local peasants, burning, breaking and destroying everything in sight. Even the recently buried had been rooted up from their shallow graves in the fort and their miserable corpses treated in the same way. The rest of the day (today) has been something of a nightmare, burying the dead, treating the wounded, feeding the prisoners, taking rough stock of the masses of captured equipment and stores, driving off looters, organising forces to cut off the escaping Italians, writing reports, distributing ammunition, questioning prisoners, shooting wounded animals, and generally taking over this place, which appears to have been a large Italian base.

Together with the guns and other things taken at Muggo, I now have enough material to equip a large army. However, I feel that the important thing is to push on while these ruddy patriots are keyed up.

As I write, sitting in a broken-down schoolhouse-cum-church which serves as my headquarters, the town is full of shouting and shots. I shall never forget the sight of the fort this evening against a stormy blood-red sky, the croaking and flapping of bloated vultures, the slush and filth and litter and the awful stench of wet, burnt-out buildings and rotting flesh. At this moment two warriors stepped past me. They were celebrating our victory by firing their carbines still slung from their shoulders. One of them failed to notice the muzzle of his weapon had slipped round and was now tucked in under his chin and the next time he pushed down the trigger, the bullet came out of the top of his head killing him instantly. The milling mob crowded round roaring with laughter. The party continued. And now, as I go to bed, some blood-drunk Habash is chanting a war song, accompanied by the whooping of hyenas and the yelping of jackals on the hill. The rain beats down, but tonight I have a roof over my head.

I wasted no time at Hosaena and very soon we were on our way again, marching towards Tambaro near the Sodo/Jima road. Duncan has set off southwards to Boditi to tweak the enemy's tail, while I blow the road and wait for them as they retreat towards Jima. Last night one of the Italian prisoners told me that they had all been given instructions to fall back on Jima, so now I shall go full tilt for the Omo bridge, where they will no doubt make a stand to cover their retreat.

26th May: 0700 at Tambaro: the enemy pulled out of Sciola just ahead of us, and our advance guard got mixed up with some unfortunate deserters whom they took for fighting troops.

The Italians then staged a rearguard action, based on a small fort situated on the lip of the great gorge overlooking the Omo River 2,000 ft below, but we cleaned this up without much difficulty, taking a number of prisoners, two light tanks, an ambulance, and miscellaneous trucks and other vehicles. Prisoners confirm that by cutting across country from Hosaena as we did, a number of Italian units have been cut off in the Sodo area.

27th May. Today with Balambaras Mengesha and about 200 of his men in the lead we ventured down into the Omo gorge. The Italians must have seen us coming down the face of the escarpment, as they retreated before us in the direction of the bridge, leaving behind a column of 45 trucks fully loaded with military supplies of every variety. With all this wonderful loot available I had difficulty in persuading my men to continue. The enemy made a stand supported by mortars and artillery in the bridge area and the tussle which followed went on till we were overtaken by darkness, and as we had no water and were short of ammunition I led the men back up the terrible, almost vertical face of the gorge, getting in long after dark.

* * * *

28th May At Sciola: The enemy have abandoned all their strong-points on our side of the river and are now well dug in on the far bank. There appears to be a general retreat up the escarpment across the river in the direction of Jima.

Together with a couple of my lads, I succeeded in finding a place tailor-made for sniping situated on slightly high ground within a stone's throw of the bridge. Directly below us was a flaming oil tanker, the black smoke blowing slightly to the side and almost completely, but not quite, screening our position, giving us a clear shot whenever there was a sign of life on the other side. The Italians were aware of my approximate position, but believed me to be about 35 yards to my right, which was fortunate for me, as that area came in for continual machine-gunfire from a bunker just the other side of the bridge.

Eventually I decided it was time to go home. We sneaked away to the place where we had left the mules. About 100 men had waited behind for me, and just as well, for the Italians put across a party to shake us up in the rear. I led the stampede in the other direction, while a few stalwarts armed with rifles and my light automatic hose-piped the bush behind us. Sadly we had three killed and the same number wounded, among them my special friend, Basha Gobana from Geto village near Indibir. Poor old Gobana. I found him lagging behind today and told him rather severely to get moving. Ten minutes later he was flattened out by a machine-gun bullet.

30th May. I went down early this morning with my men into the hot sultry atmosphere of the Omo valley. The Italians, as usually happened, had moved patrols across to our side of the river, using the partly demolished footbridge which they still dominate from strong-points on the far side. We are not really equipped to make a counter-attack on the bridge crossing itself. The Italians eventually eased back across the river and we returned to our camp on the escarpment to find that an advance party of the 22nd East African Brigade had arrived via Sodo, and with it the 22nd Mountain Battery RA, Bulgy Leach, Alf Hartigan, Bruce Wilson and Sarel du Toit who happened to be with them. This was just the sort of boost I needed. Warfare, in particular guerilla warfare, is a desperately lonely business. Loneliness was my most dangerous enemy.

4th June: Brigade moved in on 30th May and took up a position on the escarpment near my camp. Then something happened which upset me. I was told that the brigadier wished to see me immediately. Brig 'Fluffy' Fowkes was a tough, crusty old nut and something of a tyrant, loved by some and hated by others. When I reached his tent he was standing with his back to me. I saluted smartly and stood to attention. There was a long, ominous silence. Then, suddenly, he spun round and shouted at the top of his voice: "You, Millard, get out of my sight, and if I see you again or any of your bloody patriots, I'll shoot you and I'll shoot your patriots. Get out!"

I just couldn't believe my ears and stood gaping at him as his words sank in. After all, my patriots had excelled themselves at Muggo Hill and at Hosaena and here in the Omo valley we had driven the Italians off the escarpment and across the river. In addition, our casualties had been heavy and I had lost many of my best men killed or wounded. In utter disgust I turned on my heel and, without saluting, marched off out of his tent. It was then that he relented. He ran after me, took me by the arm, apologised profusely and invited me to regard Advanced Brigade as my base.

The truth of the matter was that had he got to the Omo valley ahead of me, credit for the operation on the west bank would have fallen entirely upon himself and his brigade. Instead of that, part of the job had already been completed very successfully by my ragged column, and I suppose his resentment was understandable.

Every day since this incident I have been out with my irregulars, helping Brigade with odd jobs, looking for alternative mine-free routes down the escarpment, testing river crossings, detecting and pin-pointing enemy gun-positions. Tom Henfrey with his Scouts has come up with the Brigade. Tom has disbanded his main force of patriots and is now operating like me with a smallish selected group, highly mobile and lightly equipped.

I discussed my position with the brigadier and he is not keen that I should push on ahead as had been my plan, as we are closing in on Jima and he fears congestion if my mob get mixed up with the Brigade when they finally cross the river. I decided to disband my robber band and reduce them to about 20 picked men. On the 31st, Henfrey and I did a mounted reconnaissance along the escarpment parallel to the enemy positions. The same night we moved down and camped close to the river ahead of Brigade headquarters. We called our camp "The Pig and Whistle". Next morning (lst June) we made another recce upstream with the object of finding a wading crossing for troops. All probable shallow reaches were covered by the enemy and we had to find out just how well they were being watched. Four hours of fighting through bush and wading in mud and water eventually landed us near a shingly beach in a quiet bend of the river and here we lay for some time. I was just about to slide into the water when a machine-gun opened up. We sneaked back into deeper cover. Then, after a quiet smoke in a deep shadow while we watched an Italian gunner chopping wood just across the river, we slipped away into the forest and set course for home.

On reaching the bridge area, we found that at last our troops were actually at the bridge and that three Europeans and an African had succeeded in swimming across the river and were trying to drag a cable over. There were two South African light tanks drawn up on the bank covering the party of sappers who were endeavouring to gap the broken piers with some sort of decking, and a small party of officers, including Col Hopkins of the 2nd Nigerians and Maj Carr. At this moment, the bridge area was subjected to a very heavy artillery barrage. We dived under the nearest tank, shells shattered the trees above us, Maj Carr went down wounded. The air was full of deafening explosions, dust, flying shrapnel and smoke.

Our troops were told to pull out, so I tacked on to one of the Nigerian platoons and we worked our way down the road, which by this time was receiving the undivided attention of an Italian battery across the river together with some mortars. I was worried about Henfrey and started back, but found him almost immediately.

6th June: Yesterday our troops, after two days working day and night, succeeded in getting enough men across the river to stage an attack. Although hopelessly outnumbered, the 5th KAR and the 2nd Nigerians put up a first-class show against an almost entirely European force, taking 1,200 prisoners and 16 guns, including eight of heavy and medium pieces.

8th June: At first light we rushed our horses and mules across the river on the pontoon, which the engineers have at last got going. Later we collected together the best of the mules from captured Italian pack batteries and added them to our quota. Many of their mules were so galled and miserable that we had to shoot them. We followed the road for 12 miles and this brought us to the first demolition, which was pretty extensive. It would appear that something may have gone wrong, as some of the retreating Italians were caught in this blow, and the hillside is littered with their dead and transport. We surmised that the demolition party mistook the retreating Italians for our advance troops and detonated their charges prematurely.

Meanwhile, Brig Smallwood and the 3rd Nigerians from my Indibir days had forced a crossing of the Omo, 50 miles north of us at Abalti, and they beat us by a short head to the Piccolo Gibe bridge, but we were all there for the surrender of the Italian force and decided to call it a dead heat.

So, here we are on the Gibe, just a few miles short of Jima, our ultimate objective. A regular gathering of the clans – Nigerians, Kenyans, Tanganyikans, Gold Coasters, South Africans and Brits, and Mussolini's huge colonial army, or most of it, is in the bag or on the run towards Gondar, their last remaining stronghold. In the Gondar area is Gen Nasi, a rather exceptional leader and fighter, who has succeeded in building up a substantial force from the remnants of the Italian units still at large.

Later. Today we received an emissary from Gen Bisson Milio, who has been left in charge of Jima by the Italians, stating that Jima should be regarded as "open" and requesting our immediate occupation to prevent the massacre of hundreds of civilian men, women and children by the Ethiopian patriots commanded by Fitewerari Garusa, who has had the town under siege for some time.

The GOC has replied that Jima will be left to its fate unless there is a complete surrender of all remaining military strength in Ethiopia. I feel that to use a mainly civilian community of any race, colour or creed as a pawn of military strategy is wrong, but there it is. I doubt whether Gen Nasi will surrender anyway on these terms.

The Brigadier is aware of my good relationship with Fitewerari Garusa Duki and is most anxious that I should at all costs remain with the Brigade for the time being, with a view to keeping the patriots at bay until a final decision as to the future of the town is reached. I was in daily contact with Fitewerari Garusa and the ever increasing groups of leaderless armed Ethiopians converging on the Jima area. Garusa was having serious problems with his own army of 12,000, who were restless and could not understand why we did not all pile into the town and wipe it out.

Rather as I had anticipated, the Italian High Command called our bluff and refused to capitulate, and finally it was decided that Jima should be occupied forthwith. I dashed off at high speed in a borrowed car to warn Garusa and ensure that he would keep his men in check.

On reaching our usual rendezvous, where about 100 of Garusa's bodyguards were camped, I found everyone in a frenzy. Fortunately, I had brought with me my faithful interpreter and companion, Engide Work Gebre Mariam, and very soon the full picture emerged. Garusa's men were about to launch an attack on Jima. Garusa himself had taken off ahead of my arrival for his base on the far side of the town in an endeavour to restore order and hold his men in check. Clearly it was vitally important that I should see Garusa immediately. There was not time to consult with Brigade.

Garusa could only be contacted in time by going directly through Jima itself.

With headlamps blazing and hooter honking, Engide Work and I drove full tilt to the nearest, enemy strong-point on the outer defences of the town. There was no knowing how the Italians would react, but as it happened all went well. We were taken directly to Gen Milio's headquarters, given a permit and a four motor cycle escort, and half an hour later we were at an Italian bunker on the southern boundary of the town adjacent to Garusa's base. Armed with the information I gave him, Garusa was able to persuade his army to calm down. I never told Fluffy Fowkes that I had entered the town a day ahead of him and his Brigade!

The occupation of Jima was fairly straightforward. Brigade assumed responsibility for the manning of the perimeter defences, security generally, and all matters connected with the previous military presence. As temporary political officer, I set up shop in the Vice-Regal Lodge, a very fancy establishment.

There was a large and very cooperative Greek community in the town and I was able to make use of them as special constables and replacements in the existing inefficient Italian civil service. Political prisoners were released from the large and very grim prison, and by using civilian Italians with mechanical skills the infrastructure of the town was put back on track. However, my main task, as I saw it was as soon as possible to ease suitable Ethiopians into the running of the province as a whole and with this in view to involve Fitewerari Garusa (who was destined to become the future governor of this region) in the reconstruction process. Garusa was at heart a fighter, and he admitted to me that he was not really interested in getting involved in the administration of a large and difficult area. However, I persuaded him to begin selecting a team of trusted men.

* * * *

At 2100 on the third night after the occupation of Jima, there was a telephone call from the main gate into the town. The NCO on duty said, "Sir, there's a bloke 'ere wot says 'e is the Emperor of Abyssinia. Shall I let 'im in?" The only transport immediately available was a motor cycle, which I grabbed and went roaring off. Waiting outside the gate was the great little man himself, Haile Selassie, Emperor, King of Kings, Lion of Judah and all that, and with him his son, the Duke of Harar, and a couple of retainers, all tucked into a rather tatty little civilian motor car. He could not have been more understanding and charming, and with me put-putting along on my bike I acted as guide and royal escort on his triumphant entry into Jima town!

Back at Vice-Regal Lodge, faithful old Katungi, always at his best on occasions such as this, somehow produced a substantial meal. My Ethiopian flag which I always wore wrapped round my chest as a lifesaver when in action with

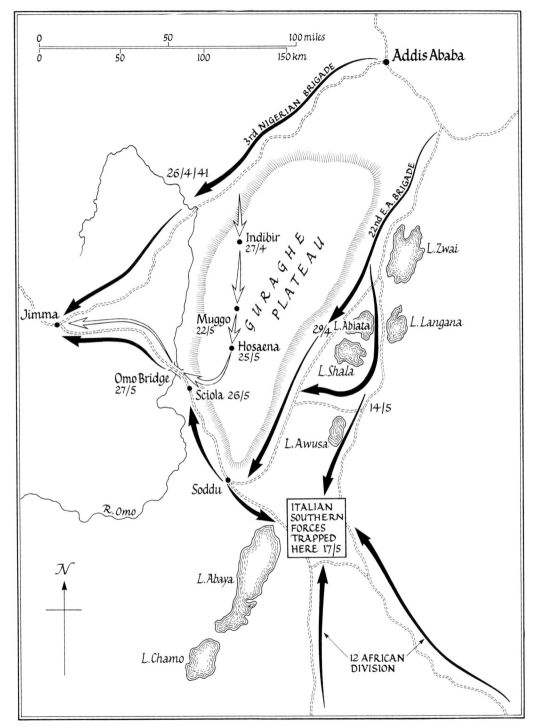

Map 2: Showing where Millard's Scouts were operating on the Guraghe Plateau and the Italian strongpoints they captured. Solid arrow = regular British units, open arrows = Millard's Scouts.

my patriots, I attached to a spear and stuck it into the wall above the entrance to the guest wing.

Meanwhile, in Addis Ababa next day all hell was let loose. The "King" was lost, did I perhaps have some news of him? "Sure thing," I replied. "The King is having breakfast with me at this moment!"

"Thank God," said the voice in Addis Ababa. "We will send armoured cars down immediately to escort him back to the palace, congratulations on finding him!"

Years later Haile Selassie paid a state visit to Tanzania, and together with the President, Julius Nyerere, he visited Moshi where I had once been DC. He remembered me and asked to see me, and we talked of Dan Sandford and others we had known, and of times gone by during the war against the Italians.

But now my time in Jima was running out. Weeks and months of hard living, continual fighting, bad food, extreme cold, dysentery and the difference of opinion I had with an anti-personnel mine had left me thin as a rake and more or less at the end of my tether. The Brigade Medical Officer tried on several occasions to get me moved out to hospital, but the Brigadier was reluctant to let me go as I was his only link with Fitewerari Garusa and the ever increasing movement of heavily armed Ethiopians into the Jima region. However, at last a replacement arrived together with instructions from Addis Ababa that I was to be flown out immediately for treatment.

I spent a few days laid up in Addis Ababa, then on to the Military Hospital in Nairobi and finally to South Africa to recuperate. My final report to Brigadier Sandford follows:-

REPORT ON THE ACTIVITIES OF THE PATRIOT FORCES OPERATING IN THE AREA LYING SOUTH OF WALSO AND UOLCHITTE AND SOUTH WESTWARDS TO THE SODO-JIMA ROAD AS FAR AS THE OMO RIVER

This report treats briefly of the period between 25/4/41 to 3/6/41, during which time patriots under my control were active over a large tract of enemy occupied territory. Owing to the difficulty of communication it was not possible at the time to give an accurate or detailed account of our movements. The patriots did excellent work in those parts and I feel that by this summary I may succeed in obtaining for them some of the recognition they deserve for valuable work done under exceedingly difficult conditions, in country where it would have been well-nigh impossible for our own forces to function.

The raising of a patriot force to cope with the Italian strongholds in the Guraghe country had not been considered, but the possibilities presented themselves to me when I visited the area towards the end of April to investigate reports of unrest among the Guraghe near Indibir. On the first of these visits it was possible to sow the seeds of what afterwards developed into a general uprising. On this occasion also, accompanied by a small force of tribesmen, I was able to make contact with the strong enemy force then occupying Muggo Mountain. The advantages of irregular fighting to cope with the enemy installed at Muggo, Urbaragh and Hosaena were stressed in my report and I was afterwards seconded to develop this suggestion and to endeavour to raise a column of scouts strong enough to keep continual pressure on the enemy and to harass them wherever possible. This was not easy as the country was only lukewarm towards the rising, and in the early stages our ranks contained a high percentage of traitors.

However, early in May of 1941, with about 1,000 patriots, mostly Guraghe under the Guraghe leaders, Fitewerari Seyfu, Fitewerari Kabid Ali and Fitewerari Rashid, we made our first serious attack on Muggo; and from that day continued to harass the garrison (which numbered 1,200 Europeans and 900 native troops) without respite. This pressure which was kept up day and night in the face of considerable gunfire from four Italian batteries, often at point-blank range and 40 machine-guns, did much to rattle the enemy and resulted in wholesale desertions by the native troops from both Muggo and Urbaragh.

On the 13/5/41, as the result of a strong enemy counter-attack, we suffered heavy casualties and lost most of our ammunition, all our heavy equipment and my own personal supplies and baggage. We continued to fight on until all ammunition was finished, but it was obvious that without reinforcements and a further supply of ammunition and more machine-guns we could do nothing except make matters very uncomfortable for the Muggo Italians. Occasionally we were able to entice patrols into areas where they were not covered by their own gunfire and it is true that very few of these patrols returned, but more arms, ammunition and men were required. At last on 19/5/41, reinforced by 800 patriots led by Akim Balcha, Balambaras Mengesha, Balambaras Kebede, Balambaras Amonya, Lij Haile and others, we marched on Muggo. About this time the enemy, in view of the Italian defeat suffered at the hands of the 22nd East African Brigade in the lakes area and our continual pressure, were preparing to move from Muggo. Urbaragh had been previously vacated. Hoping to catch them before they left Muggo we pushed on with all speed, marching day and night in an effort to encircle them but in this we were only partly successful as most of the enemy got out just ahead of us leaving one battery of medium calibre guns and a few European and native troops.

At Muggo we were joined for a few days by 2/Lt Duncan with a small force of irregulars and a patriot band under Shaykh Bakala from the neighbourhood of Buttagiari. That same day, thus reinforced, we marched to Hosaena, where we succeeded in surrounding the enemy rearguard.

By this time our combined force numbered some 3,000 riflemen. The enemy was estimated at 400 Europeans and 300 Eritreans and they were installed in the two forts on the summit of Hosaena hill. On the evening of the 21/5/41 we moved into position under the cover of darkness and rain, and at dawn on the 22nd the attack was opened. By noon the enemy had been driven from the lower fort with heavy losses to themselves, and during the night they fought their way out of the main fort during a rainstorm and scattered in all directions. It is impossible to say how many were killed as many had been buried before we occupied the forts, but about 100 prisoners were taken, mostly Eritreans, many of them wounded. Twelve Europeans were found dead in the fort and others were discovered later, buried or lying out dead in the forest to which they fled. Our own casualties were

20 killed and about 30 wounded. During these two days the patriots stuck to their positions, in spite of intense cold, rain and continual machine-gun fire. Twenty machine-guns were captured and much gun ammunition, tractors, lorries, small arms ammunition and foodstuffs. Two days march following the retreating enemy brought us to Sciola on the Sodo-Jima road. Here were met a small enemy rear-guard, who surrendered after an hour's fighting. 2/Lt Duncan with part of his force had in the meantime departed in the direction of Sodo (at the time we did not know that a British force was operating in that area). On the 25th the march was continued, and the enemy, who were holding the escarpment above the Omo River, were driven down into the valley leaving a number of Europeans and native prisoners in our hands as well as three armoured cars and 15 lorries.

The same day a patrol under Balambaras Kebede moved forward to the Omo itself and found the enemy holding strong-points along the west bank (our side) of the river. On the 26th we again attacked and drove the enemy across the river. They left behind them 45 lorries, most of these loaded with war materials, and other equipment. Our losses in this operation were 25 killed and about 35 wounded. (Many of the wounded have since died.)

Three days later we were overtaken by the 22nd Brigade advancing from Sodo towards Jima, and in the course of the next few days the patriot force with me was disbanded as I considered that its usefulness in that area was over. I myself, with a small party of picked men, continued to scout for the Brigade and acted as liaison officer between it and the patriot forces under Fitewerari Garusa Duki during events leading up to the surrender and occupation of Jima.

I would like in conclusion to mention my interpreter Engide Work Gebre Mariam. This man remained with me throughout and did more towards holding the men together than any of the Ethiopian leaders. He also took part in all actions and was always at my side even in the most unpleasant and awkward situations. It is impossible to make special mention of any particular patriot leader. All of them fought well on occasions, including the Guraghe tribesmen.

Signed

J.F. MILLARD Capt. G.R

(*note:* the spelling of the place names was as I perceived it at the time, and may not be exactly the same as in Map 2)

CHAPTER 6

THE ITALIAN DEFEAT

D URING my absence in South Africa, Gen Nasi, a rather exceptional soldier, together with 30,000 hardline remnants of the Italian forces, had
retreated northwards and were now established in the heavily fortified Lake
Tana and Gondar region. When I got back to Addis Ababa on 15th October it
was to find that there had been a number of changes. Dan Sandford was now
Political and Military Adviser to the Emperor and Lt Col Ord Wingate had
assumed control of irregular forces previously under Sandford.

Wingate divided the formations available to him into two sections: himself
keeping the larger southern force and diverting the remainder northwards to
Gondar. Ben Tarleton, based in Addis, was responsible for patriot affairs in the
north, and required me to proceed immediately to Gondar and act as liaison
officer between the patriots already there and the regular troops converging on
Lake Tana. I am to set off immediately with a convoy of 54th Field Coy with
ammunition, medical supplies, pack saddles, shells and 900,000 Maria Theresa
dollars, for the patriot commanders and their men who have not been paid for
some time.

There are two main groups: Dougforce under Major Douglas of the
Highland Light Infantry, and with him, Mark Pilkington, Billy McLean, Carl
Nurk and the Belgian patriot leader, van Veen; and some 1,500 men under the
command of Fitewerari Biru, the Emperor's special representative and one-time
Minister of War. Douglas and Biru are marking time and camped on the eastern escarpment well away to the east and out of touch with the enemy concentrations. For some reason Douglas and Biru have fallen out and Tarleton wants
me to resolve the quarrel and get them moving towards the enemy.

Just before leaving Addis I was informed that for some obscure reason I had
been awarded the Military Cross,* but when the official list was published this

---

* Subsequently I was awarded a military M.B.E., but so far as I can remember it had no
connection with the Abyssinian period.

had been reduced to a Mention in Dispatches. Anyway, here I am back on the job once more, fighting fit, beard gone, dysentery gone, no lice in my hair, a stone or two heavier, and in time for the last battles that remain against Mussolini's Great Colonial Army in East Africa.

18th October. As I write we are benighted on a bleak pass high up on the plateau between Debre Birhan and Debre Sina. A more cheerless place would be difficult to find. There is no firewood and no suitable camp site. The lorries are drawn into the side of the road and five feet from the verge is a sheer precipice into the valley below. An icy cold wind blows, and mist sweeps down on us from the ridge above. It would appear from the map that we are between 9,000 and 10,000 ft above sea level.

19th October. We were away soon after sunrise and plunged almost immediately into the famous Mussolini tunnel. One emerges on the far side to find oneself on the edge of a cliff, which is in fact the wall of a colossal escarpment. Far below was the village of Debre Sina with its morning fires smoking, and the road, a tiny white thread zig-zagging forever downwards.

I reported to the senior officer in Dese just before dark and was provided with a fatigue party to assist in the unloading of the coin and the ammunition, a job which took two hours and was achieved partly in the headlights of our lorries in pouring rain.

It was here, at Dese, that the South Africans, assisted by Campbell's Scouts, did so well against a force three to four times greater and in the face of terrific artillery fire from Italian naval guns in concrete emplacements and well dug-in fortifications on the heights overlooking the approaches to the town. Eventually, the South African gunners wheeled up their 60-pounders and one of their ranging shells landed in the township. This was too much for the Italians: they came out at such a speed to discuss terms that their infantry, thinking we were staging a blitz from the rear, fired on their own emissary. The final bag in Dese was 10,000 prisoners, 52 guns, 250 machine-guns, 40,000 rifles, 40,000 gallons of petrol, 250 military transport and a mass of other equipment.

23rd October: Transport forward was not easy to come by, but I am now on my way and heading for Debre Tabor. To get this far I have had to traverse some stupendous valleys; in each case it was necessary to drop down to about 4,000 ft above sea level and then climb up to 9,000 or 10,000 ft, perhaps more. The valley walls are almost sheer and the road is nothing more than a track.

My little convoy of trucks is camped with the most forward pioneer unit on a great bluff with views surpassing anything I have ever seen. The road or track which the pioneers are in the process of pushing through to Debre Tabor is lined with gorse and bracken with a cliff of about 1,000 feet up to the road edge. The cliff then falls away a little off the vertical for another 2,000 feet, after that the slope loses itself in a labyrinth of gorges and castle-like hills and a thousand small valleys. About 80 miles away is a huge massif, which I presume is the high point marked on the map lying northwest of Gondar. Storms are raging here and there, between them great blotches of golden sunlight, the whole a patchwork of blue, mauve, purple and black. I had to dash for shelter as a storm came sweeping in from behind us. Now I am sitting in the cab of one of the lorries as I write, with rain drumming down, but with the setting sun trying to break through.

Sunday 26th October. The column is at a standstill for the 20th time during the last couple of hours. Two of our lorries have buckled their track rods, and several others are bogged down in a sea of mud and quaking bog. What a relief it will be to get back to pack mules and horses. It's a magnificent crisp morning. The slopes of the hills are ablaze with yellow Meskel daisies, so called because they are in full bloom round about the feast of Meskel* when the Ethiopians deck themselves in daisies, and even the most evil-looking of them are transformed into something moderately attractive and romantic.

27th October. This morning, in blazing sunshine, we ploughed our way through to Debre Tabor, not a bad little place, situated on high ground overlooking the great escarpment which falls away westwards to Lake Tana, the source of the Blue Nile. There are a few modern Italian houses and, set on prominent hilltops overlooking the town, are the two Italian forts recently stormed and captured by a column consisting of Skinner's Horse, irregulars, and patriots.

28th October. T'ereg Iman, an unattractive little Ethiopian village, is perched on a high col astride the main road. Ahead is Kulkabar, the heavily fortified barrier range on the outer perimeter of the Gondar defences, the enemy positions clearly visible. It's a grey afternoon and I am very tired after the long trek; none the less it is good to have shaken off lorry transport and to be back again in the familiar atmosphere of mules, horses, wood fires, patriots, and the untidy jumble and smell of a guerilla encampment. I have been joined by Lt King, an excellent lad, and he will act as my adjutant. With us are about 300 patriots. Yesterday an Italian CR42 aircraft came in and shot up my happy home good and hearty, killing four wounded who were in a shed on the roadside and wrecking some of the tents. However, now there is a lookout on a nearby hilltop and three shots in rapid succession is the signal which puts everyone into slit trenches in a twinkle. Most of the day spent zig-zagging up from T'ereg Iman to the plateau above and now, at last, I am camped together with my small bodyguard in a new world of cedars, brambles, and sweet-smelling clover grass.

---

*   Meskel is Amharic for cross, i.e. the cross of crucifixion and the Meskel Feast commemorates the day the cross was found.

We have made a detour of the Kulkabar positions and are now able to look down upon them and along the whole length of the ridge as it lies at right angles to the eastern escarpment and stretches away from us till it eventually peters out on the lake shore. It is this ridge that I must now try and organise the patriot forces to help take. And it is perhaps worth reminding the reader at this point just how varied the forces aligned against the Italians were. There were regular army units drawn from all over the British Empire. Some had entered Ethiopia from Kenya in the south. Others had come in from the Sudan in the west. There were remnants of the regular Ethiopian army. There were irregular units of that army. And least disciplined and organised of the lot, though tough fighters none the less, were my bunch – the patriots. Given the variety of units it is scarcely surprising that liaison between them was difficult. I had no radio, for example, and once I was away from Addis Ababa was quite literally on my own. To a high degree I really was independent. In these circumstances odd characters turned up, seemingly from nowhere. There simply was no time to enquire much about their backgrounds and, when the fighting was over, we went our respective ways knowing little of one another – other than what we had learned on the battlefield. Such was young Lt King who I had arbitrarily appointed my adjutant: I don't know how he came to be in T'ereg Iman or where he went to afterwards. He was simply there to be used and was an excellent lad.*

Another unusual but first rate man whom I met for the first time at T'ereg Iman was Sergeant Morrow from Ireland. He had three captured Italian artillery pieces hidden in a cave and for which I had brought him ammunition from Addis Ababa. Periodically he wheeled out his guns and, with the help of several Patriots, shelled the Italians in the plains below. The guns would be then wheeled back into the cave until the next urge to fire at the enemy took him. I never ascertained from whence he came, how he acquired the artillery, or on whose orders, if any, he was carrying on his lonely campaign. I assumed that in some way he, too, had originated in '101' mission, and that the weapons had been captured by patriot forces from the retreating Italians. Suffice it that he was an independent after my own heart and very useful.

Yet there was little of this in my mind at the end of the day I had first reconnoitred Kulkabar. Then my thoughts were on Lake Tana which I found just a shade disappointing. I had always imagined that the lake was flush up against the mountains. In fact, although it is surrounded by immense mountain masses, the highlands lie back from the lake, which has receded through the ages, leaving a wide level plain on most sides.

30th October: at Degoma: this evening, after a glorious march through high wheat fields and patches of forest, we reached Degoma. Douglas and Fitewerari

---

* I assume King originally came into Ethiopia with Brigadier Sandford's '101' mission from the Sudan.

Biru have been parked in this area for some time now and their men have been like a swarm of locusts upon the land. My intention is to insist that Douglas moves down to the plain between Kulkabar and Gondar, as his Degoma position has no strategic importance. His argument against this is that the troops get sick and his mules die, but if the enemy installed on Kulkabar are to be ousted this sort of thing must not deter us. Douglas and his boys certainly look the part. They all have beards and long hair and Douglas wears a long Swahili-style kanzu . He does not appear to have any stomach for action despite the fearsome appearance. Their camp is on the rim of a great horseshoe cliff with terrific views to the northeast.

I confess that I was not impressed by the Dougforce encampment. The whole area was a stinking shambles, and the commanding officer's H.Q. was dilapidated and filthy. By contrast, the immediate vicinity of Fitwerari Biru's command had some atmosphere of order and discipline and Biru himself was a man of dignity and charm.

In contrast to their commanding officer, Lieutenants Billy McLean[*] and Mark Pilkington of Dougforce were cooperative and on the ball. In my discussions with them I got a good idea of the general situation and of the conflict between Douglas and Biru. I decided that I would have to deal with these two officers directly if I was to get Dougforce to play an active part in the impending battle against General Nasi.

I met with Biru and Wolde Emanuel (a guerilla leader) and other patriot leaders and think that I have convinced them to close in on the Kulkabar defences.

1st November: Dead weary, and back at T'ereg Iman. Then rode over to where Sgt Morrow has his captured guns. With me on this occasion was Major Peter Molloy M.C., later to become Chief Game Warden of the Anglo-Egyptian Sudan and later still the Director of Tanganyika's National Parks. Peter was anxious to have a taste of guerilla warfare and his companionship at a time like this was invaluable. From Morrow's gun positions we could see Asosa, another key point, and its aerodrome, but out of his guns' range. I told Morrow to move his 65mm guns further along the ridge closer to the Italian defences. If he gets directly above Kulkabar the Italians will find it difficult to elevate their pieces sufficiently to retaliate, and provided he is screened by Biru's patriots he should be able to lob stuff over the edge in comparative safety. Biru has promised to

---

[*] Billy McLean had joined Dougforce some time prior to my arrival and it is interesting that Xan Fielding in his biography of him (One Man in His Time – The Life of Lt Col N.L.D. Billy McLean D.S.O.) recorded Billy's impression of his commanding officer was not very favourable. He found him lying half naked on a rug in a clearing littered with paper, dirty plates, flasks of Tej (a beverage made from fermented honey but more intoxicating than ordinary mead) and a miscellaneous collection of weapons. His personal presence, straggling beard and unkempt hair matched the surroundings.

The redoubtable, solitary, Sergeant Morrow with a captured 65mm gun who kept three artillery pieces hidden in a cave above the Italian position at Kulkabar. Periodically he wheeled them out, let fly a volley of shells, then disappeared back into his cave with his guns, before the retaliation commenced.

supply 200 men to manhandle the guns to a suitable position. Before leaving we wheeled out Morrow's guns and sent two or three brace of shells screaming over to Kulkabar, and then made tracks for T'ereg Iman, camping en route near the rim of the escarpment, in a delightful little valley with a brook and big trees and pretty woods round about. An old man and his wife who lived in a nearby dwelling came out early this morning with a gift of eggs and honey.

Peter Molloy accompanied me on my next visit to Dougforce and Biru. Douglas seems reluctant to move despite it being essential that he should establish himself astride the road on the north side of Kulkabar. The Italian position will then be cut off from Gondar except by water via the little Lake Tana port of Gorgora, which is still held by the enemy together with Chelga as part of their outer ring of defences. My problem is that Douglas is a major and I am only a captain, but I have a gut feeling that I will win in this contest.

Biru, as expected, has agreed to move his camp and to take up a position between Amba Mariam Hill and the escarpment and despite the lack of enthusiasm I hope Douglas will make a similar move in good time.

3rd November: We know now that the idea of forcing the door to Gondar from this, the Debre Tabor, side has been abandoned owing to the condition of the Dese/Debre Tabor track. The main offensive will now be down the Asmara road, while a small column known as Southforce is to shake up Kulkabar from this side. An advance party under Col Collins arrived at my camp an hour or two ago. As Southforce will be making the main offensive against the Italians before us, I attached myself to it to ensure my patriots' coordination. It seems that we will have the unenviable task of endeavouring to put up a good show on the south side of Kulkabar with inadequate troops and supporting weapons.

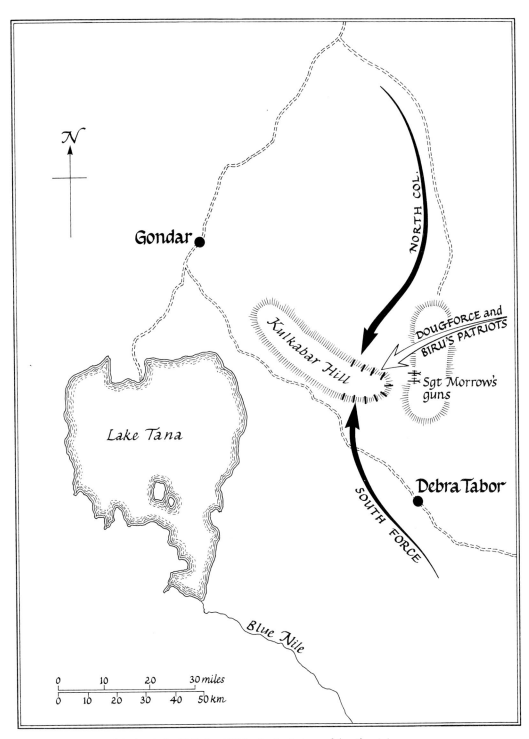

Map 3: A diagram of the battle for Kulkabar Hill in the final phase of the Abyssinian campaign.

Reconnoitring Kulkabar ridge from the east with Colonel Collins of Southforce.
Sergeant Morrow's artillery was concealed a little way to the left of this picture.

6th November: Three very full days of hard patrolling and one final rushed trip up to see Douglas, put him in the picture and try to get him to move forward.

My camp is well forward in a little saucer-shaped valley near a delightful stream with thickly wooded banks and a stone bridge. The bridge is registered by the enemy guns and the area surrounding my camp is pock-marked with shell craters, but the camp itself is in dead ground and fairly safe.

I am hanging on to 60 of the Welo Banda, who are part of the enemy force which surrendered at Debre Tabor. The Welo are tough hillsmen from the neighbourhood of Debre Zeit. The fact that a few months ago they were fighting for the Italians against us doesn't seem to be on their conscience at all, and they are at present among the most reliable of our irregular troops.

Charles is our tame Italian, and a souvenir of the Debre Tabor haul. His previous line of business in life was bootlegging in the States. One day he and two of his buddies were making a quick getaway and unfortunately bumped off a policeman in the process. After that Charles had to make himself hard to catch. He worked his way back on a tramp steamer to Italy, where he was immediately roped in to do his military training, and afterwards, much against his will, he was shipped to Eritrea to take part in the Italian/Ethiopian war of 1935, as a transport driver. His opinion of Mussolini and his views on Fascism do not bear repeating. He knows a little about most things and a lot about diesel engines, and is worth his weight in gold.

7th November: Like me, some of the South African sappers who are now with us are longing for more action. Yesterday, three of them went down towards the lake to where a Gladiator fighter was shot down over a month ago. They found that there was little damage apart from a shot-away oil feed pipe and that there were 20 gallons of petrol in the reserve tank. One of the sappers knew something about flying, so damn me if he didn't patch up the machine and fly it off! Not satisfied with that, he zoomed low over the Italian positions and then did a perfect landing on a better piece of ground near my base camp.

The same lads have been amusing themselves making huge bombs; they crawl up with these at night close to the Italian positions, then light the fuse and skip it. Ten minutes later there is a flash and a roar and every Italian for miles around bounces out of bed, looses off everything he has into Africa and stands to for the rest of the night.

10th November: At dawn came a message from the CO Southforce telling me to be ready to go forward on a recce with him to a high point known as Hill 9, well up against Kulkabar ridge. Col Collins is anxious to get a close-up view of the layout and then decide just how and where the patriots and regulars should attack when we make a trial assault on Kulkabar from this, the south side.

Our approach was overlooked by the Italians, so we split up into three small parties and made our way forward independently. We reached the summit of Hill 9 first, and the others trickled in during the next hour or so, sweating and bleeding after battling through the high grass and thorns. The view from Hill 9 was excellent and we were so close to the Italian machine-gun positions that here and there we could see their weapons glittering in the sun. Kulkabar ridge from close up is terribly broken, and it took us two and a half hours to decide upon a plan of attack. Two well-defended hills on the left flank of our proposed line of approach are the main snags, but the gunner who came with us thinks he can deal with them. My job now is to give Douglas an exact picture of what is going to happen from this side and to make sure that he understands his task, which is to attack on the north side of the ridge when we launch the Southforce assault. His lack of enthusiasm is striking and with the greatest reluctance he agreed that Mark Pilkington with a small but specially selected formation would be well placed to support us when we open our assault on the southern defences. Fortunately we can rely on Mark to do his best.

12th November: As I write, Southforce, consisting of two KAR battalions and a battery of South African medium guns, is assembled close up against the southern aspect of the enemy stronghold of Kulkabar. On the other side of Kulkabar, to the north, is Dougforce. Tomorrow at first light we, Southforce, together with Dougforce, will launch a simultaneous combined attack in an effort to try out the Italian strength and, if possible, split the defences, establish ourselves on the ridge, and hold this position, while 25 and 26 Brigade groups,

J.M., H.E. Fitwereri Biru, and Colonel Gilbert Collins, C.O. of Southforce before the battle for Kulkabar ridge.

approaching from the north via Adwa, close up on Gondar itself. I am with the Southforce commander, Col Collins, and with a small detachment of my own will cover his headquarters and be well placed to liaise if necessary with the patriots should the joint attack succeed.

14th November: I joined Collins at his bivouac near Hill 9. At 2200 hours we checked watches, and the first troops started off in single file. At about 0230 the moon came up, and this helped, but as dawn began to break we were still behind schedule and found ourselves in a saucer-shaped clearing overlooked by the enemy defences.

Finally, in the grey light of dawn, it became necessary to throw discretion to the winds and scramble for it. There was a low escarpment just ahead and our sudden appearance on top of it took the Italians by surprise. We were able to establish ourselves well up the hill, but in a rather exposed position. From the noises off on the other side it was clear that the patriots were in business, but by now the enemy had sorted themselves out and we were under continual machine-gun and mortar fire from strong-points on either flank.

After two or three hours things started to go wrong. The Dougforce patriot attack began to tail off and no doubt the enemy realised that we had less in the field than they had estimated. We had to ease back from our initial position, which was now being pounded by exceptionally accurate shellfire. There was a low granite ridge just ahead of us which gave some protection, but sent stuff ricocheting over in a most unpleasant manner. Then the enemy mortars got busy and we really began to cop it.

At this point the CO asked me whether it would be possible to get the patriots on the other side to stage a second attack. I had to point out that once a patriot attack fizzles out they normally fade away. I was of course prepared to give it a go myself, but warned that my chances of getting through were minimal, as the area just ahead was covered by several Italian strong-points and no doubt mined and booby-trapped.

Michael Blundell with his sappers was nearby and I asked him for two volunteers to go with me to help with the inevitable mines. I added my best light machine-gunner to our little kamikaze party and then went off to question some prisoners who had just been brought in. When I got back I found to my enormous relief that the CO had decided against attempting a breakthrough. Our wounded were under shellfire while being moved and we were down to our last reserves in ammunition, mortar bombs, and water. Well, it's something to have fought in a battle where, for once, one was not top dog! A small force remained in position till the last moment to cover the evacuation and we got back to our bivouac area about midnight. It had been a clear 40 hours without sleep, except the sort of sleep one falls into as soon as one sits down or relaxes for a minute or two. What a game this is. I can't recollect getting to bed this morning. All I remember is taking a shot of neat whisky from my flask and lying down. My orderly must have undressed me and zipped me up in my sleeping bag.

16th November: It seems that the pretty substantial Northcol force under Brig James has succeeded in cutting across from the Asmara/Gondar road and is working towards us along the plateau via Denk'ez . Thank goodness they have at last realised that Kulkabar is too tough a proposition for Southforce to take on short-handed. Col Collins and I are required at a rendezvous in the neighbourhood of Denk'ez tomorrow evening to liaise with Brig James of Northcol.

17th November: At Denk'ez, tired, hungry, and cold. Our march last night to reach Northcol went wrong. We got hopelessly lost in the labyrinth of valleys and broken country at the foot of the escarpment. Eventually, we decided to give up the unequal struggle and settle down for the night among the stubble of a newly-reaped wheat field. With the first streak of dawn we pulled out, struck the path almost immediately, and trekked solidly all through the day. We arrived at the rendezvous just before dark and a bit ahead of the Northcol advance party, who have just clocked in even more tucked up and miserable than ourselves.

18th November: Our meeting with Brigadier James took place this morning, and he informed me that Douglas had been relieved of his command. I am to assume control of Dougforce as soon as possible and move to the northern

Gondar sector. Collins was kind enough to protest strongly, but it would seem that this decision has been made and is final. Douglas has left the operational area and is now at Rear Brigade H.Q. The other major decision made at our meeting was that there is to be a simultaneous final attack on the Kulkabar defences by Southcol and Northcol with the co-operation of all available irregular units now concentrated in the area as a whole.

Nightfall – at Morrow's Camp: Biru is camped nearby. It was necessary to put Morrow and Biru in the picture and to get details of ammunition requirements for the coming battle. Biru's task will be to take on the enemy's eastern flank and to keep that end thoroughly occupied while Collins and his boys make their dirty rush in from the direction of Amba Mariam, going straight for Pimple Hill and the guns, across the road and then up the slope beyond. Peter Molloy is still with me for this final phase of the campaign and has agreed to attach himself to Biru's patriot force, who will tackle the eastern face of Kulkabar, enabling me to be with Mark Pilkington, van Veen and Karl Nurk and the Dougforce patriots for the final attack on the northern Kulkabar defences.

19th November: The escarpment is killing the mules, and this particular bunch will never manage another ascent. The anti-tank rifles have been especially troublesome; they are a most awkward length to pack on a mule and we have continually had to stop to fix them. There have been air strikes on Kulkabar this morning. The Kulkabar ridge lies at right angles to the escarpment, and from where we are at the moment one has a magnificent view down the whole length of it. Almost directly below is the enemy eastern flank. Some of Biru's patriots have already moved down and taken up a position behind a small ridge about 600 yards from the barbed wire perimeter of the nearest enemy fort.

Since I started writing, the enemy have suddenly opened up on them with shrapnel, but, as usual, it is bursting high and the patriots appear to be quite unconcerned about it. Camp-fires are smoking away happily, horses, mules, and cattle grazing peacefully. Beyond all this is Pimple Hill and the enemy gun positions near the road. Above that is the main defended locality, which occupies the central and highest portion of the ridge, about seven miles of heavily-defended high ground. We have them well and truly boxed up now.

20th November: Darkness overtook the column when we were still some miles from Biru's camp. I tried to get a guide from a village filled with crowds of heavily-armed half-drunk patriots. I have seldom seen a more evil-looking mob of ruffians. There was a big fire blazing in the centre of the village, and no doubt the effect was exaggerated somewhat by the dancing firelight striking the whites of their eyes, their teeth, and the rows of gleaming cartridges in their bandoleers. Some of them began to get tough with my bodyguard and for a moment it looked as if there was going to be some shooting, but at the crucial moment more of our men, hearing the row, arrived on the scene and the party began to sober up. A miserable villager was reluctantly produced as a guide, but I refused to take him and insisted almost at the point of my pistol on two of the armed men accompanying us. The mule pack-train loaded with gun ammunition for Sgt Morrow got in some time before us, so he had news of our progress and was waiting with great mugsful of steaming sweet tea laced with rum. Morrow is now well supplied with ammunition and cordite and I have given him his piece, which is to get busy with the two 75mm guns and the little 65 mm, first on the enemy battery near the road, then lifting to the Machine-gun Nob and any other visible targets on that slope as the attack develops.

22nd November: After leaving Morrow's camp we marched hard and fast, locating Brig James late yesterday afternoon under a huge wild fig tree. We ran through the operational order which I had brought with me from Southforce, and was able to give him a picture of the layout and Biru's role. Brig James gave the plan his blessing. The next morning just before sunrise Mark Pilkington and I and about 80 patriots established a headquarters base on a small hill directly below the ridge held by the enemy, while our assault force worked its way across the open country ahead of us towards Red Hill. The enemy had located our approximate position and our front was coming in for a good old plastering from gunfire, mortars and machine-guns.

In the middle of all this, a flock of guinea fowl, terrified by the awful din, came screaming overhead and settled in a nearby thicket, well out in no-man's land, about 200 yards from where we crouched. Lying next to me was Deresa, Mark's Ethiopian orderly, and I noticed that immediately the birds came into view he riveted his attention on them, watching hawk-like as they settled. Then, with a final glance to make sure of their position, he grasped his rifle and wriggled away, crawling where cover was lacking, crouching, running and dodging. By this time we had lost interest in the battle and all attention was focused on Deresa and his birds. The shell-fire was creeping in his direction, and one and all were terrified least the next burst would flush the birds. Crash, and a shell pitched slightly off to his left. Deresa flattened himself to the ground. A moan of disappointment from us as one of the birds took off noisily. A moment later a sharp crack, followed almost immediately by a second shot. There was an excited babble of voices from the Ethiopians behind me as Deresa, throwing discretion to the winds, sprinted across the final 50 yards to the thicket, collected two guinea-fowl and, with rifle slung and the birds still jerking convulsively in his hand, he strolled back towards us over the same ground, handed over his bag to Mark's cook and carefully wiped a fleck of blood from the barrel of his beloved Mauser.

Elsewhere, especially to the northeast, where the regulars were in action, things were going more or less according to plan, though our Air Force nearly kiboshed the whole shooting match by dive-bombing our own troops, wound-

ing and killing some and driving them off a hard-won strategic point, which
was not regained till some hours later after hard fighting.

However, it was all over by 1500 hrs and the whole of the Kulkabar ridge was
ours. I went in on the Red Hill sector. There was much to do, evacuating hundreds of prisoners, attending to the wounded and generally directing operations
in a not too savoury atmosphere of corpses, flies and the usual mess of battle. It
was not till after dark that I found Mark and then set off for the advanced dressing station with the most seriously wounded in a captured truck driven by one
of the Italian prisoners. It was a hell of a trip over rough country, no road apart
from a sort of a trail blazed by our three South African tanks through the thick
bush and grass. I was thankful that I had morphia with me, as I was able to give
some of the wounded temporary relief; even so, four of the poor devils died en
route. To cap it all, just as we were nearing the dressing station, the lorry crashed
into an antbear hole and I had to walk in and arrange for ambulances to be
sent out. Then, at long last, I stumbled back through the frightful scrub to my
little camp and to bed about midnight. Patriot casualties were about 30 killed
and 80 wounded. The Italians got what was coming to them. The Shewan patriots took few prisoners and the Nandi regulars of the KAR, after being bombed
by our own aircraft, were in no mood for clean fighting. One Italian commander said to me that he thought our troops were very cruel. This from one of a
breed capable of such atrocities as the Graziani massacres,* struck me as being a
bit off beam.

* * * *

24th November: The enemy are holding a strong line along the Megech River,
extending from the lake to Gondar. Most of the defences are on low bare hills,
difficult to get at in that there is very little cover. They have plenty of artillery
and long-range mortars and, contrary to what we thought, they still have one
CR42 Fiat fighter.   Yesterday, in the hope of ambushing it, I took my special
bodyguard of four Eritreans armed with their ancient Lewis guns up the Asosa
road and penetrated as far as I dared towards the Italian perimeter defences in
the hope of getting a low-level shot at this fighter plane while in the process of

---

* Italy invaded and annexed Ethiopia in 1935. Yet though the Ethiopians had been quickly defeated in an open combat, guerrilla resistance continued up to and after the outbreak of World
War II. At a public meeting in Addis Adaba a bomb was thrown at Italian General Graziani,
wounding him and killing some of his entourage. The Italian response was prompt and
extremely savage. Nine thousand men, women and children were shot on sight in Addis
Adaba and many homes burned down. Ethiopian aristocrats in neighbouring provinces were
executed. Monks were dragged from their monasteries, shot and pitched into mass graves. All
Ethiopians known to have received a foreign education were killed or deported. It was a fore-
taste of things to come in Europe and is remembered annually in Ethiopia as a martyr's day.

take-off from its hide-out in a cave near the aerodrome, but it failed to appear.

We visited the same area this morning, again drew a blank and were peacefully bumbling back to Brigade in a borrowed vehicle when suddenly we were subjected to a hail of tracer followed by the roar of the engine as the aircraft pulled vertically out of its dive, did a perfect stall-turn and was diving into a second pass at us before we had our wits together. It's amazing how fast one moves on occasions like this. In a twinkle we skidded to a stop and dived for cover in a nearby culvert. Further down the road travelling ahead of me was the Brigade Major Michael Biggs and with him Lt-Col John Ormsby, the Brigade Artillery Officer. The enemy fighter plane having dealt with my vehicle then pounced on Michael riddling his vehicle with tracer bullets. Sadly John Ormsby was killed, but, by the grace of God, Michael survived.

26th November: The ring round Gondar is closing and the Italians, now almost completely surrounded, are fighting back and we, in particular the patriots, are having casualties, mainly from mines, booby-traps and mortars. I have been forward most of the time with the patriots and have come in for some nasty shelling, in particular in the so-called Tada Ridge area, which will be our sector in the final assault on the Gondar defences. As I write my Dougforce patriots are in the process of moving up into their positions. I have briefed Mark Pilkington and Karl Nurk and they can be relied upon entirely.

According to the plan of action I was to base myself at brigade H.Q. in order to coordinate the patriots activities with those of the regular army units. On this occasion, however, it seemed more important that I be with my Dougforce men in person as a great deal was being asked of them. I suggested that Peter Molloy should take over my liaison role during the battle – after all he now knew us quite well. To my delight Brigadier James agreed to this.

The patriot task is a tough one. We have to scramble down a 1,000 foot escarpment, where every yard is registered by the Italian artillery and mortars, then make for the Fanta Forts, which are really just series of low hills honeycombed with defensive positions, barbed wire and mines, and finally over a long defended ridge to Asosa, where we should meet the regulars, swing right and gallop into Gondar, which at the same time will be under attack from the north by the 21st Brigade.

29th November: On the night of the 26th at 2230 Morrow and I moved up the guns. It took time to drag them up behind lorries by the light of a fast-setting watery moon, but at last we had them somewhere near enough to the OP, and while Morrow was digging the guns in, I went off to lay the telephone line to my lookout which was on a very exposed cliff about 400 yards forward of the guns with a magnificent panorama of the Italian strong-points immediately below.

Just at my feet was the little defended hill called Iridibida, and while I was

putting the finishing touches to my camouflaged OP an Italian bugler suddenly blasted out the alarm. The next second every machine-gun and all the hand
grenades and rifles in Africa seemed to open up. For a moment I thought that
somehow or other it all concerned us; then I remembered that Mark
Pilkington's men were making an early morning attack, so I stood by and
watched. It was all over in quarter of an hour, but then the trouble started as the
enemy in the flanking positions and to the rear of Iridibida, suspecting a major
attack from that direction, opened up with mortars and field guns on the low
gap in the escarpment where Morrow and I were lying up. Shelling by day is not
so good, but at night it's sinister and by now the moon had set. At last, dawn
began to break. We had not dared to fire before, as in our exposed position the
flashes would have given away the gun position. The battle on the plain was
going ahead full blast. The regulars on our left were moving in on their objectives with fixed bayonets and light automatics blazing, and the patriots and
irregulars at the same time came swooping down on the Fanta Forts, hand-
grenades flying, machine-guns chattering, all with such speed that it became
difficult to keep our gunfire ahead of them. The Italians for once fought like
tigers for a short while, but we moved too fast for them, swept over their forward defences and on. The Shewans under Karl Nurk on the extreme right took
a bit of a crack. They successfully occupied the bluff overlooking the two smaller Fanta posts, but were then blown off it by accurate mortar fire from the big
fort of Maldabar, which was really one of the objectives of the regular units
attacking from the northeast; but they stuck to their positions on the lower
slopes in spite of casualties, and eventually overran the bluff once more and later
got Maldabar as well.

By noon we were in Asosa, and a couple of hours later the irregulars were
fighting in the streets of Gondar. At the last moment, we carried forward the
little 65 mm pack gun and set it up right on the edge of the cliff near my
OP, where we would have command of the whole plain below. Sgt Morrow by
this time was cheering in broad Irish, his great red beard flying in the wind,
shaking a colossal fist at the one enemy battery which still continued to plaster
us on the ridge.

Gondar was a shambles, the previous air bombardment, shelling, and the
subsequent street fighting and looting having fairly wrecked the place, and even
as we came in there was a tidy little battle raging. No lights were on and, except
for blazing buildings here and there, everything was in pitch darkness. The
streets were littered with corpses, dead mules, and stray dogs, and the racket
was awful. Rifle fire and bombamanoes always seem to make twice the amount
of noise at night, more especially in half-empty streets, where the reports seem
to echo from building to building. So Gondar has fallen at last – the end of
Italian resistance in East Africa, and with it the end of a unique and fascinating

campaign.

The Ethiopian campaign took place at a time when Britain was fighting for survival. Dunkirk, the Desert War, and the devastating advance of the German armies in Europe dominated the media and the minds of people throughout the world, and it is only natural that what was happening in the jewel of Mussolini's colonial empire attracted little attention. And yet, in its own way, this was an epic advance, involving a running battle over a distance of nearly 2,000 miles and the liberation of an area as large as France, Britain, Italy and the low countries put together. Our invasion force of only 100,000 men virtually routed an army of 300,000 trained troops from the Italian mainland and the colonies, well equipped with modern weapons, armour, and aircraft and with every possible strategic advantage. Had that Italian army been available to be sent to North Africa, its impact would have been devastating. As it was, we had them pinned down in Ethiopia.

I disbanded my remaining patriots, said goodbye to the Brigadier and many other good companions, found myself an excellent captured vehicle, an Italian army Fiat, and set off for Addis Ababa, dreaming of the fleshpots of Nairobi. I thought that for me, this was the end of a chapter. Instead, Brigadier Sandford called me in and explained that the Galla tribesmen were becoming a serious threat to our lines of communication in northeastern Ethiopia and that the General Officer Commanding required that I should proceed immediately to the trouble area, base myself at Mekele in the Tigre province and assess and report upon the rapidly deteriorating situation in that region.

NOTE BY BRIGADIER SANDFORD ON THE REPORT TO BE MADE BY CAPTAIN MILLARD ON THE WAJIRAT & AZEBO GALLA SITUATION
Ever since the defeat of the Italian forces, the Wajirat, Raiya and Azebu Gallas and other tribes in N.E. Ethiopia have been a constant source of danger to public security and a permanent threat to the line of communication in the North East.

His Majesty the Emperor asked the General Officer Commanding to employ British troops in punitive operations against these people, but the General Officer Commanding was unable to accede to his request. His Imperial Majesty thereupon asked me to ascertain whether British aircraft and tanks could be loaned to him in support of operations undertaken by his own irregular troops. I recommended, however, that before making this request the General Officer Commanding should be asked to detail a military officer to make a full report on the whole problem involved. The General Officer Commanding agreed to this suggestion and by arrangement with the Deputy Chief Political Officer, Captain Millard was detailed for the purpose.

The report should cover the following points:-
(1) Details of the tribes and communities which are causing trouble – numbers, habitat, chiefs, estimate of rifles, etc.
(2) Nature and objects of the raids made by them.

(3) Whether the unrest amongst them is due to grievances which can be met, and whether in any case their potentiality for trouble can be neutralised by means other than military punishment.

(4) If a punitive expedition is necessary and Ethiopian irregulars are the only troops available what plan or plans should be followed to inflict such punishment as would be likely to deter the trouble-makers from creating further trouble and to "draw their teeth" for the future. In preparing these plans the opinion of Ras Seyoum and other leading chiefs should be sought and account should be taken of the local forces available. If Captain Millard considers that the local troops will not be adequate for the purpose he should state what reinforcements, and of what nature, he required.

Sgd. D.A. Sandford. Brigadier
Addis Ababa   3rd January, 1942

* * * *

And so it was that I set off the very next day on the long and hazardous journey to the far north. I decided to base myself at Mekele and was just settling in when I was signalled to proceed to Alamata, 130 miles to the south in the heart of the badlands, to investigate a rumoured massacre of an Ethiopian army unit by Galla tribesmen.

I found the remnants of an Ethiopian company behind barbed wire, well dug in with a troop of armoured cars standing by. They had moved down from their original position at the far end of the Alamata aerodrome and were now concentrated near the petrol point. An old bomb dump had been turned into a temporary fort and sangars and outer defences had been hastily built with empty petrol tins filled with sand. The Commanding Officer was badly wounded, they were low in ammunition and water, and in a rather desperate situation. Just after I arrived an unfortunate driver from one of the wrecked trucks staggered in. He had been dragged from his vehicle, castrated, and then made to walk in the direction of our bunker. The atmosphere was extremely tense.

What had happened was this: Three days previous to my arrival, the Officer commanding the Abyssinian Army unit guarding the aerodrome and petrol supply at Alamata aerodrome decided to put an end to Galla hold-ups and harassment of the military convoys using the main highway between Asmara and Dese. He hopelessly miscalculated the strength of the Galla, who were based at Cobbo Village in the Alamata area, and the ensuing battle had been a disaster.

The day I arrived, there had been another attack by the Galla on an unsuspecting convoy. Several vehicles were destroyed and looted, but a few got through and were able to report on the situation.

That same evening a relief convoy with armoured cars arrived from the army base in Dese. They had orders to attack the Galla hide-out at Cobbo and to arrest the leaders. Frankly, I doubted whether any useful purpose could come of this, as the Galla would be aware that reinforcements had arrived and without doubt by now they had faded away into the hills and would merely keep a low profile till the dust settled.

I made an immediate signal to Brig Sandford stating my views, namely, that 1) the attack against the Cobbo stronghold should go through as planned but that I doubted its value, 2) the leaders would not surrender, 3) there were 34,000 rifles and other weapons among the Azebu and Araya Galla, most of them distributed by the Italians previous to their surrender at Gondar, 4) unless the teeth of the Galla were drawn by totally disarming them no amount of punitive expeditions and aerial bombardment would effectively reduce their capacity for raiding and trouble making, and 5) disarming could only be achieved by fighting, and that the regular Ethiopian army not British troops, should be used in any future operation. The next day I attached myself to one of the armoured cars.

I found the whole operation distasteful, feeling that while there was a real war raging we were wasting time and risking British lives on what was properly a domestic responsibility of the Ethiopians. A few shots were exchanged and a dozen or two mortar bombs loosed off. Then the troops got busy with petrol and matches and soon the sun was blotted out. The people of Cobbo retired to the hills, and then several thousand of them set out to raid the Danakil. Other tribes in northeastern Ethiopia, egged on by the spectacle of the Galla, began raiding here and there and playing at highwaymen on the roads.

* * * *

28th February 1942 at Mekele: I am all packed up and ready to leave Mekele tonight. A week-old message arrived yesterday stating that in view of the unsettled state of the country and the fact that all regular troops were being withdrawn, I was to close down the station and return immediately to Addis Ababa.

My function during the last few weeks has been to liaise with Ras Seyoum and with his assistance to keep our lines of communication open and the Galla tribesmen at bay pending our final handover to the Ethiopians themselves. Among numerous other things, I have been keeping a fatherly eye on the civil prison and the welfare of the 100 odd toughs interned there. Somehow or other the news of my probable departure penetrated the prison walls, and this afternoon the inmates, rather than face the horrors of an entirely Ethiopian-run jail, decided to make a break. My office, a ramshackle affair, is situated just across the square and when the firing started I had the big steel safe moved across the window. I partly opened the heavy bullet-proof door and watched the battle in complete safety.

From the start, the guards did not have a chance. One joker, having killed the storeman and lifted a light machine-gun, succeeded in establishing himself on the high wall overlooking the main courtyard and the gateway. With one burst he cleaned up the guard at the gate, wounding two and putting the rest to flight. Then, by the way of a change, or by accident, he playfully sprayed the roof of my office, sending tiles flying and putting my Asian clerk to ground under the bottom shelf of the safe. I could not see what was happening elsewhere, but there was much shooting and shouting, and the next moment the prisoners began to bail out and scatter towards the outskirts of the town, those who had acquired rifles keeping up a running fight through the streets. As there is always shooting and shouting going on in Mekele by day and night, the firing was not suspected as anything special and there was a certain amount of delay before the alarm was given, by which time the fugitives were well on their way.

As I write, my two vehicles are packed up ready to leave. I got back to Addis Ababa to find most of the East African Command gone, including nearly all my friends. Asked by Sandford to stay on as an administrative adviser to the Emperor, I emphatically refused, and was saved from further argument by a signal from Command telling me to report back immediately to Nairobi.

That day an old man who had been with me during the fighting around Hosaena stopped me in the street to say that my lorry, which I had been forced to abandon near Muggo, was still intact except for a few bullet holes and was being cared for by the people of his village. I had long since given up hope of salvaging the vehicle, but now decided to bring it in and at the same time to visit for the last time Fitewerari Garusa Duki, Rashid, Seyfu, Gobana and others in those parts.

Armed with a Greek mechanic, a new battery and a drum of oil, I journeyed back over the old familiar road to Indibir and beyond, feted at every village with embarrassing enthusiasm. The old lorry, as if determined not to be left behind in a strange land, sprang to life with very little encouragement, and three days later we were back in Addis Ababa.

I was now prepared to say goodbye, but had been dreading parting from my two ponies. At the last moment I decided to take Addis, the grey half-Arab. My friends said I was crazy, that no horse could possibly stand up to such a long journey over terrible roads. This made me all the more determined. An Italian carpenter built a horse-box just aft of the cab, and on March 15th I was bowling down the Adama road, Katungi and an Ethiopian syce perched on the top of a huge load of baggage, miscellaneous loot, bales of hay, and drums of spare petrol. On the seat beside me was Bullet my bull terrier and, Addis, ears pricked and snatching at his hay-bag, riding perfectly happily in his padded box behind me. Six days later we were in Nairobi.

CHAPTER 7

MADAGASCAR

M Y H O P E S of a long overdue leave were shattered by the news that I had been recalled from Ethiopia for special duties. In Nairobi I was told to report to Col Bettington, the GSO I(O) at GHQ East African Command.* He asked if I was prepared to volunteer for a rather tricky job outside Africa. The idea of refusing did not occur to me. He then told me, I and Capts. Clive de Paula, van Veen the Belgian guerilla leader and five selected NCOs were to form a small commando unit and link up with a group of Free French partisans in Madagascar. We were to proceed immediately to Dar-es-Salaam, where we would receive further instructions. In due course we learned that we were to be part of S.O.E's Todd Mission. Its goals were to link up with the Free French in Madagascar, obtain military intelligence from them, and help them carry out acts of sabotage. My group's special role related particularly to the latter and the use of explosives. All this was part of the build up to the British capture of Madagascar from the Vichy French.

Van Veen I knew, as he had been with me as a guerilla leader in Ethiopia. De Paula had arrived recently from the West Coast, where he had served in Col Williams' mission with the Free French. At the last moment three more NCOs were included, also Capt Alan le Brocq Royal Marines and Lt Commander Wilfred Hancock RN.

We carried tentage for the party, provisions for five weeks, light machine-guns, grenades, various other weapons, several tons of explosives, time devices and other horrible things. After a brief sea voyage, we arrived in Dar-es-Salaam on 27th March and from that day on we were dogged by misfortune. An officer of the S.O.E's Todd Mission temporally based in Durban had flown in to brief us, but he proved to be so dedicated to secrecy and so full of his own

---

* Bettington had held a similar post in Ethiopia and it was he, with Brig Sandford, who helped me in the early days when my Ethiopian patriot movement was in its infancy.

importance that we had to prise information out of him. This was that our "probable" role was to set sail immediately for an island off the northern tip of Vichy-held Madagascar; then, after a brief period of intensive training in explosives, proceed on the schooner "Lindi" to Madagascar and team up with certain Free French agents and sabotage bases and installations under Vichy French control. This would precede a major operation to be carried out by a British seaborne task force designed to put to an end, once and for all, to the support being given by the Madagascar Vichy French to Japanese submarines and other craft which at that time were taking a heavy toll of shipping on the Cape route to the Middle East and the Western Desert war area. Le Brocq had gone ahead of us on the "Lindi" prospecting suitable landing sites on Madagascar and contacting our agents. A few days later he returned and we sailed on a small schooner, the "St George", in company with the "Lindi".

Unknown to me at the time, Michael Macoun CMG OBE was Director of Intelligence and Security in the Tanganyika Police and had played a prominent part in the planning stage and the build-up of the S.O.E. Todd Mission operation in Madagascar. Had we known this, much of the time we wasted in our dialogues with the Mission based in far away Durban may have been avoided.

Mwakatumbi was an isolated and uninhabited island, and by the time we had spent a week or two there we knew something about explosives and a number of sabotage devices and tactics. A signal from Durban then instructed van Veen and Sgt Tannerhill to set off in the "Lindi", to land near Majunga, pick up five Free French agents and then establish themselves at some inconspicuous point on the rugged northern coast of Madagascar. Le Brocq, de Paula and I were ordered to fly to Durban immediately and report to the Todd Mission before 24th April. The remainder of the party sailed off to Durban in the whaler "Sondra", which was due to arrive on the morning of the 25th.

It seemed that no one really had a clear idea of what was wanted of us. In Durban we were told that we would either go back to carry out our original mission or possibly be switched to creating a diversion at some other point on Madagascar. However, as the "Sondra" was late, events overtook us. The British invasion of Madagascar was already on its way and we were to be part of it. De Paula, le Brocq and I were each assigned to a task force troop carrier as guides to the beaches west of Diego Suarez.

* * * *

At sea we looked terrific: two aircraft carriers, a battleship, two cruisers, about a dozen destroyers, 10 troop carriers and a swarm of light naval craft. Most of the troops had been training for this sort of operation for the past two years. Those on my carrier were the 2nd Royal Welsh Fusiliers commanded by Col

Hugh Stockwell and No 5 Commando. I was to go in with the first wave of assault troops. Stockwell and I get on very well together and he has asked me whether I will join up with him after this show as his Staff Captain.

May 12th 1942: 0215 hours found me with several officers and 60 other ranks being lowered over the side of our troop carrier in a landing craft. By 0220 we were heading for the beaches 3,000 yards away. Gradually the black line of the coast came out to meet us. Suddenly we ran aground, the gates crashed down, and with weapons held high we plunged chest deep through the surf to take up a position on the ridge above the beach. Other craft were beginning to land and success signals were going up, but moments later the enemy began to open up on us. On the far side of the island one of our cruisers was causing a diversion at extreme range, shelling the Diego Suarez harbour and installations.

No 5 Commando who landed with us were making a direct assault on the so-called "Windsor Castle" batteries. It was not long before their success signals went up, but they still seemed to be bumping into quite a bit of resistance.

Our first objective was Mangoakay village, a few miles inland, but the landing was being seriously held up owing to the steepness of our beach. I knew of a more suitable area about half a mile to the south, so contacted the CO and suggested a recce. Col Stockwell told me to take a sweep along the beach myself and report back to him as soon as possible. I decided I could move faster alone and set off down the beach armed with my old Thompson machine-gun and soon met up with a party of engineers, who had also been sent off to look for a better landing. They said they had been unsuccessful, but I told them to follow me. As I had surmised, there was a landing. Two dhows were anchored in a narrow channel cut through the mangroves and there was a village, a couple of warehouses and a good road, presumably leading to Mangoakay. I rushed back to the original landing point and, having told the beach master to send down an adequate force to clear the village and then to divert all landing craft, I set off in pursuit of the battalion, who were now pushing on towards Mangoakay.

By this time the world was beginning to wake up, our first aircraft were in the air and the noises-off were developing into a racket. Following the tracks of our headquarters party, I plunged on through the thick bush and grass. There was a certain amount of shooting going on. I was watching my left flank with one eye, Tommy-gun at the ready, and also keeping an eye on some of our lads who were working their way along a hillside to the right. The sun was just rising. Our troops, new to this type of country and new also to the business of real fighting, were on edge and jumpy and making slow progress, so it was not long before I began to outflank and pass them.

In this particular battle, as is often the way in close country, a percentage of our casualties were caused by our own crossfire, and that's how I got mine, together with another poor fellow quite near me. What I felt was a terrific blow, as if I had been struck by a cricket bat. I was lucky: the bullet grazed my shirt front and smashed through my wrist watch and up through my left arm. My first reaction was to drop for cover, but then I realised it must have been one of our own bullets, as it came from the right. I was overcome by rage and got up to yell to them to hold their fire. These troops were new and probably the sight of a lonely figure traversing rapidly and silently across the hillside in the half light had been too much for them. They came plunging towards me through the long grass, but by this time a few signallers had overtaken me and I shouted to them to push forward and to give my message about the beach to Col Stockwell. All this had taken about two minutes and, although I realised I had been fairly badly hit (as far as one can be up the arm), I had not yet given it much attention. I supported myself against a rock and inspected the damage. I found to my annoyance that I was drenched in blood from head to foot, and when the rest of the signallers arrived, they nearly passed out with horror. It was obvious both bones were gone, as the arm below the elbow was limp and sagging and streaming blood. One of the signallers, after gaping at me for what seemed like hours, pulled himself together and got busy with my field dressing and a piece of dry wood as a splint.

After that I don't remember very much, except that someone gave me a shot of morphine and I was carried into a field dressing station and laid out with other wounded in the shade of a building in the very village I had recommended as a landing point. The beach and village were now in our hands and the offloading of carriers, tanks and troops was going on apace. There was a shortage of stretchers, so I got the bearers to help me up, and with the assistance of two stalwarts I was able to walk slowly out across the beach.

By the time I had waded to the landing craft and had been half-lifted halfdragged aboard together with a dozen or so other casualties I hadn't much fight left. The day was hot as hell, and there was a choppy sea running. Soon we were all drenched by flying spray. We did not know where we were being taken and didn't care. Eventually we pulled up alongside the Polish hospital ship Sobieski. In spite of the sultry heat most of us were now shivering with cold and shock. Stretchers were sent down the gangplank, but what with the ship rolling and our boat rising and falling eight feet in the swell, it was impossible to transfer us by this method. After awful delays, however, lifeboats were lowered alongside and we were hoisted aboard.

Then at last we were under warm blankets, drinking hot tea in a long ward of double-decker cots with many other wounded. Later that day I was carried into the operating theatre, given a shot in my right arm, told to turn my head to the left and count slowly. 16 is the last number I remember. I woke up back in bed, my arm and shoulder all boxed up in plaster and feeling not too bad.

Scraps of information from the shore trickled in. We really bumped into the

French that first evening and they definitely got the better of the first round, fairly pasting our tanks with their 75s and doing a lot of damage with hidden machine-guns and mortars. By the evening of the second day, nine of our precious tanks were out of action and most of the officers killed, including the CO. On the second day also we lost a minesweeper and other shipping was damaged. How most of our large fleet of 52 ships escaped the mines in the approaches to Ambararata Bay is a miracle. The French aircraft did not stand much of chance against our Hurricanes and Martels, but we lost all of our Swordfish. Thirteen of our aircraft were destroyed, mostly bagged by the French ground defences. Our troops, who in my opinion were too laden, took some nasty cracks, and casualties were unnecessarily heavy. It seems to me that we broke through at all the points which were most obviously held, and with undue haste. Having once lost the initial momentum and initiative, maybe we should have spent more time locating the enemy gun positions and strong-points and then systematically eliminating them with our longer-ranged 25-pounders. Furthermore, our tanks showed the greatest reluctance to move anywhere except on the roads and tracks, which were of course, mined and registered to the nearest yard by the Vichy French 75s and covered by machine-guns set in pill boxes. One wounded tank officer I spoke to said: "Well, you see old boy, we have been training for two years, and somehow in England with Ministry of Agriculture restrictions and all sorts of other regulations one gets into the habit of moving only along roads."

Meanwhile casualties among our troops fighting their way towards Diego Suarez were building up, and some of us in the Sobieski were transferred to the British Hospital ship Atlantis. We were told that we were destined for the military hospital in Durban, and very soon were on our way. Five days later the Natal coast appeared on the horizon. Newspapers in Durban had got wind of our arrival and in banner headlines announced "Heroes of Madagascar arrive today on hospital ship 'Atlantis'!" The dockside was thronged with cheering crowds and beautiful women. This was too good to miss, and with an eye to the future those of us who could walk, hop or crawl on all fours attempted to cash in on this wonderful reception. The hospitality of the people of Natal towards the brutal and licentious soldiery on the Cape route to the Western Desert and the Middle East was legendary.

Getting my arm straightened out took a few weeks, but I was soon able to move around, and in one way and another my time in hospital was to become relaxation after Abyssinia and the build-up to Madagascar. As it happened Sandra Gage was one of the young doctors on the hospital staff and had a house in Durban, and during my convalescence I moved in with her. Sandra had been married to Jack Gage, the great rugger international and my old friend of Basutoland days. We were together for a while in the Abyssinian war but in

1942, Jack was parachuted into Yugoslavia. While there with Tito's partisans he fell in love with a beautiful girl, Diana, and with Sandra's approval married her. The war over, he returned to South Africa and remarried Sandra. Then, some years later dear Sandra died of cancer, and in due course Jack married Sandra's best friend Connie, and Connie and Jack lived happily together till Connie was killed in a road accident. At one time Diana, Sandra and Connie and old Mrs Gage, Jack's mother, all lived as great friends in the Cape. Jack loved them all and they in turn worshipped him.

Finally my time in Durban came to an end. General Smallwood who had assumed command of what was known as Islands Area, which included Madagascar, Mauritius and Reunion, asked me to join him there as his ADC until my final medical clearance and arranged a passage for me on a destroyer, HMS Arrow. On the voyage over we were instructed, aided by a couple of Catalina anti-submarine aircraft, to hunt down a Jap submarine in the Mozambique channel. We failed to locate the sub and eventually I joined the general, who was based at Diego Suarez. During my time with the general we visited military formations, mostly East African troops, covering the occupation of Madagascar. In due course most of these formations were destined to go to the Far East, where they would be faced by well-trained, fanatical, and ruthless Japanese. I was not impressed by what I saw of their training, equipment, and arms, nor by the sort of education and instruction they were receiving. I am only a civilian soldier and this sort of thing was not my line of country, but one day I plucked up sufficient courage to speak to the general about it.

Smallwood's reaction was immediate. He told me to take a few days off and to prepare a memorandum with notes and illustrations covering the general subject, including clothing, rations and weapons. This led to my immediate release from ADC duties and orders to proceed to the swampy forested area of Madagascar south of Antsirabe and there to set up a jungle training centre through which he would channel certain selected officers and other ranks,

Unit commands were instructed to give me every support and any necessary equipment and as from now I would be responsible to Smallwood as GOC and him alone. This was a fascinating assignment. A few senior commanders resented my direct contact with the GOC. Others objected to the fact that for some of our training exercises I used live ammunition, but in spite of this the project was well supported and most of those who went through the course enjoyed it. African personnel in particular entered into the spirit of the thing, and were absolutely first class at inventing booby traps, pitfalls, trip wires and other lethal tricks and devices based, no doubt, on their childhood upbringing in the African bush, perhaps with a bit of poaching thrown in. I discovered also that a man will succeed in moving along a shallow muddy ditch efficiently and at speed and with mother earth very close to his chest if there is a Bren gun firing on a fixed line a few feet above his backside.

Anyway, the course was a success, and was fun, as was Eileen, a beautiful Free French fighter who claimed to be in love with my General for whom she had her pet name, which was the French for "Twiggiewig", sometimes "darling Twiggiewig". General Smallwood seemed pleased!

Eileen's brother, Percy Mayer, was our leading Free French contact during the build up to the invasion of Madagascar, and during the Todd Mission assignment. Unfortunately Percy was betrayed, arrested by the Vichy and sentenced to be shot as a traitor and spy, but was saved at the last moment by the timely arrival of the British invasion force.

Finally, we all returned to East Africa. With my background I feared that if I remained with the East African Command I might get bogged down as an administrator in ex-enemy territory. Furthermore, I was desperately anxious to move to the Middle East sector. I wrote to Brigadier Lush, with whom I had served in Abyssinian days. Maurice Lush was on the 8th Army Staff in Cairo. Three weeks later I was in Cairo, and moved on from there with the 8th Army in their great advance following the Alam Halfa battle and Alamein, resulting in the final defeat of Rommel's Afrika Korps.

CHAPTER 8

NORTH AFRICA, ITALY
AND EUROPE

F ROM TUNIS we moved to Malta, and finally during the early days of
June, the 8th Army and the Americans invaded Sicily. Italy and mainland
Europe lay ahead. On the Catania plain in Sicily we came up against fanatical
German resistance, and the 8th Army was held up near Lenteni. My billet was
a farmhouse on the reedy banks of a swamp flanked by two aerodromes recently evacuated by the Germans and immediately taken over by the Desert Air
Force. That first night the airfields were heavily bombed by the Luftwaffe and
our farmhouse was directly at the end of the bomb run. Very soon the happy
home began to fall apart. We grabbed a couple of bottles of whisky and streaked
for an old Roman aqueduct, where we spent the night drinking and singing
while the bombs thundered down and the skies were lit up by enemy flares and
laced with our flak and tracer. Here we were fairly safe from the bombs, but not
from mosquitoes.

Shortly after this incident, the Germans cracked and most of them withdrew
across the Straits of Messina. The 8th Army moved up behind them and I decided to shift my own headquarters to Messina itself, where my driver and I were
informed by the Town Major that all billets had been taken. There was, however, excellent accommodation along the sea front. I sensed a snag, asked why, and
was told there was a certain amount of shelling going on from across the Straits.
Kelly, my driver, who had a sixth sense in these matters, was consulted and
opted for a seaside villa. The house was perfect. There were books, pictures,
linen and even a grand piano. I took a room with a double bed. Hours later I
woke, vomiting, my bones aching, and shaking like a leaf. I knew the symptoms: malaria. There was no alternative to getting to the nearest field dressing
station 25 miles away. Having told Kelly what to do next day, I set off in the jeep
before I flaked out.

By then the doctors in Sicily knew how to handle malaria and when Kelly
found me 24 hours later I was over the worst. He said, "Cor blimey, sir, you 'aint
'arf lucky."

"Lucky?" said I. "You call this lucky?"

"Yes, sir, you are. Lucky to be here with the malaria, I mean. Two minutes after you left a shell came in through the window, hit your bed and blew it into the house across the street."

At this time I was a major in charge of the military government organisation at Corps level under Gen Dempsey. I had a small headquarters staff of hard-working young men, as well as detachments in the forward areas and on our lines of communication. Those in the forward sector had to go in with the assault on enemy-held urban areas, and under unremitting pressure from enemy shelling, mortar attacks and bombing had to endeavour to control panic-stricken populations and restore order. My transport consisted of a jeep and an armoured car. Kelly and I were forever on the move, visiting our various detachments, sleeping where we found ourselves when darkness fell, often under a wall or in a grove of olive trees, sometimes in the rubble and stench of a ruined town. One night we dossed down in a minefield and when daylight came spent a tense hour extricating ourselves.

As we penetrated farther into metropolitan Europe, military government operations were becoming increasingly important, for it was vital that our advance and lines of communication be kept clear of refugees, the civil population fed and rehabilitated, and essential services in devastated towns restored.

This travesty of Kipling's "IF" composed by one of my officers, was used by me as a sort of Operation Order to my men on the job while in Italy.

IF you can land along with our invaders
And go straight to the Police and deal with them
IF you can guard the Banks and all their papers
And just as much look after food and men

IF you can communicate with F.S.P. blokes
And also meet and talk with C.M.P.
IF you can fraternise with all of these folks
And work with them in perfect harmony

IF you can see the Mayor and his officials
And make them see the very light of day
IF you can mark his cards with your initials
And show him that you mean to pave the way

IF you can muster all the blooming transport
Be it carts or bikes or taxis even trams
IF you can get men working at your Base Port
And make them go according to your plans

IF you can post the flaming proclamations
And note the time you did this dirty deed
IF you can put an end to disputations
Of these poor folks whom you have now relieved

IF you can ration foods and fix your prices
To put a stop to markets that are black
IF you can rid the land of all these vices
And then provide provisions which they lack

IF you can close the Banks and use their money
On matters of extreme emergency
IF you can get the Railway system running
To expedite the cause of S.A.C.

IF you can make a note of all the clothing
And medical supplies and H_2O that's clean
IF you can clear the roads of mess of bombing
Repair and fill the craters that are seen

IF you can safeguard all the local records
And close the schools to all the little ones
IF you can straighten out all irritating discords
And make use of chemists, doctors, midwives, nuns

IF you can get the blooming Health fraternity
To open up a centre of First Aid
IF you can deal with sickness and maternity
And dodge the booby traps and mines delayed

IF you can get the Siren system going
And black the "Black-out" as hell
IF you can stop the Jerries' fire from glowing
And get your fire prevention working well

IF you can fill each day, each hour, each minute
With work, toil, sweat, ad infinitum
Yours is the earth and everything that's in it
AND – which is more – you may be a C.A.O. my son.

The 1943/44 winter dragged on with snow, slush, extreme cold, and hard slogging battles against crack German formations. In the Adriatic sector of the Italian mainland the Sangro front was probably one of the roughest. Every road, in particular those round Ortona, had been registered to the nearest yard by the German 88mm guns. Fortunately, we had the New Zealanders on the ground and the Desert Air Force overhead. When the weather was fine (which was not often) the Germans, who had turned Ortona into a fortress, were compelled to lie low, but all the same our casualties were heavy. I was lucky with only two of my men wounded from shellfire when their vehicle copped it on a stretch of road we called "the mad mile".

The Sangro front was bitterly cold, dismal and depressing, so I was pleased when orders came posting me to Second Army (Planning) in the UK: planning for the second front, D-Day and the invasion of the European mainland.

* * * *

This was my first experience of Britain at war. I was shocked by the drabness of the dim, dreary, wet streets, the black-out and the shattered buildings. But this was offset by the cheerfulness and friendliness of everyone we met. England was full of Americans, Canadians, Free French, Poles, you name them, and things were on the move, our tails were up and in spite of the bombing raids, the flying bombs, the V2 missiles and the resulting tragedies, it was good to be alive, and London for us was a glamorous place to be in. We worked hard by day and sometimes through the night. The coming invasion of western Europe was all one thought, talked, and dreamed about, and the end was in sight at last.

Throughout the time I had spent on the fronts, that had been my world. I had lived absorbed by my job, men, the enemy, and the daily business of survival. London was different. It was a joy to talk to English girls again, and it was not long before I found my own special companion. She was Penelope, a WREN, and personal assistant to an admiral in Planning. In her uniform she looked attractive, efficient and smart. Out of uniform, at the Dorchester, where we often danced, she was a wonderful partner.

We were spending a weekend in the Cotswolds, when suddenly I went down with a recurrence of the malaria I had collected at Lenteni in Sicily. Penelope managed to get me to the home of a friend and nursed me until an ambulance arrived to cart me off to hospital in Oxford.

After that, I did not stay long in London, as formations were already moving to their assembly areas, mostly in the south of England. Now a Lt. Colonel I was posted to the staff of XXX Corps. I knew from my planning experience that this meant a ringside seat in the punch-up we were about to embark upon. We were moved to a top security camp near Ipswich. The great day was drawing nearer and one could sense the tension and excitement, and the relief that the show was on the road. An entry in my diary seems appropriate here.

> Frankly, I am glad to be here and I am not unduly apprehensive. I have travelled a long way since the outbreak of this war, made wonderful friends, and have had excitement and experiences the memory of which I shall cherish for so long as I live. This war has taken me through the deserts of Jubaland and Somaliland, the highlands of Abyssinia, Madagascar, the Western Desert, Sicily and Italy, and finally England where I have spent about three months on the planning staff of

Second Army. And now I am here and playing a small part in what could be the final and greatest battle of all, and the eventual end of this long and dreary war.

What follows includes extracts from a sort of log or diary written just before and while actually onboard craft during the voyage across to the Normandy beaches, partly to pass the time, and partly, I must confess, to keep my mind off other things.

At last we move to our concentration areas; myself to a big barbed wire-encircled security encampment near Ipswich in the estuary of the Orwell River. We await orders to embark. The excitement grows as the days, glorious sunny days, slip by and we lie about under the trees near our tents relaxing and waiting - training a thing of the past – ready now for the real thing. Officers are briefed and everyone is in the picture, only the vital 'place' is still unknown to all except a few who have been involved in the planning.

Eventually, on the night of 2nd June my ship's party was called upon to embark. We leave camp near midnight and on 3rd June at 0100 hours I ride aboard a LCT (Landing Craft Tank) on a Sherman tank and we slide off down the Orwell River with a host of similarly loaded ships to await orders to move on. And now, as I write, on the evening of our third night of waiting, we are lying, one of a vast mass of invasion craft, in the channel of the Orwell, our's loaded to the last square foot of space with tanks and men. Continual high winds have kept us congested and pinned down to the shelter of the river and we presume there will be no move until the weather shows some improvement. We were to have been off this morning, but that was cancelled at the last moment.

Life is far from comfortable – these vessels were not built for pleasure cruising. The men are sleeping on and under the tanks. Officers do likewise, or like me rig up some sort of a bunk on tarpaulins in the lee of the bows. There is nothing to do except read, smoke, gamble and eat. Eating seems to take up a lot of our time and the food is fairly good and plentiful. An endless source of amusement are the antics of the barrage balloons. In the gale which is blowing continually they behave in a crazy manner, many breaking loose and zooming heavenwards to collapse eventually when the pressure within them becomes too great. Some with damaged fins dive and plunge around like enormous crazy tadpoles till they bash themselves to death and explode against the mast or superstructure of a ship. The day drags by, punctuated by endless brews of tea and large meals cooked on primus stoves between the tightly-packed tanks.

Language becomes worse hourly, but spirits are high and, as usual, rumour is rife. Everyone now, including the embarked troops have been briefed. Strangely enough, they thought we were heading for Norway (why Norway?) or Belgium, but these hardened old tank men, many of them from the Desert and Italy, don't really give a damn – one bloody country is much the same as another, and there ain't much difference between Krauts, Wops, Wogs and Frogs! They have all drawn £1 in French money and gambling debts are paid for in francs as if they had been doing this for months. I am the senior officer on the craft but the OC ship is one of the Tank Officers, which is as it should be as mine is a comparatively small unit. The ship's officers are hospitable and friendly and I spend some of my time in their tiny wardroom, but not much, as I know how easy it is to offend if one exploits rank, especially on occasions like this when everyone is a bit keyed-up. This evening the gale is stronger than ever and shows no sign of letting up. My bunk is perched up on three large bins of rockets and explosive material, and below that are the ship's fuel tanks of high octane fuel, so if we get hit I'll disintegrate quite rapidly!

Monday 5th June. 1010 hours: Well, this is it. At last there is a fairly clear sky and the sea after yesterday's gale, is rough, but nothing really to worry about. We are stretched out in an endless line of shipping following in a lane cleared of mines through the muddy Channel sea. Our craft is second in line of the LCTs, but ahead of us are some big LSTs (Landing Ship Tanks) and a few escort vessels. We have been going since 0800 hours and so far no problems. News of the fall of Rome came through last night. We are beginning to roll and plunge a bit as we hit the more exposed seas, but the tanks are lashed down and riding well. Everyone is glad to be on the move after all the waiting and preparation. All this now seems very unreal but in my experience it is always like that before an attack.

12 noon: Now we are ploughing through a very nasty sea. Gone is the blue sky and sunshine; instead it is drizzling, and exactly every eight seconds a sheet of yellow salty water washes over our bows and the spray is whisked back by the wind along the whole length of the open barge-like craft. As I write I am huddled into a corner of my home-made bunk, covered to some extent by a waterproof fabric salvaged from a wrecked barrage balloon. Some of the tank men look very green and unhappy, others have gone to ground in their tanks. Looks as if this is going to be a rough ride. However, it could be worse I suppose. Still no enemy action, no E boats and no Luftwaffe attack; it seems too good to be true as we are a sitting target, a vast fleet of slow-moving, not very seaworthy ships wallowing along on a fixed bearing in the mineswept lanes. However, we are riding the sea O.K. and the tanks continue to stay firm. We hear that H hour off the beaches for us is 0735 tomorrow (6th June) and we are due to beach on the next tide – sometime tomorrow evening I guess. I am reading Arnold Lunn's "Mountain Jubilee" so spend much of my time in the high Alps or on some fantastic ski-run. Something to look forward to after all this will be another expedition to Austria or Switzerland. I am not seasick funnily enough, but so far as I can see I am on my own in this respect!

1345 hours: The sea is getting wetter and wetter, but somehow the tank crew with whom I feed managed to get a brew of tea going. This was good, but some-time later they heated up some soup which was 10% paraffin, and that was not so good! There is speculation as to whether we will be shelled by enemy long-range guns shortly as we are entering that part of the Channel where we will be within range from the French coast. The weather shows slight signs of improve-ment, occasional patches of blue sky appear between scudding low cloud. The sea is as lively as ever.

2100 hours: There is a really nasty sea getting up. The bows are plunging into the waves and sheets of water and spray are showering us continually. My bunk in the rocket bins is still fairly dry, but if we change course I'm in for a bit of trouble. Still no enemy action, though we are well into the straits of Dover. Maybe they are waiting for darkness. I wouldn't call this the best sort of inva-sion weather, but it's all we've got. Black clouds hang low on the sea and it's cold. I have been trying to skip but there is not much room for deck games – only six feet by four to be exact. Had tea with young RNVR skipper in his tiny ward room and now, after a final mess-tin of soup and a mug of cocoa, I'm for a kip while the going's good.

6th June, Tuesday "D-Day". 0800 hours: The landings on our beach, Gold, started less than an hour ago. We ourselves are still ploughing through heavy seas under leaden skies; waves breaking over us every minute and it's impossible to keep dry. The night wasn't too bad and the wind seemed to drop a bit towards midnight. All the same, it wasn't exactly calm and I decided to keep my Mae West firmly secured. I don't know how Mae West herself coped in bed, but per-haps after years of practice she developed a technique for stowing her bosoms and found a comfortable lying position, but I failed miserably. All the same I slept pretty well and am feeling fine this lovely morning!

1000 hours: ....and all's well. Weather improving, patches of vivid sunshine, but the sea has taken a turn for the worse if that is possible, and this tub is buck-ing about like a two-year-old in a sea which would have ranked as very rough on a normal Channel crossing in a luxury Channel steamer. Most of the men and some of the officers are having a really bad time, but at last we have turned southeast and we are now running straight for the Normandy beaches. News from ahead is good but very sketchy – we have got a footing and it remains now for us to pile manpower and equipment into the bridgehead. As for our section of the convoy, we are still unmolested, but it is becoming almost too good to be true. We are the leading LCT and the flotilla leader is with us. The LCTs and other craft stretch away behind as far as the eye can see in an endless double line, and ahead are about thirty LSTs and big transports, but I gather we are to move past them shortly and C Squadron of the County of London Yeomanry with whom I am travelling are to go into action immediately on arrival. My old friend, Bob Crisp DSO (South African) is in command and I was able to bum a ride with him as Tac HQ XXX Corps main party are, I believe, on one of the big transports and are more than likely to be delayed. My plan is to go in on one of Bob's tanks together with my sergeant and as soon as possible on landing, gather together my personnel who are distributed on three different landing craft. One section, or detachment as it is called, of thirty-one men from 218 PoW unit and some doctors, is to set up a Refugee Camp and PoW cage immediately on landing. The other detachment takes over Bayeux town if it is already in our hands. I shall see them into position and then set up shop myself with Tac HQ XXX Corps when they arrive and can be found, but of course everything depends on how this little party develops and it would be most unwise to make too cut and dried a plan. All I have in the way of transport as this stage is one motor cycle, and my sergeant and I carry all we have in the world on our backs. When our heavy vehicles will get ashore, is anyone's guess.

2100 hours: We are lying just off the beach and have been for what seems like a very long time. It's dusk, and the general confusion is as it always is on these occasions. The congestion on the beaches is fantastic and we are all standing by awaiting our turn. Lots of bangs, smoke, noise and shouting. The Luftwaffe is being troublesome, and the sky is lit up with tracer. An enemy plane was brought down a moment ago in the sea nearby, in fact it's becoming quite exciting. Plenty of flashes, smoke, flares and explosions and with our tin hats well down over our ears we are having a ringside view from a little way out. It's getting very cold and the sea is as rough as ever. I'm off now to try to snatch some sleep if I can find a dry patch and if the racket permits. Our Gold Beach does not seem too awful, but on our right is Omaha Beach in the American sector and the Yanks are having a bad time.

Later: Now we are pulling in towards the beach. It's cold and grey and the Luftwaffe was overhead bombing this vast armada of ships and strafing the beaches, but now some Spits are on the job, they appear to be pulling out in no ordinary hurry. We are edging in closer towards the shore but the crush is terrific and vehicles are disembarking in five to six feet of water – this is not good. Here and there are drowned tanks and trucks, some with their crews perched on the highest points and even then up to their waists in water – waiting to be picked up. Others try to swim ashore. This is an amazing spectacle, one of the most unforgettable things I have ever seen. We are not supposed to waste time pulling half-drowned guys out of the water, but of course one does when one can.

Later still: After several attempts we eventually got near enough to the beach to have a go at a landing. I rode in on the turret of a Sherman. The waterproofed tank was submerged and waves were breaking over us, but we made it. One of our nine tanks got drowned and four of my men and the tank crew had a near shave but got ashore, having been picked up by another landing craft closer in.

Then there was the rush for the inshore dunes along the white-taped mine-cleared lanes. Sniping from somewhere and occasional shell bursts. Wonderful feeling to be on land, but after four days on the landing craft the world continued to roll and sway. We assembled about three quarters of a mile inland in some dead ground and brewed up tea. Naval shells from the battle-wagons offshore rip up the air as they scream inland just over our heads. Dead Germans here and there, dead horses, dead cows, much smoke and much noise. I confess that I found Gold Beach itself a rather unattractive seaside resort, but all things considered it was an interesting trip, if a little uncomfortable.

* * * *

D+1, I decided to push forward cautiously and assess the chances of getting the unit into Bayeux. As usual, no-one seemed to have a clue as to what was happening ahead, but the battle was clearly in full swing and very close. Anyway, my sergeant and I eased forward slowly on the motor cycle through the close bocage country. Troops moving slowly forward, others digging in, but so far no actual combat. Then, suddenly, we find ourselves on the perimeter of Bayeux itself – fighting in progress on the outskirts and at the railway station end, and much noise. Mortars on the go on the left flank and the familiar sound of Schmeissers mixed up with the slower and louder beat of our Brens. It was now obvious that we had arrived at the sharp end and at last we were able to get first-hand information from troops who were actually in contact with Rommel's men. It seemed that the Germans were easing out round Bayeux and that our chaps intended to by-pass the town and press on if possible.

Keeping our heads down we moved forward a couple of hundred yards to find a mob of townspeople, including the mayor, huddled under and around a small bridge on the outskirts of the town. I explained to them briefly that I was in command of a small detachment of specialists in military government and that were coming to assist them during the initial invasion period. They then gave us a welcome which was all rather embarrassing and completely out of step with what was going on all around us. We, who had done nothing except force ahead where we really should not have been in view of the activity all around us were treated like conquering heroes! I was presented with an engraved sword and we were led by back streets and alleys to a pub, where much drinking of Calvados, back-slapping and handshaking ensued. The fighting seemed to die down as darkness fell and my sergeant and I, on the principle of "Where we dines we sleeps" accepted the invitation of the hotel keeper to doss down in the hotel. We lay down together on a big double bed upstairs fully clothed. At about 0100 hours, we were woken by our host who announced in a hoarse whisper the Huns were back in town, and on looking out of the window I was horrified to find a half track fighting vehicle full of Germans drawn up in the street below. There was nothing we could do other than to lie very doggo, and soon, by the grace of God, they moved on. At dawn all seemed to be quiet, so we crept out, collected the motor bike and wheeled it through the deserted streets to the bridge along the route by which we had entered, and then scurried like a couple of scared rabbits back towards our bivouac.

Later in the day the Germans moved out of Bayeux and I was able to bring my detachment into the town. On this occasion a war correspondent came with us, and a picture of me standing on the cab of a lorry which had been rigged up in the market place with red, white and blue bunting receiving a bouquet of flowers from a little girl while I was addressing the assembled populace through an interpreter appeared the next day (9th June) in England in the Evening Standard! What a war, what a caper! My sergeant, meanwhile, had collapsed from fatigue and strain (and possibly too much Calvados), and was moved to a field hospital. One is apt to forget that a majority of the troops involved in this invasion have never heard a shot fired in anger and no doubt for them it is all rather disconcerting. Personally I am just scared stiff the whole time, but I guess I have got used to it! That evening I located Tac HQ XXX Corps, who had landed the previous afternoon, and I settled in with them in an apple orchard. Quite a nice place (the sort of place my driver in Italy used to refer to as good courting country!), except for the occasional shelling by day and the bombing by night. We sleep in slit trenches, which are really quite comfortable once you get used to them. A soldier with whom I spoke today said that he always slept in his slit trench with a tin plate over his face and his steel hat over his private parts – he was convinced he had got his priorities right!

Allied air activity goes on by day and by night. Over the bridge-head the enemy air attacks by fighters and fighter bombers are of the hit and run variety, except at night when our fighter cover is less effective. Caen is still in German hands. Our grip here is on a thin narrow strip, just a toe-hold really, but we are here.

On D+4 an American airman from a flaming Fortress bomber landed on top of me in my slit trench. The first thing he said as he hit the deck was: "Got any souvenirs buddy?"

I gave him my newly acquired sword in exchange for his beautiful fur-lined flying boots, directed him to the nearest headquarters, and off he went, sword in hand and in his socks. His parachute made a comfortable mattress for me and the boots accompanied me to within a few miles of Berlin.

My driver, Simon, had been a wall of death rider. Near Villers-Bocage we came tearing round a corner at a T-junction and ran slap into the back end of a German Mark V tank. Fortunately, the turret with its dreaded 88mm gun was turned away from us. In a split second Simon had the jeep careering backwards,

On D+2 upon the liberation of Bayeux, I found myself paraded on top of a vehicle.

round the corner and down the road. Meanwhile, I watched with consternation as the 88mm swung round and began to zero on our jeep. We ran into dead ground just at that moment and were able to make tracks.

The German Panzer formations were equipped with Mark V and Mark VI Panthers and Tigers armed with 88mm guns capable of outranging the 75mms on our Shermans and Churchills. I think that on the whole they were better tanks than ours, though about this time we did develop a 17-pounder gun and a high-velocity armour-piercing shell, which was most effective. Also, rocket-firing Typhoons were now being used to search out and attack Panzer concentrations. Once, while lying with my nose and eyes over a bank, I watched three Typhoons take on four German Tigers. All the tanks were brewed up in one minute.

For several days after the landings we had no RAF fighter base on the French mainland, but the sappers worked non-stop until they laid down a strip half a mile from our Corps bivouac area. Then, in came the fighters, together with none other than Robin Johnston. Robin wanted to know where the war was and suggested we went off and had a look-see in a two-seater reconnaissance aircraft. The shooting down of artillery spotting and reconnaissance aircraft was a sport also enjoyed by the Germans, so I was instructed to keep a sharp watch through the back windshield. Suddenly, out of the corner of my eye, I had a glimpse of a streaking black shape, obviously a German 109 fighter.

"Down," I yelled. We zoomed earthwards and dodged about among the apple trees for a few minutes. "How are we doing?" yelled Robin.

"All clear," said I, and off we went again into the setting sun. Before I had time to get my bearings, there was that black shape again. We dived down into a small valley, and it was only then that I squashed the fly in the back windshield.

With a view to getting my own back just a little, I suggested Robin should get his men to dig a few holes. "What the hell for?" "Shelling," I said. I was told the RAF simply don't make airstrips within shelling range.

That night we were woken by heavy shelling coming from the new strip. When I visited it the next morning, shovel loads of dirt from down under were flying in every direction.

Meanwhile, the battle for Caen raged on, and fighting along our perimeter continued unabated. To the north and west in the American sector another key battle was being hammered out. With their speed, enthusiasm, and confidence, the Americans completely confused the Germans. The American Ninth Division in particular seemed to be here, there and everywhere, continually bypassing opposition, sometimes by accident. Cherbourg fell and 80,000 cases of brandy were found in a Wehrmacht store. The fighting around St Lo was bitter, but the German divisions in that area were being systematically destroyed and the same was happening around Caen.

Caen should have fallen to the British and Canadians on D+2, but German resistance was based on the knowledge that the area was being used by the Allies as a pivot for the bridge-head battle. It fell on 9th July and there followed a series of hard-fought battles to the south and southwest of the city. For the first time heavy bombers were used in close support of our infantry and tanks; the Germans merely went underground and were still there to face the follow-up thrust by our forces. However, enemy casualties in men and equipment were still considerable. Any movement of men or supplies by day was doomed, as by then we had almost complete air superiority. German morale was beginning to founder.

The great break-out, when it came, was costly. Two hundred British tanks were lost within a few hours and we gained only a mile or two, but the relentless momentum of the attack did not falter. Likewise around St Lo, the Americans were on the move, fanning out at high speed in all directions. Suddenly there was a complete collapse of the German Seventh Army. Our tanks broke out into the Falaise plain and the enemy became wedged in the Falaise Pocket.

Falaise was one of the greatest military defeats of all time. In this pocket the survivors of 30 or 40 German divisions were captured, killed or maimed at the rate of several thousand daily. Since D-Day the enemy had already lost nearly 500,000 men.

Few of us had ever imagined slaughter on such a scale, such devastation, such chaos. The Germans made extensive use of horse-drawn transport, and one aspect of the scene at Falaise was the hundreds of dead and maimed horses. I used my revolver to put some out of their misery, but hundreds did not get a kindly bullet in the brain. There were thousands of discarded steel helmets. A defeated army in full flight gets rid of everything, rifles, grenades, shells, rations, cooking pots, photographs, silk stockings and women's underwear lay everywhere, and paper – paper by the ton. Never had I imagined there could be such desolation and squalor. A gunner in command of a battery of light Bofors anti-aircraft guns told me he had fired over open sights into a fleeing German troop concentration but had been forced to stop when overcome by a fit of vomiting, the horror of it being more than he could endure.

* * * *

We now turned our march on Brussels, and the march soon became a gallop. On one day the leading formations covered over 60 miles. The remnants of the German army were on the run, and on the American sector it was the same. Paris fell and was occupied by de Gaulle and le Clerc during the last week of August, and on 3rd September we entered Brussels.

That day was the fifth anniversary of the outbreak of war. The reception we received made the liberation of Paris look like a funeral. The whole of Brussels turned out. The crowd went beserk with joy. We were showered with flowers, brooks of champagne bubbled and every vehicle was loaded with cheering, laughing and shouting Belgians. A young man on my vehicle said, "Please come to our house and bring friends." Three of us were directed to a posh residential area. On the way, our guide asked us to stop while he picked up his "governess". She was a dazzling popsy. The great house we reached was a paradise, the family delightful, the hot baths unforgettable and the banquet which followed, heavenly. Then two elderly retainers carrying picks and crowbars led us to the cellar. Well-stocked racks on the way were ignored. The men commenced demolishing a blank wall at the far end. Soon light shone through a great hole on row upon row of rare wines, brandies, champagnes and liqueurs, which had all been sealed off from German eyes till the great day, this day, the day of liberation! Friends called in and the celebration extended into the early hours of the morning. It is said the birth rate in Brussels nine months later was up by 15%.

The Allied advance into Europe was by-passing the coastal ports and the strength of the British and Canadian formations along our line of advance was now considerable and we were running short of supplies. Hitler had put out "last round last man" orders to the garrisons still holding out in the Channel ports as the longer our lines of supply, the more difficult our continued advance became. The result was desperate resistance. While the Germans pulled back from most of Antwerp, they stayed entrenched in the port area, realising that it was the key to our supply problem. Until the German garrison in the port was expelled it was no use to us and, as the railways were still wrecked, supplies had to be road-hauled all the way from the Normandy beachhead.

I had a couple of detachments in Antwerp and paid frequent visits there. I hated the place as it was continually targeted by V1 flying bombs and casualties both military and civilian were extremely heavy. There are few things more sinister than the put-put-put of an approaching V1. Suddenly the engine cuts, silence as the projectile stalls and plunges earthwards. Then the shattering explosion followed by the crash of masonary mingled with screaming and the wails of ambulance sirens. The glamour of the Allies' impetuous progress towards Germany tended to obscure the cost of numerous rearguard actions, particularly where the coastal port civilians were concerned.

On 10th September the Irish Guards, commanded by Lt-Col "Joe" Vandeleur succeeded in crossing the Meuse-Escaut canal at Hetchel, thus punching a hole into the German line, which for several weeks had been blocking the Allied advance northward into enemy occupied Holland. The crossing point was dubbed Joe's Bridge. Sixty miles ahead, at the end of a narrow road through a scrubby heath and five bridges large and small, was Arnhem.

It was near Joe's Bridge, six rainy days later, that I joined the Guards Armoured Division. My task was to enter Arnhem with the Guards Armoured and once there to join up with the Civilian Administrator Lt-Cdr Arnoldus Wolters who was on the staff of the Dutch Government in exile in London. Wolters had escaped to England with his mine-sweeper and crew when the Germans first occupied Holland.

My other Arnhem contact was Col Hilary Barlow, second in command of the First Air Landing Brigade, who was destined to become Town Commandant in Arnhem after its capture. Both these men came in on the initial drop, but sadly Barlow was killed soon after landing in the battle for the bridge over the Lower Rhine – his body was never found.

The Guards Armoured had taken up a position partly sheltered by tall buildings and mine dumps on the canal near Joe's Bridge. There was a football match on the go on a bit of wasteland when I reported to divisional headquarters, but just then mortar bombs began to fall on the general area and we all had to run for cover. Early the next morning after a rather disturbed night, as the enemy were very close at hand, I scrambled up one of the mine dumps to chat up the

The H.Q. Staff of XXX Corps, in Belgium 1944.

machine gun crew dug in on the summit. They were having a brew-up of tea and I joined them. One of the gun crew suggested I should have a bash at the Jerries. They pointed out a likely enemy hide-out and I loosed off the best part of a belt in the general direction. This was just what I wanted to let off steam, and I came down relaxed, ready for breakfast, and with a gut feeling the day would go well for me. The date was September 17th, D-Day for operation 'Market Garden'.

By 1400 the XXX Corps Column commanded by Lt-Gen Horrocks had formed up and at 1415 pm exactly we began to roll forward, covered for the first few miles by an artillery barrage of 350 guns moving slowly ahead of the column. Overhead were swarms of rocket-firing Typhoon fighters. Almost immediately, in spite of the artillery cover and the Typhoons, the column was attacked by hard hitting battle experienced German units, including armour. Three enemy tanks emerged from the woodlands adjacent to the road and destroyed nine of our tanks before they themselves were demolished by the Typhoons. By nightfall, our leading section had reached Valkenwaard only five miles along the 64-mile single track road to Arnhem. Already we were well behind schedule.

At Eindhoven the next day the entire town turned out to cheer us on, rejoicing and dancing, only to be bombed that night by the Luftwaffe and suffer considerable civilian casualties. At Eindhoven we joined up with the American 101 Airborne Division, which had been continually in action against an increasing enemy presence along our line of advance. My section of the column reached the great Grave bridge captured and held by the American 82nd Airborne at daybreak on the 19th, and that day we entered Nijmegen. It had been a battle, and a tough battle at that, for every mile, every yard, all the way. At Nijmegen we found the bridge over the Waal in enemy hands. Arnhem was still 12 miles further on and the situation for the formations in Arnhem itself was becoming desperate.

Eventually we got control of the Nijmegen bridge, but the build-up of enemy resistance between the Waal and the Lower Rhine had been immediate and movement in the area across the bridge difficult in the extreme, this due to the presence of a panzer formation lodged in the forest adjacent to Arnhem. It was this enemy concentration which had been detected by Maj Brian Urquhart (the intelligence officer of the First Airborne Division) from aerial photographs during the last few days preceding the onslaught of our airborne formations on Arnhem on 17th September. The Dutch Resistance also reported this enemy presence, as did Gen Dempsey's staff, but for some reason Montgomery, Boy Browning and those concerned with the final planning chose to ignore Maj Urquhart's findings and saw to it that he was declared medically unfit and pushed out of the way.*

There were other very strange miscalculations in the 'Market Garden' plan, for example the planners hopelessly under-estimated the ability of the Germans to recover, regroup and reorganise so soon after the Normandy break-out and the Falaise debacle. Added to this was the non-usage of the Driel ferry giving easy access to Arnhem and which was still in use by the Dutch at the time of the invasion.

They also failed to recognise or make full use of the amazingly efficient and highly organised Dutch Resistance. Some of us, including the Dutch population generally, could not understand the reluctance of formation commanders to co-operate with the Resistance. I can speak Netherlands Dutch after a fashion and talked to numbers of ordinary people and Resistance personnel and some even suggested that had HRH Prince Bernhard for example (who was, so

---

* Long after the war Brian Urquhart rose to great heights in the United Nations, and as an Under Secretary-General came to East Africa on an official visit together with his wife and son. I was asked by the UN to take them on a safari to the Serengeti National Park in Tanzania and we got to know each other well. Later when he joined the Ford Foundation I stayed with him on two occasions in New York. It will always be my view that, had his warning as to the presence of panzers in the vicinity of Market Garden drop area been accepted, the whole tragedy of Arnhem could have been avoided.

far as I remember, in Nijmegen with us), given the go-ahead as late even as 'Market Garden' D-Day itself, this would have released within a matter of hours a vast force of dedicated resistance fighters capable of causing havoc along enemy lines of communication, roads and bridges, and restricted the movement of German formations converging on Arnhem itself.

I myself experienced in a very small way how easily an uprising of this sort could have been set in motion. Gen Horrocks ordered me to contact the mayor of Nijmegen and if possible arrange for 25 resistance men to go immediately to a point near the village of Elst only half a dozen miles from Arnhem, where one of our infantry units was holding a position on a railway embankment, and there to bury a number of German corpses. The mayor was co-operative and literally within half an hour came back to say that he had 200 volunteers clamouring to go with me. I agreed to take only 30 as the position was under fire and the company commander feared that a larger concentration would attract additional enemy retaliation.

It was on that day while I was with the company commander on the railway embankment that we saw an act of extreme heroism by a formation of RAF aircraft engaged in a supply drop on our paratroopers in Arnhem. For the sake of accuracy these aircraft flew into a grey blanket of enemy anti-aircraft fire at about 500 feet and, while we watched, three of the aircraft were shot down while others on fire or disabled pulled out and finally crashed. Sadly, as it happened, this was all to no avail as our men had been forced to abandon that particular position.

The history of 'Market Garden' and the great battle for Arnhem is well known, and I won't dwell upon it. What I have written is merely a brief record of my own experiences and impressions at that time. The fact remains that Montgomery's ambitious plan to cross the Rhine and by one lightning stroke to bring Germany to her knees and end the war failed.

Allied casualties in Market Garden were even greater than those suffered in the D-Day landings in Normandy. The bravery and sacrifices made, and tenacity of allied forces involved in this tragic operation will never be forgotten.

Eight thousand paratroopers, some of our best soldiers, fighting desperately for survival in Arnhem, were totally isolated. It was not until 26th September that 2,000 of them managed to get back across the Maas in boats and barges, some even by swimming, but the rest were lost.

There followed one of the severest winters ever. The Germans had their backs to the wall, their homeland just behind them. Their morale, which had been low after Normandy and Falaise, was now restored. On their own doorstep, they believed themselves to be invincible.

* * * *

By the beginning of December there were rumours of an enemy build-up in the Aachen area opposite the Americans. Suddenly, in the dawn mist and snow of 16th December 1944 under a low cloud base and in extreme cold, Field Marshall Karl Gerd von Rundstedt attacked along a 40-mile front with a 250,000-strong force and 2,000 tanks. His objective was to surge through the Ardennes, cross the Meuse and crash on to Antwerp.*

The initial impact of the attack on the American 1st Army was devastating. By the evening of the 17th December the German bulge extended as far as Malmedy and Stavelot. Then, just as the situation began to look desperate, isolated American concentrations began to fight back with unparalleled ferocity.

Meanwhile on the 22nd, Eisenhower put Montgomery in overall command of the battle. Without delay, Montgomery set about regrouping and coordinating formations in the Ardennes sector, while the divisions under XXX Corps closed in on the Meuse to prevent any German break-through between Dinant and Liege.

On the morning of the 19th December, my assignment was to proceed immediately to Dinant to clear all roads of refugees and civilian traffic to enable Corps formations to move forward unimpeded. I also had to post men to towns and villages, and work out alternative routes for the evacuation of civilians should this become necessary.

I drove into Dinant in the jeep, just me and Simon my driver. The few people we met were furtive and scared. Everyone believed the Germans would arrive at any moment. At the bridge we found a single British reconnaissance vehicle. The lieutenant had his binoculars trained on the terrain across the river. He said he had been told to find out how far the enemy had penetrated, but how the bloody hell could he do that alone in his little tin car? I saw that maybe the only way was to cross the bridge and have a look round. We then drove his armoured car over the river and a mile or two up the road. Suddenly, from a distant ridge, there was a flash. We swerved into the shelter of the road embankment and simultaneously a shell landed on the high ground above us. So now we knew what we had come to find out and wasted no time in making ourselves scarce.‡

The German Christmas assault on Bastogne where the American 101 Division were holding out against enormous odds was foiled by Patton on Boxing Day. From then on the German offensive began to falter and the weather cleared sufficiently for Allied air reconnaissance and attacks. But in the final

---

* Had it succeeded, the attack would have split the Allied armies and cut our supply lines. It would have prolonged the war and perhaps influenced the terms offered to Germany.

‡ It is probable that this was an isolated German commando unit. Subsequently we learned that dressed as Americans they had infiltrated small parties of English-speaking scouts deep into the Ardennes ahead of their main line of advance.

analysis, it was the stubborn resistance and magnificent fighting spirit of the Americans, in particular at Bastogne, which put paid to the attack. The Yanks were magnificent! Thus Hitler's last great gamble failed.

Back in Brussels, after a fortnight's leave, I managed to get a lift with a party of American officers. We travelled through the night and by sunrise were approaching the Ruhr. Ahead of us was an irregular range of sand-dunes glowing yellowish-brown in the winter sunshine. But as we drew closer it became apparent that the dunes were in fact the remains of a great industrial city. I had never witnessed such total destruction. We drove along a track which had been bulldozed through the ruins. A few tottering walls and an occasional church spire still reached skywards, but around these lay acre after acre of dust, rubble, and pools of water. Power cables and telephone wires overlaid the shattered buildings like giant cobwebs and there was an all-pervasive stench of rotting flesh, dust and smoke. Streets had disappeared, while the human survivors shuffled about like zombies, picking up firewood and bundles of loot, searching for food and water. That smell and the feeling of the terrible futility of that city's destruction still haunt me.

I found XXX Corps in a heavy stand of timber, well camouflaged and in dead ground. The Germans were nearby and there was the usual sound of battle. It was cold, and rain was lashing down relentlessly. Snow lay in the gullies and the slush was ankle deep. Much of our contacts between formations could now be made by assault boats, as the Germans had flooded the low lying land in the area, the Polder.

Gradually, as the Germans gave ground, we moved towards the Rhine. Our plans for crossing it into the heart of the Fatherland were now well advanced. We were glad to be out of that dark, dripping forest.

The first town we reached was Kleve, at one time in history the home of Anne of Cleves, whom Henry VIII called his Flemish mare. The ground offensive had been preceded by aerial bombardment. When I entered the town with my driver, fighting was still in progress and the contents of most houses and shops had been blasted out into the streets. We came upon a life-sized mannequin of a girl in evening dress, golden hair, blue eyes and a smiling mouth and I propped her up in the back of the jeep. As we drove, her hair flowed in the wind. The shouts and whistles of the troops accompanied us all the way back to Corps headquarters, where she was immediately christened Gretl.

On our staff was Tony, a brave and efficient but also very strait-laced officer. He was still out, so we put Gretl to bed in his caravan. She looked so enticing with her golden hair spread across the pillow, her shoes by the bedside and her underclothing scattered about the floor.

Tony arrived exhausted after a heavy day out in the cold and it needed several stiff tots of brandy to get his circulation going again. He then walked slowly to his caravan, opened the door and switched on the light. But instead of enter-ing, he retreated rapidly to a tree, where he stood for some time, visibly per-plexed. Then, to our amazement and delight, he smoothed his hair, straightened up his battledress and returned to the caravan. Moments later, the door flew open and Gretl, accompanied by a stream of obscenities, came hurtling through the air to land in a nearby puddle. Next morning Gretl was in bad shape, with her dress in tatters, but she was still smiling as if she too had enjoyed the joke.

On 25th March 1945, the crossing of the Rhine on our sector was preceded by a devastating bombing attack by British Lancasters on the far bank. 6th Airborne Division's drop some miles behind the German forward positions fol-lowed. However, the dropping zone was heavily defended by the enemy, and our casualties were grave to the extreme. The Commandos crossed at Wesel and I went over in one of their assault boats. By the evening of that day, we were well established across the Rhine, on German soil.[*]

* * * *

The fighting which followed marked the beginning of the end and towards the last days of April we closed in on Berlin. We could have taken it without much opposition had it not been for the arrangement that the Russians were to occupy it. I believe we would have gone in regardless but for Gen Bradley's belief that an Allied assault on Hitler's last stronghold could have cost the Allies 100,000 lives.

Large German formations retreating before the Russians from their positions along the Oder River were surrendering to us, only to be handed over later, by previous agreement, to the Russians. The entire land was recoiling in terror from the Russians – city dwellers, farmers, factory workers and hundreds of thousands of foreign slave workers, bedraggled, leaderless, frightened and hun-gry, all on the move like an incoming tide. I found myself feeling sorry for this broken and demoralised nation. Then I remembered Sandbostel, a small con-centration camp we had overrun on the outskirts of Bremen. The Corps doctor and I climbed through the barbed wire around one of the cages holding sever-al hundred half-naked, emaciated inmates and piles of corpses. They spotted the doctor's little terrier and, like a pack of African hunting dogs, pounced on it. Then, as it struggled and squealed pathetically and we stood watching helpless-ly in fear, they tore the dog to shreds with their bare hands, fighting among themselves for scraps of its bleeding carcass.

It had been agreed that the River Elbe would be the stopline between the Russian advance and our own. American and British formations reached the

---

[*]   Nearby, on our side of the Rhine, on a hill near Xanten, Churchill himself watched the
    crossing operation.

river ahead of the Russians. Magdeburg was partly occupied by Americans, but as it was in our Corps sector I was instructed by Gen Horrocks to be present when the area on the west side of the river was taken over by a British formation.

I flew to Magdeburg in a light communications aircraft piloted by an Army Air Force captain based at our headquarters. The city's aerodrome was so riddled with bomb craters that landing was impossible. There was, however, what appeared to be an airstrip a few miles beyond the far bank of the river and my pilot decided to have a look at it before attempting an emergency landing on our side. Suddenly we were set upon by two Mig fighters. We tried to turn back, but they forced us down to the airstrip by firing tracer past our wings.

On landing we were dragged from the aircraft by very unfriendly soldiers, who removed our side-arms and pushed us roughly to the administrative buildings and into a room occupied by a senior officer. All the Russians were short and stocky, slit-eyed and draped about with assorted weaponry. Their clothes were in tatters. They stank like a litter of polecats. Their only transport consisted of horses and ox-wagons. Except for a rice ration, they appeared to be living off the land.

We were interrogated for hours, no one understanding a word. We were then pushed off with guns in our ribs into a building surrounded by barbed wire. Here we were guarded by a sentry outside the single window, another outside the door, and one more sitting on a chair between our beds. Strangely, the beds were equipped with sheets and blankets. In the morning we were marched off and shaved with a large cut-throat razor by a thug. For meals we were taken to a mess room, where we ate rice and meat with the senior officers. Never for a single instant were we left unguarded.

The window of the mess room overlooked the main street of a village still occupied by German civilians. During meals, whenever some miserable German was spotted in a back garden drawing water or trying to cross the street, all the officers jumped to their feet and loosed off with pistols or any other handy weapon. Every time a German collected a burst and crumpled to the ground, a great cheer went up, followed by clapping and roars of laughter.

During the whole of the first two days I kept my satchel containing a Leica camera and a few papers and letters. No one had attempted to take it away from me. It occurred to me that its contents might help our captors identify us for what we were. Before we were paraded for shaving next morning I left the satchel in the room having removed one or two documents which could have been regarded as confidential. When we got back it had been done over, but left in my corner. Not long afterwards we were told by signs that we could go.

We landed at the first American airstrip we came to, tumbled out of the cockpit and fell asleep immediately under the wing of the aircraft, just where it came to rest. So ended the awful days of extreme stress as at one time we seriously believed that they might shoot us out of hand as spies.

A few days later, on 4th May, all officers of field rank were told to assemble at Montgomery's Tactical headquarters on Lueneburg Heath. That beautiful spring afternoon we watched five high-ranking German officers in their long grey coats, led by Admiral Hans Georg Friedeburg, being shown into Montgomery's conference tent. Minutes later they signed the single sheet of paper which formally ended the Second World War for most of those of us present.

All gun-fire ceased, no aircraft flew overhead, not a tank moved. For the first time in many months I became conscious of birds singing, the wind soughing in the trees and the sound of distant voices.

* * * *

The period immediately preceding the outbreak of the Second World War and during the war itself, was a sad time for us as a family. My mother died at a comparatively young age, and my beautiful and talented sister Barbara, who was married to Gervas Hughes, a Rhodesian farmer and rancher, was killed in a fall from her horse. Joan, my dearly loved younger sister took over Barbara's two young children and dedicated herself in the prime of her life to the care of the children and our father, who was unwell and losing ground. At the time Joan was engaged to the be married to Brian Freyburg, but he was made a prisoner of war while serving with the South African Division in the Western Desert. Brian escaped on two occasions from his PoW camp but was not reunited with Joan till towards the end of the war. Meanwhile, Barbara's husband Gervas remarried, and he and his wife were both shot and killed by terrorists during Ian Smith's 'War of Independence'.

My father died while I was still in Italy in 1943. Doctor Crichton-Miller, a well-known psychologist, and my father's greatest friend wrote from England to my sister Joan.

> To me he is still the cheerful, genial, humorous adventurer, full of zest for life, scorning dependence, ever alive to his responsibilities to life, dominated by a simple vision of eternal things that kept him gentle in all things, valiant in action, steadfast in adversity and you and John are left with an inheritance of a home background permeated by that atmosphere of security and serenity which can only be generated by parents who live in perfect harmony, adjusted to triumph and disaster, living for their children and encouraging independence through it all. Will you please give a special message to John? Tell him from me that how-

ever unattainable may seem the goal he must never relinquish the aim of being a better man than his father. There is no hope for human evolution unless each generation accepts the challenge of excelling the previous one. Only so can we contribute to the progress of our race from the monkey to the God.

CHAPTER 9

TANGANYIKA AGAIN

T HE Colonial Office had arranged my immediate release from the army when Germany capitulated and Robin Johnston flew an Anson from Tangmere fighter base in England to Hanover to pick me up. He brought two other well-known RAF fighter pilots, Keith Hampshire and "Doc" Stanford. This distinguished aircrew announced that Copenhagen had just been liberated. Our mutual friend, the great fighter ace, Johnny Johnson, had moved in with a wing of the new Meteors, and we had been invited to be his guests.

Our sojourn in Copenhagen may have lasted three days. I remember it only as a haze of parties, beautiful blonde blue-eyed women, dancing in the streets, good food and drink and great rejoicing. The city, young and old, was crazy with joy and relief at the departure of the Nazi regime.

Johnny Johnson had liberated a hotted-up Mercedes sports car from the head of the Gestapo. After we arrived, Johnny and Robin took the car out for a gallop on the autobahn. On the way back and driving at 100 mph a roundabout loomed up. It was too close for braking, so they flew over the top, made a perfect three point fighter landing – and crashed into a fishmonger's shop. Bleeding a little, but not unduly damaged, they began clearing glass splinters and frozen fish and lobsters off the front seat when a Danish policeman insisted on taking them to the nearest hospital. By the time they got there, the policeman was well smeared with the blood of his reluctant charges, who then, with great presence of mind, each grabbed an arm and ushered him into the casualty section. As he protested violently, a nurse, assuming he was in serious shock, dragged the policeman off to the nearest ward, whereupon Johnny and Robin made tracks for home. The RAF salvaged the car and compensated the fishmonger, and that afternoon Johnny, with a slab of plaster covering a cut above his eye, escorted the Queen of Denmark to a charity air display he had arranged.*

---

* Just before the capitulation of Germany, the RAF staged a precision strike on the Nazi headquarters in the heart of Copenhagen. The operation called for a deadly accurate rocket and bombing strike on the upper portion of the building, as the basement housed a number of

Returning to England then, was an anticlimax. My years of active service had served to boost my self-confidence to the degree that I felt capable of dealing with almost any situation. But that was war; faced now by the prospect of normality, I suddenly felt unsure of myself.

The compartment of that normality I had chosen for myself was the Colonial Service. Shortly before the end of hostilities in Europe, Sir Ralph Furse had asked me to help him select key administrative personnel for the post-war Colonial Service. Although I was longing for Africa, I had agreed.

The day I took up my appointment, I asked Furse who would be on the job with me. He invited suggestions. Robin Johnston was immediately accepted, and Robin proposed Max Newman of the Fleet Air Arm, one of the then youngest Naval commanders. We were appalled by the task before us. There were about 10,000 applications. It took a month to sort through stacks of files. At the end of it we put the applicants into three categories: the obvious choices, the obvious duds, and those in the grey area between best and worst where every individual had to be investigated. At the end of each fortnight or so we would select 15 or 20 to be put before a board chaired by Sir Maurice Holmes, Permanent Secretary to the Ministry of Education.

I never fully reconciled myself to working at the Colonial Office. The routine, the red tape, the caution applied to decision-making and the bureaucracy weighed increasingly heavily as time went on. We tended to ride roughshod over regulations and refused to sign ourselves in and out of the office as required. Robin's last entry in the office attendance book read: "Time in 9.30 a.m. Time out 10.30 a.m. Went home, but thought about the colonies!!"

One morning a work party barged into my office to remove my easy chairs, desk, carpet and bookshelf. They said an officer of my grade was only entitled to a table and two hard chairs. Infuriated and humiliated, I asked the telephone operator to track down the person who had given the orders and to put me through to him. She said his name was Lloyd and put me through. I told him our section was competing against big business and important services throughout the UK, and that anyone being interviewed should at least be impressed by my office, if nothing else. I called him a blasted saboteur. In the end I asked: "Who the hell are you anyway?"

He replied that he was the Under Secretary of State for the Colonies. Furse was delighted. I got my furniture back and with interest.

Allied POWs. The attack was successful, but by terrible chance one of the aircraft crashed into a convent. The follow-up aircraft, flying low and at full throttle, mistook the blazing aircraft and convent for the target, so this building too was subjected to a devastating bombardment, resulting in the deaths of many children and adults. The charity air display was staged to collect funds for the victims.

* * * *

It was now September 1945, and it was at this point that past events caught up with me. Early in the war I had met Joy O'Rourke, one of those attractive and vivacious dark blue-eyed Irish girls. Joy had been struck down by polio in Cairo while serving as a FANY and evacuated to a hospital in Nairobi. She later moved to her godmother's farm in Kenya near where I happened to be on a training course. When I first met her she was bedridden without much hope of recovery. I decided that somehow I was going to get her off that bed. She had been a keen horsewoman, so I got her a horse, and before long she was riding again, laughing and facing up to life. Then I was posted and did not see her again for three years, although we corresponded occasionally and a bond of sorts had been forged between us, because somehow she believed that but for my efforts she would never have walked again.

In the winter of 1944 I had been given a fortnight's leave, but when I got to London I did not know what to do with myself. Joy was by then in Dublin, so I telephoned her that I was on my way. Unknown to me, Joy had just become engaged to a naval officer I knew. When I telephoned, she was convinced that I was coming to propose, which was in fact not the case, as I had decided not to get involved with anyone until after the war. Anyway, Joy took immediate steps to take my eye off the ball. A decoy, one Corinne Odlum, was approached. Corinne, Joy's best and most trusted friend, was at home in County Kildare on leave from WVS duties in London and due to go hunting with her father's pack on the day of my arrival. She told Joy point-blank that she would have no part in the plot. However, the elements

The decoy - Corinne Odlum.

Corinne.

Robin Johnston was my best man.

intervened: it snowed. The 'Killing Kildares' hunt was cancelled and Corinne doomed, and so was I.

My next meeting with Corinne took place immediately following my return from Germany via Copenhagen. By now Corinne was employed as personal assistant to Arthur Rank's senior film star medical officer in London and was expecting me to pick her up from his office in Park Lane. Our reunion was perfect, except that I ran into intensive flak when she detected smudges of Danish lipstick on my battledress collar.

Corinne and I decided to get married. The wedding took place at the Odlums' country home in County Kildare on 22nd September 1945. Robin Johnston was best man. Everyone knew everyone at the wedding except the groom and his best man. Corinne was superbly beautiful, the champagne flowed, the sun shone, and even the birds in the garden did their stuff. It was a very grand occasion, but it did not last long. Corinne's father had himself contrived that the wedding should coincide with a race day, knowing that by so doing, she and I would be allowed – and indeed encouraged – to leave sharp at 1400 hours so that everyone could be off the place in time for the first race at 1430 and we would get to Connemara and our destination, Inver, before dark.

On the 22nd September 1945, Corinne and I were married.

Joe McQuirk, one of the oldest and most trusted drivers, was to take us, but when the time came Joe was nowhere to be found. He was finally run to ground buried under a pyramid of empty champagne bottles. For the sake of appearances Robin bundled Joe into the driving seat of the black Wolseley and then, accompanied by the usual cheering and jeering, we zig-zagged our way down the drive. Over my shoulder I watched guests rushing indoors to collect their hats and coats.

We then put Joe in the back and I took over the driving. At dusk, as we approached the west coast we ran into heavy rain and high winds. It was no ordinary storm. Trees were falling and our pace was reduced to a crawl. A huge tree across the road finally brought us to a standstill. It was dark, rain pelting down, the wind screaming through the trees. Joe, who had been singing all the way down, was now snoring, Corinne's corgie in his arms. We tried backtracking, but as we turned another tree crashed down and we were trapped. About 100 yards away we caught sight of a glimmer of light and a dark shadow, which could be a big house. We pulled on our waterproofs and battled our way as far as the front door, which we beat upon frantically. It opened a fraction and an elderly maid wearing a black dress and frilly white apron and cap peered at us from behind a candle. We explained our predicament, and were ushered into a hall hung about with family oils and old hunting prints, dimly lit by a hurricane lamp as the power lines were all down. The maid's strident voice announcing our presence in the next room told us that our hosts were very deaf. We were then invited into the drawing room, where the old couple were having supper on a tray in front of a turf fire. Delia, the maid, was told to prepare a room ("the haunted room, because it has a good fireplace"), and to bring food. An hour later we were led up a creaking staircase.

The room was large, as was the four-poster bed, and a fire burned in the grate. Delia was sorry about the smoke, but explained that neither the room nor the fireplace had been used in 10 years. At least we were now dry and warm, and by opening the window a fraction some of the smoke filtered out.

Corinne gave the bed a dummy-run and found it as damp as a flowerbed, so we decided to camp in front of the fire. This was a good idea until a half-smoked, half-roasted jackdaw tumbled down the chimney and fell at our feet, followed by a smouldering nest and a further brace of jackdaws.

Next morning was clear. The gale had blown itself out. I went off at dawn to sort out poor old Joe, but the car was empty. After asking around, I eventually found him shacked up with a schoolmistress, who, as it happened, had once lived near him.

At Inver we banged on the ploughshare which was used to summon boats from the lodge on the island and at last, the steward, unshaven and sleepy, rowed across to pick us up. A banquet had been prepared for us the previous evening, but the champagne was still on ice and the steward and the maids, who had waited for us until dawn, joined us to celebrate our wedding and arrival.

After spending a few days at the Inver Lodge we moved to our well-equipped little granite lodge, also on an island, in Curreel Lough. Each day the head ghillie came with his donkey loaded with dry turf, milk and vegetables. We fished for sea trout in the solitude of the blue hills in a silence broken only by calls of curlews and greenshanks.

Memories of where one spends one's honeymoon are likely to last, but the large estate of Inver captured our hearts. Its beauty and all that it had to offer made it a permanent part of our lives. Inver had been bought by Corinne's father, Claude Odlum, in 1941. With 13 sea trout lakes and 28,000 acres of shooting, a main lodge, a gate lodge, the house on the island in the lake and a fish hatchery, it was the sort of estate one dreams of. It never entered our minds in those brief ten days in 1945 that one day we would own part of it. To run ahead of my tale, it came about like this.

For all that it was a wonderful place, Claude Odlum's responsibilities in commerce and as a Governor of the Bank of Ireland meant that he could not live there. As time passed it became progressively more apparent that it was not possible to administer the estate satisfactorily from a distance. At the same time Guinness & Company, among whose directors Claude had many friends, was looking for additional fishing waters within reach of its own properties. Unknown to us at that time, he made a deal: provided Guinness & Company assumed responsibility for the administration and services connected with the estate during his life-

J.M. at Inver, our home from home in Eire.

time and that of his wife, then when both died or vacated the place, Guinness would assume full ownership of Inver. For Claude and his close friends and associates in Guinness, this was an ideal arrangement. Yet it did not take long for Corinne and I to realise that there could come a time when we would have no stake in the property.

As it happened, Alan Lennox-Boyd (Lord Boyd) had been Colonial Secretary during part of my service life in Tanganyika and had become a close friend. I approached Alan, who was then Chairman of Guinness & Company, and explained our dilemma. The long and the short of it was that he agreed, at minimal expense to ourselves, that we could there and then become owners of the eastern portion of this huge property. It is a tract containing the lodge itself, the gate lodge, the fish hatchery, the shooting on 12,000 acres and the fishing rights on the four main sea trout and salmon lakes. So it was that we had the great good fortune to become the owners of this remote but very beautiful property. In a very real and deep sense Inver became a second home to us outside Africa.

But to go back: our honeymoon ended and reluctantly we returned to London, the Colonial Office, and to our first small, but comfortable, home in Ebury Mews.

My task at the Colonial Office ended in 1947. It was winter, and Robin and I were homesick. Corinne too had fallen under the spell of our mood and was now ready to start a new life in Africa.

* * * *

Thirteen days later, the three of us were standing at the rail of a Union Castle liner as the familiar outline of Table Mountain appeared on the far horizon. Friends were on the dockside to meet us. We took delivery of our previously ordered new vehicles and a few days later headed north. For me it was a joy to be back again in the land I loved, and to share it with Corinne. The flower-mottled veld was green. I had almost forgotten the astounding blueness of the highveld skies, the clarity of the atmosphere and the almost limitless visibility. As we moved on beyond the Victoria Falls and the Zambezi we camped each night under the stars, first in the sandy bushveld and mopani forest of Northern Rhodesia, then in the high cold country of the Southern Highlands Province of Tanganyika.

Our safari passed smoothly and now we were back to the old tempo, Africans pleased to see us as were many friends of all races. After nearly eight years of exile I had expected to have been forgotten. We had come home.

Our new headquarters was at Handeni in the Tanga Province. The boma (boma is a Kiswahili word that literally means enclosure or stockade – usually for livestock – which was adopted as the term for district headquarters, probably because the first headquarters were enclosed) was a fort built in German times astride one of the old slave routes between the coast and the interior. The Germans had converted the route into a military road to Kondoa Irangi and onwards to Tabora and Lake Tanganyika.

The fort was a Foreign Legion type building with massive crenellated walls and corner turrets. There was a central courtyard with shade trees and huge underground water tanks. The living quarters were high roofed and airy. Corinne soon had the fort shipshape – walls in the living quarters cleaned and painted, the bats, lizards, bush-babies and snakes removed and the garden manured, reshaped and planted. My job was to reopen the district, which had been lying fallow during the war, and to re-establish an administration.

A page from a memo pad reads: "Repair all buildings, schools reopen, bridges reconstruct where necessary, roads, arrange self-help programme with headmen, establish district courts, running of and procedure. Appeals from courts, review. Start up produce markets and fix prices. Boundary disputes, visit areas and settle. Wells and water points, investigate and develop. Indent for gelignite, cortex fuse and detonators. Build new police lines."

"Wells": before long the local headman and I were at the bottom of a 25 foot shaft. I was tamping down charges, cutting the cortex fuses and sorting out the detonators when I suddenly sensed we were not alone. Sure enough, there, in a corner, partly hidden by a pile of rubble, was a six-foot Egyptian cobra, head raised, tongue flickering, looking agitated and angry. I climbed the ladder like a startled monkey, closely followed by the headman. There was no way of driving the cobra out, so I had to blow it apart with my shotgun.

Because of tsetse flies no cattle could survive at Handeni. Milk was available only at a Wakwavi village seven miles away. From there a woman came every day with two bottles in a basket balanced on her head. The shilling she was paid for each trip was good money in those days, bearing in mind that my own salary was £750 a year.

An Asian shop in the village stocked sugar, salt, tea and maize meal. If you needed mutton you bought a sheep and if you liked beef you bought a bullock. A meat safe with charcoal lined sides drip-fed from a large can of water served as our refrigerator. The cooling principle was evaporation from the soaked charcoal and the contraption, widely used throughout East Africa, was surprisingly effective.

Soon after our arrival, a bowman from a distant land fell foul of nearby villagers. He killed two men and wounded a woman with poisoned arrows, after which he was arrested. Murder, arson and rape were crimes beyond my jurisdiction as magistrate. However, I recorded in the preliminary inquiry that as this man was violent and likely to go berserk, he should be carefully guarded and segregated while on remand. I then passed the case on for hearing by the high court.

My recommendation was ignored by the European prison officer at Morogoro and while on extramural work there, the man murdered the officer's young wife with a carving knife and escaped into the bush. The DC signalled me that he had earlier vowed he would kill the magistrate who had committed him for trial and that he was believed to be heading for Handeni. On the principle that attack is the best form of defence, I decided to set off on foot with several policemen to hunt the man down.

I left Corinne a long-barrelled .45 Colt revolver and put double day and night guards on the boma. We failed to locate the fugitive. It was rumoured that he had been hunted down by the young men of the village where he made his original killings, but then lions, some of them man-eaters, were plentiful in the sparsely populated country between Morogoro and Handeni.

Latham Leslie-Moore, who I had first met early on in the war when we were both rounding up Germans on Lake Nyasa, was the agricultural officer and was the only other European employed in the district. He spent his entire life moving around in the bush. Latham had served as a page-boy to Queen Victoria and was alleged to be a son of Edward VII. He was gassed in the First World War and given six months to live, but he went to Canada to work in a logging camp and made a miraculous recovery. Later he drifted to East Africa. Tall and good-looking, dedicated to his work, he was much respected by the Wazigua tribesmen. He was however, eccentric in his appearance, wearing only a kikoi (loincloth), sandals and a monocle in his left eye. A mission on our border wrote to me complaining that his near nakedness was having an adverse influence on the girls at the mission and the people of the district. I showed the letter to Latham. Without comment, he picked up the office Bible and opened it unhesitatingly at Mark Chapter 1, verse 6.

"It's about a joker called John the Baptist" he said, "a man held in high esteem by these Bible-bashers. Perhaps in your reply to these blokes you could say that this John the Baptist lived in the wilderness like me, wore only a loincloth and, like me, ate locusts and wild honey. Suggest that what was good enough for J the B is surely good enough for Latham Leslie-Moore."[*]

Most of the Handeni district was arid and lacking in fertility; pockets of good land were widely separated. Crop damage caused by wild animals was a recurring problem. Great herds of elephant, buffalo and antelope roamed everywhere, and because there were too few game scouts we could not give the Wazigua peasants the protection they needed. The elephant population was increasing rapidly, there was little poaching, the price of ivory was low and shooting for sport was restricted. Thus it was that on occasions as the DC it was also my job to deal with raiding herds of elephant and buffalo and prides of lion – even man-eaters at times.

It used to be believed that when about to die from old age, debility, or wounds, elephants gravitate towards a particular venue. Large numbers of elephant skeletons, sometimes still carrying their ivory, have indeed been found concentrated in one place, but the graveyard idea is a myth. This I proved to myself while tracking an elephant in an uninhabited part of Handeni district.

[*] After retiring, Latham acquired M'simbati Island off the coast of southern Tanganyika, where he spent the happiest years of his life. At independence, he declared himself Sultan and applied to the UN for permission to secede. Of course nothing came of this and a year later he was brutally evicted from his old Arab house by the Tanzanian authorities and lost everything dear to him.

The footprints led into a depression surrounded by dense thorn bush and stunted forest. It was a dried-up swamp, its surface baked hard by the sun, covered with rotting reeds and other vegetation, and on it, wherever one looked, there were bleached elephant bones and crumbling tusks, broken and yellow with age, many half buried. It was clear that for centuries in times of drought, elephants had been coming there in search of water. In their efforts to reach the last remaining pools they had got bogged down in the mud of the black cotton soil and died from starvation and thirst.

Although I am a passable shot, I have never been a hunter at heart. But hunting, like it or not, was an essential component of life. On safari you shot animals to feed the porters and also for workers on projects off the beaten track and out of touch with food supplies. Inevitably thus, I learned a good deal about wildlife, the wilderness one lived in, the signs and signals of the bush and the hazards of dealing with dangerous animals.

I believe that every man to be worth his salt needs to experience and learn to surmount real fear. Unless this comes about by chance, he must develop a desire for challenge, something to put his character to the extreme test. It is because of this that men climb rocks, steeplechase, ski, fly aircraft, rally drive – and hunt dangerous game.

For some of us in the Colonial Service, such challenges lay in the bush, deserts, and forests of the countries in which we served, and in the majestic elephants who sometimes crossed our path. Old giants with 100 lb tusks on either side were regarded as the ultimate, but anything over 75 lbs a side was acceptable, for this would meet the costs of licence and safari with a clear £100 or so left in your pocket, good money in those days. You could take your tusks to any bank and get cash on the spot. But to bring to book a really worthwhile animal one had to reckon on about 100 miles of tracking.

On one occasion I was accompanied by my PC, a famous old elephant hunter. We picked up the spoor of a small herd of five bulls; one had enormous feet and because this usually indicated a big elephant with heavy tusks, we decided to follow them – this was on the Wembere Steppe, tough, difficult country, so we travelled light with one porter, a tracker, a couple of blankets, a kettle for making tea, and a small haversack of food. It seemed that the herd was aware of our presence for it moved steadily away ahead of us. However, about midday on the second day we saw the elephants at last, tightly grouped in the shade of a thicket of thorns. We were crouched down-wind about 40 yards from them.

The big fellow was there all right, his enormous near-side tusk gleaming in the dappled shade of the thorn trees, every ounce of one hundred pounds, perhaps more. I was about to edge my way forward when the old timer grasped my wrist.

Anything over 75 lbs a side was acceptable for this would meet the costs of licence and safari with a clear £100 or so left in your pocket.

"Take it easy laddie" he said in a hoarse whisper, "Let's just first have a look at the other side of his face." It was about an hour before the old Jumbo changed position and by this time I was shaking like a leaf from anxiety and nerves. Finally, the massive head turned slowly to face us and, on that side there was nothing, absolutely nothing except an eight inch stump of a shattered tusk. I could do better than this, and so we said "goodbye and thank you" to the herd, this time at the top of our voices and it went pounding off in great confusion and a cloud of dust.

We found a shady tree, brewed tea in the old black kettle, and that evening, as an enormous yellow moon rose above the eastern horizon, we set off for base, marching through the night and finally arrived back at our camp at sunrise for a bath, breakfast and sleep, glorious sleep.

Handeni, although situated on the perimeter of the Maasai Steppe, was influenced by the warm weather pattern of the coastal belt and was desperately hot and muggy before the break of the rainy season. Near our home, however, was a hill with a small stand of forest on the summit, and in this beautiful little grove we built a banda, a small chalet of poles and thatch, where on occasions we spent weekends. Up there it was cool, with tremendous views in every direction and superbly beautiful dawns and sunsets. But now Corinne was pregnant, and the long climb up the hill was becoming too much for her. I discussed the situation with our staff, who normally came with us and enjoyed the expedition as much as we. Our old cook (who incidentally had been struck by lightning and survived!) said in so many words: "No problem, we will blow up an inner car tube and pull mama up the hill," and this is exactly what we did. Corinne would hitch the tube round her waist and we, Kibanga, Mpishi and me taking turns with a rope over our shoulders, myself singing the Volga Boat Song, would lug her up the hill. It worked like a charm, and ultimately Corinne was in this manner dumped on the summit as fresh as a daisy in the spring.

But as time went on I decided to send her by boat to South Africa, to my sister Joan who was an experienced nurse, had five children of her own, and was in touch with good hospitals and doctors. In normal circumstances this would not have been necessary, but Handeni was way out in the bush, and because of giraffe and herds of elephants the single telephone line was mostly flat on the ground. Further the road was always impassable after heavy rain. So finally Corinne sailed southwards from Tanga on the east coast and for a while I was on my own.

It was the time of the north east monsoon winds and the big ocean-going dhows from the Persian Gulf and the Horn of Africa were beginning to arrive at the nearby ports of Sadani and Bagamoyo, loaded with Persian rugs and other exotic merchandise. Corinne was due back from South Africa shortly, so I decided to make an expedition to Bagamoyo and buy for her two Persian carpets as a home-coming present.

In those days the arrival of the dhows was an exciting annual event, hard bargains were struck and much legitimate and a good deal of illicit merchandise, such as ivory, gold, diamonds and other precious stones changed hands. Young girls were hidden, sent inland, or locked up, as the abduction of children, in particular girls, by the Arab sea captains and crews was not uncommon.

The history of Bagamoyo dates back to the earlier days of exploration and trading along the East African coast. In comparatively recent historical times it was one of the main slave trading centres and the gateway into the interior of the continent for the early explorers, missionaries, and travellers. It was to Bagamoyo that the body of the great David Livingstone was carried for nearly 1,000 miles and then shipped back to England for final burial.

In due course Corinne returned with a beautiful bouncing blue-eyed daughter: Pippa. To me this was a miracle. I know that having babies is quite a common feat among the opposite sex, but that my Corinne should achieve this, just off the cuff as it were, was to my mind a superb performance on her part!

At about this time the western region of Tanganyika was in the grip of one of

Pippa, Corinne and J.M.

the worst droughts ever. The Nzega district in Sukumaland was the hardest hit, and I was instructed to proceed there immediately and take over this area, where a near famine situation was developing. I had an excellent staff of administrative officers, vets and doctors and was able to arrange at once for three trainloads weekly of cassava (a starchy tuber) to be delivered from Kigoma on Lake Tanganyika. Due to over-stocking and over-grazing and the added impact of the drought, cattle were dying by thousands, so we bought hundreds of these miserable hat-racks and slaughtered them for food before they fell. By these and many other methods the situation was brought under control and very few lives were lost, in spite of the fact that at one time we were feeding 135,000 souls.

There was no Bob Geldof in those days, no Band Aid, no shiploads of grain and powdered milk from an opulent and sympathetic outer world, no great fleets of trucks and no air drops of essential medical supplies. In spite of this, people did not seem to die by the thousands as they do these days!

As an aftermath of the famine the district was fraught with problems, but the Wasukuma are a sensible and attractive tribe and they cooperated to the full in our efforts to get the district back on its feet. Then at last good rains fell. Suddenly the bare parched veld blossomed with flowers, almost overnight there was a freshness in the air and a showing of green and very soon Sukumaland returned to normality.

I remember an interesting case which came before me while at Nzega. A case which could have made a good 'whodunit' story. A man had been murdered. I knew, and the village elders knew full well who had committed the crime, but of course he, the accused, denied all knowledge and no dead body had been found, so no case. In the interest of the safety of the suspect, who would without a doubt have been knocked off by the victim's clan if he had remained in his village, I arrested him. I could not, however, hold the man indefinitely and was about to release him when one day a wrinkled old stranger who said he was a bee keeper called on me and that he had seen a very strange thing. At this stage I should explain that bee hives are made from hollow logs or rolls of bark several feet long and these are suspended in trees fifteen or more feet above ground level. I asked: "What is this strange thing you have seen?"

"Well it's like this," he said. "There is a hive in a tree near mine and no bees are entering the hive."

"The hive may have been abandoned," I suggested.

"No, the hive is occupied, but by bluebottle flies," he said. Of course we found the body in the hive and the accused confessed!

In due course our tour came to an end. In spite of the famine and a certain amount of ill health and hardship, the work had been interesting. We would gladly have spent longer in this district where we had made many good friends.

* * * *

By 1950 we had signed on for another tour, this time at Moshi, the most sought-after posting in the country. It was a district of about 2,000 square miles and embraced the entire massif of Kilimanjaro with a population on the lower slopes of over one million Chagga people.

Our house was on the mountain's southern slopes overlooking the town, with distant views of the blue Pare Mountains and the escarpment beyond the headwaters of the Pangani river. Towering above us, with the summit only 19 miles away as the eagle flies (a crow couldn't make it to that altitude!) was Kilimanjaro 19,340 ft above sea level. The ice-cap and the glaciers on the southwest side are spectacular and the view from our house and the town itself dramatic beyond description.

I found the Chagga intelligent and certainly the most industrious of the Tanganyika tribes, and trade in produce such as coffee, sugar, timber, maize, hides and skins, sisal and other crops was booming. The markets and cooperatives were efficiently run, and due to the fact that the district had been seen heavy missionary activity since German times at the end of the last century, a high percentage of the population were educated, with literacy generally way ahead of anything I had encountered elsewhere.

I had a large and experienced staff, and local government – under the guidance and supervision of the Mangis (chiefs) in close cooperation with ourselves – worked well. The Chagga Council included hereditary chiefs and elected individuals and was responsible to the Chagga for the proper running of affairs. All problems affecting life on the mountain were initially thrashed out and decided by the Council. We seldom interfered and always provided funds and technical staff for the implementation of any reasonable resolution adopted. Administrative officers were continually on the move, each with his own region of two or three Mangiates. In this way they became familiar with local problems and districts, the people and their leaders.

When I arrived, however, I sensed a negative undercurrent fostered by radicals demanding change. They wanted a Mkumbi, a sort of dictator, to head the tribe. This ambition diametrically contradicted the Council system which we were promoting. Surprisingly, the new movement was joined even by the most enlightened members of the tribe. In the end we capitulated, believing that the trend was unlikely to last due to the changing attitudes beginning to prevail countrywide.

The intelligent young Thomas Marealle, a senior member of the mountain's leading family, was unanimously elected Mkumbi, and Sir Edward Twining, the Governor, came up for the 'coronation' of King Tom as he called him (he also gave me the title of 'Kingmaker'). As expected, Tom soon saw which way the wind was blowing. He gave up, got a good job with the UN and went to live in Rome.

There were other important moves. On arrival, I had been confronted by a high-powered Government team engaged in acquiring land for landless of the Chagga tribe. This was the outcome of the Wilson Report, which recommended buying up tracts of land from white farmers in the heavily-populated area on the southern and eastern slopes of the mountain. These were mainly former German estates and mission lands with original titles dating back to the beginning of the century. The Report's proposals were sound in principle. We successfully took over thousands of acres and compensated the title holders who were evicted or had their holdings reduced.

Yet this policy had its negative aspects. Once the Chagga believed that Government would try and find land for the landless, thousands more than we could accommodate tried to climb on the bandwagon. Where once virtually everyone in Chagga society had farmed and fed themselves, now they had a relatively developed and complex society in which traders, timber merchants, carpenters, shopkeepers, boot makers, builders and a host of other categories, constituted a landless middle class. Such a situation greatly complicated the business of determining who were deserving claimants and who were undeserving. Then the whole issue was exacerbated by population growth. So densely was it settled that Chaggaland was virtually a huge, straggling township extending

Sir Edward Twining and J.M. (D.C. Kilimanjaro) installing Thomas Marealle as Paramount Chief of the Chagga tribe, 1951.

from the mountain's forest edge down into the plains below. In no way was it possible to provide land for all those living within the district boundaries. The situation was complicated by Chagga reluctance to move out of their traditional coffee and banana belt on the mountain slopes. We managed to persuade some to settle in the corridor of higher ground between Mounts Kilimanjaro and Meru to the west, but the majority had little enthusiasm for these cold and windy grasslands. Being in the mountain rain shadow, they were rather dry and not very fertile. Perhaps important too, they were adjacent to the land of the Maasai – traditional enemies to the Chagga. To my relief the powers that be recognised that space for the landless Chagga would have to be found elsewhere and those engaged in this quest were transferred away from my district.

On Kilimanjaro's northwestern slopes I was concerned by the state of the forests. Annually in the dry season, fires would sweep up from Amboseli and the Maasai lands below and burn the trees, progressively pushing the forest edge higher up the mountain. What was needed was a buffer between the Maasai and the forest edge. A band of well run farms would provide this and at the same time boost development in the District. With the support of some of the European farmers to the west of Kilimanjaro, I proposed that the lower edge of the forest reserve between the 6,000 and 7,000 ft contours be degazetted (most trees in it had already been burnt) and divided into farms. They could accommodate some of the disgruntled farmers who had been dispossessed when their land further round the mountain had been taken to resettle landless Chagga. The area was known as Ol Molog, meaning "the place of the pimples" in Maa, the language of the Maasai. The pimples were the many small craters and volcanic blow-holes that dominate the landscape. My proposals for Ol Molog were approved by Sir Edward, the Governor.

I was now instructed to lay out a number of economic farming units below the 7,000 ft contour on the northern and northeastern slopes of Kilimanjaro. The country was rugged. The patchy forest and even the grassy glades teemed with wildlife. Surveyors would often get lost and the only way to get one's bearings was to climb a tree or get onto the cab of a vehicle. Rhino were the main problem, and the area was full of them. There is nothing like an encounter with a rhino to get the adrenalin surging. Suddenly, just ahead of you, sometimes behind you, there is an explosion of sound – branches crack, snorts and snufflings as the beast spins round, facing first in one direction then another as he tries to get your wind. He is purblind and relies mainly on his acute senses of smell and hearing. Effectively, you too are purblind in the dense bush. With luck the rhino will take off, but usually he crashes in your direction. You start running, as do your companions if you are fortunate enough to have company, in the general direction of the vehicle or the nearest tree. The trees on these occasions are inevitably as flimsy as beanstalks or bristling with thorns. Your hat goes flying and your shirt is in shreds and you (if you are me) lose your head entirely! Meanwhile the rhino is huffing and puffing, now on your left, now behind you, now on your right until you can dive into the cab of your vehicle, shaking. You pull yourself together and start shouting to your companions, who have gone through the same performance. There follows much back-slapping and nervous laughter as each tells his tale while a fire is kindled. You brew up, eventually stop shaking and the work goes on.

There was a water-hole where the Engushai spilt out of the rain forest and ran for a few hundred yards into a glade below the tree belt. That was the site of our base camp. There our tents were pitched in a circle round a great camp fire, which was cheerful and more than welcome, as the nights are cold at this altitude.

We carved out eight new economic units from that tract. Unit No 8 was one of four I personally marked out with beacon poles and blazes on trees. In due course pipelines carrying a limited supply of water were laid, one from the Engushai and another to the west at the Londorossi spring. Take-off points were established on each unit.

A boundary fence was erected between the farming block and the Maasai grazing areas below. Above, a rough track was hammered out along the forest edge perimeter and each unit had an exit through the boundary fence below to the so-called road at the foot of the escarpment upon which the farms were situated. Then finally the farms were ready for advertisement, occupation, and development.

The Kilimanjaro district was always a challenge, and seldom did a day go by without some amusing or interesting problem. One day for example Alec Rogers our Magistrate came in to tell me that a strange case had come before him: a Chagga tribesman from the Rombo subdistrict on the far east side of the mountain on the border between Kenya and Tanganyika claimed that he had been forced by the Kikuyu forest workers in the Talakea Glades to take an oath, and that he had been seriously beaten up when he refused. Illegal oathings and secret societies are not unusual among the Kikuyu tribe of Kenya. I was immediately interested and decided to investigate.

John Maruma, the Mangi of the area, was a good friend and we travelled together. What we found was that the Tanganyika Forest Department had given out work permits to several hundred so-called workers on a big afforestation project in the glades, and it was clear to both Maruma and myself that the workers involved were a highly organised and disciplined community. Most of the males were between the ages of 20 and 30, but there were also older men, probably leaders. In addition there were teachers and schools. We both went away with the impression that something unusual and rather sinister was on the go in this place.

On my return to Moshi I contacted my Provincial Commissioner (Page-Jones), told him about the oathings and my impression that something was amiss. PJ and I were never on very good terms, and he took the opportunity then and there to pour cold water on my story. His reaction left me feeling very frustrated, so I arranged with the Chief of Police for a temporary post to be established at the Glades with a good man in charge who would be able to report back if he detected anything untoward happening. At the same time I

Naturally while based on Kilimanjaro's slopes I took every opportunity to climb the mountain. The doyen of the local climbers, however, was the Reverend Dr Richard Reusch who climbed it at least 50 times.

wrote a personal letter to Sir Philip Mitchell, the Governor of Kenya, whom I had got to know during the war in Ethiopia when, as General Mitchell, he was the senior political officer in charge of enemy occupied territory. I had a friendly reply from Mitchell, but he made it quite clear that in his view I was talking through the top of my hat. He went out of his way to say that rumours of oathings and the seeds of unrest and an uprising in Kenya were a lot of media nonsense.

This happened in 1950, two years before the Mau Mau rebellion broke out in Kenya in 1952. I was unable to follow up the issue, because during 1950 I was transferred to a more senior appointment in Bechuanaland.

I returned to East Africa on leave two or three years later to find Kenya on a war footing and the Mau Mau rebellion in full swing. It is just possible that if the symptoms of unrest in the period leading up to the holocaust had been taken more seriously early on, some sort of solution or compromise might have been reached. I am convinced that the Talakea Glades stronghold was a Mau Mau training centre, just outside the Kenya government's jurisdiction.

Naturally, while based on Kilimanjaro's slopes I took every opportunity to climb the mountain and came to know it well. The doyen of the local climbers was The Reverend Dr Richard Reusch – the famous "Old Man of the Mountain". He was one of the legendary figures of Kilimanjaro. As a Lutheran Pastor based at Marangu at the foot of the mountain, he made an average of two ascents each year between 1925 and 1950. And in 1926 it was he who discovered the famous frozen leopard on the crater rim, and to this day the inner crater, which is still slightly active, is named after him.

Richard Reusch was Chairman of the Mountain Club and I was Vice Chairman. One day in 1950 Richard asked me to accompany him on an expedition up the mountain to celebrate his 50th ascent on his 60th birthday.

We took two porters and set off in moonlight after dinner from the hotel at Marangu. We slept the first night at the hut just above the forest (then the Bismarck, now Mandara Hut) and the next day continued via Peters' Hut (now Horombo) to Kibo at the foot of the final scree. That night there were high winds and a very heavy snowfall, and climbing conditions looked dismal, to say the least. Anyway, at 3 a.m. we sent the porters back to wait at Peters' with our loads, and commenced the ascent to Gillman's Point in a bitter wind, swirling mist, and flurries of snow and sleet.

In spite of this we made good time to Gillman's Point on the crater rim, but from then onwards we had problems. The new snow was knee deep and beneath it the ice was rough and steel-hard; the weather was awful and visibility poor. By the time we reached Hans Meyer Point, Reusch was in a state of collapse, blue in the face, staggering and frequently falling down. Fortunately, perhaps, I was going well that day, but as we crawled on towards the summit, now only a few hundred yards away, I became increasingly concerned about my companion. For one thing he was kitted up like an early German explorer in knickerbockers, leggings and a tweed jacket, and he was obviously completely done in.

I decided that to continue any further could result in both of us losing our lives, as he was a heavy man and in no way would I be able to drag him down. At over 19,000 ft (5,800 m) I found it very difficult to work out a strategy to cover the situation, what to say, and what to do. However, in the end I said, "Richard, I think you are very tired and completely at the end of your tether. No doubt we could ultimately reach the summit, but having done so, you might collapse and I would not be able to carry you down; indeed you might even die up there."

There was a long pause while he coughed and spluttered and then in a croaking voice he said "But you see, I vont to die up there." I was completely confused by this answer and was at a loss to know how to handle him. Anyway, we staggered on for a while, and by now Reusch was mostly on his hands and knees. Finally, words failing me, I took his arm, turned him round and pushed him slowly downwards ahead of me.

Somehow we reached Peters' Hut that night. Next morning Reusch suggested that we should give the summit another go, but I refused point-blank, and we returned to Moshi. He never really forgave me, but I know for sure that he would not have survived had we continued.

During our time at Moshi I explored the rapidly receding glaciers on the north west face. One place I never visited but explored to some extent years later from my aeroplane was the Great Barranco, the awe-inspiring 7,000 ft (2,100 m) crack in the eastern face of Mawenzi, Kilimanjaro's second peak. Derick Pritchard made an epic but unsuccessful assault on this place and got to know it well. So far as I know it has never been climbed and it will always remain one of the greatest challenges on this fascinating mountain. For nine years I was closely associated, together with Sir Donald MacGillivray, Kenneth Matiba, James Foster and one or two others, with the Outward Bound Mountain School at Loitokitok. We ran this as a charity, and under Derick Pritchard, who was a superb warden, the project was an enormous success.

Our tour in Tanganyika's Northern Province was marred by a disaster. Corinne, riding her swift little bay gelding, fell while leading the field in a ladies' race at a local meeting. She was overrun by the following riders and the base of her skull fractured. For days it was touch and go as we feared she would never regain consciousness, but slowly, very slowly, she recovered sufficiently to be flown to England. There, over a year or more, most of the damage, which affected her eyesight and hearing, was patched up. Philippa was cared for by the wife of one of my district officers, and by virtue of the kindness and sympathy of our friends in the district, I managed to battle through this period. My leave was nearly due and soon Philippa and I were able to join Corinne at Inver in Ireland.

CHAPTER 10

BECHUANALAND

I STILL have amongst my papers the copy of a dispatch from the Secretary of State for the Colonies to the Governor of Tanganyika requesting my transfer to the Bechuanaland Protectorate.

The appointment was on promotion. I was now Divisional Commissioner administering the northern and western half of the territory. For administrative purposes Bechuanaland was to be divided into two with a senior administrator in charge of each portion, both directly responsible to the Resident Commissioner who was the senior official for the Protectorate and actually based at Mafeking in South Africa.

My area embraced the whole of the territory lying roughly between the rivers Zambezi in the north and the Limpopo in the south. A vast and fascinating tract of country made up of six administrative centres, each with its DC and supporting services and including 11,000 square miles of the Okavango Swamp; the great Makgadikgadi pan, Lake Ngami and the Kalahari desert wastelands inhabited by the little yellow Bushmen. To the far west was South West Africa and in the east the Rhodesian border. The total area was roughly two thirds of the protectorate as a whole.

The key district at that time was the Bamangwato Reserve with its head-quarters at Serowe. I wish to make special mention of this area, because Seretse Khama, the hereditary heir to the chieftainship in this the leading tribe in the Protectorate, became engaged to and subsequently married an English girl, Ruth Williams, whom he met in London.

Seretse's marriage to a white girl had repercussions throughout Africa. Racialism was still widespread. Whites in both Bechuanaland and southern Africa generally were scandalised. Locally the Bamangwato, of whom Seretse was head, divided into two factions, namely those against the marriage and those who accepted it. The opponents, known as the Rametsana Group, were led by Tshekedi Khama, who was Regent while the young Seretse was in the United Kingdom. The local administrators were so alarmed by the schism that developed in the country's biggest tribe that they believed it would lead to civil

Exiles: Seretse Khama and his wife the former Ruth Williams in Britain. Their marriage caused
a political crisis as it was opposed by some traditionalists among the Bamangwato as well as by
racialists in southern Africa.

war. Their alarm prevailed all the way to Whitehall and was so convincing that Britain's Labour Government, antiracialist as it was philosophically, decided to prevent Seretse from returning to Bechuanaland and forced him to stay in Britain as an exile from his homeland. For his part Tshekedi Khama himself went into voluntary exile at Rametsana in Bechuanaland. The Protectorate was now thoroughly unsettled and divided. At the root of the problem was inept administration. Perhaps the racial prejudices that were so prominent in South Africa had unduly influenced the officials in Bechuanaland and it was this which led them to give greater credence to the idea of civil war than it warranted. In due course, calmer minds prevailed in London. Clearly a manifestly unjust decision had to be reversed and calm restored. Whitehall's wisdom was that a new broom was called for and I was chosen. Perhaps the fact that I was the only D.C. in the Colonial Service who spoke Afrikaans had something to do with it.

This then, in a nutshell, was the situation as I found it when one rather warm day (the shade temperature was 100°F) I arrived at Francistown in Bechuanaland having motored down some 2,000 miles from snow-capped slopes of Kilimanjaro in Tanganyika, accompanied by Hamisi, my faithful old friend and servant, and Tito a bull terrier.

Many things I learned in the army, but one of the most important was man-management and that the well-being and welfare of your men at any time and in any situation was paramount. For this reason I was surprised and saddened that no provision whatsoever had been made for my arrival, no house, no letter of welcome from the Resident Commissioner, the most senior officer for the Protectorate and my immediate superior, no instructions or suggestions as to my duties and, as for the British High Commissioner in Capetown, he appeared to be unaware of the appointment.

On arrival I called on the DC in Francistown and he offered to try to find me a room at the drab little hotel in the dusty main street of the town, and when I demurred he rather reluctantly suggested that perhaps I could stay with him. In the circumstances I chose to move with Hamisi and my hound into the inadequately equipped rest-house.

It did not take me long to discover the reasons for the cold reception. For a certain type of officer in the Protectorate this was a cosy service in which you climbed slowly but steadily up a ladder, and provided you did not put a foot wrong and kept your nose reasonably clean, you arrived eventually at the top, or near to it, with a nice pension, some sort of honour or award, followed by a happy retirement to the Cape of Good Hope, or you even went "home" to dear old England! For these characters it was a nice, comfortable, unhurried life style, everyone knew everyone and had done since the year dot, and old traditions and procedures were sacrosanct.

For this type of officer too, the arrival of a new boy in a senior position, with new ideas, and perhaps a fresh approach to a long established pattern of living was a bore. The situation had been aggravated somewhat in recent times in that when India was dismantled from the Empire in 1948, a few ex-India Imperial Civil Service (ICS) Officers and other outsiders, John Millard for example, had been posted to the Protectorate and this was resented by some of the old timers.

Later on, when I had been in the country for a while, made friends and had got to know and respect many of my fellow officers, one of my DCs, who had a flair for this sort of thing, gave me a jingle he wrote, which I think describes very sufficiently what I have tried to express above:

BOMBAY HOUSE
We're Imperial Cold Storage, superior grade,
And nearly as perfect as fellows are made.
We can't understand all this blather and fuss,
The Colonial Service are coolies to us.

To live in the B.P.'s a terrible bore,
We'd rather go back to Bengal or Lahore,
But Mafeking's chummy and natty and nice,
Where I.C.S. cluster like Travencore lice.

Go out in the districts. Of course we won't go.
We'll sit in Headquarters, say "Yes" and say "No".
We'll draft regulations, send circulars through,
Instruct all the Districts in King's English too.

Oh, it's lovely in Butlin's with buttons and bells
And never a trace of sour African smells:
We call up the typists to take a few notes,
And nark the departments by changing their votes.

We run all the Customs, grant permits or not:
Our algebra fractions are specially hot,
Two "x" over "y" equals "k" over "l",
Where "x" is unknown and others as well.

We've got Bamangwato affairs on the hook,
We've read little Izzy Schapira's big book,
The troubles created by ignorant men
Are solved by one touch of a capable pen.

The Africans – bless them – are pretty good chaps
We'll go on shikari and take a few snaps.
We haven't yet seen them - at present we're due
To scrap all the systems and start them anew.

Tshekedi Khama: a great man by any standards.

How did things get managed before we came here?
New forms are the answer, so be of good cheer;
We'll sit in our office with hundreds of files
And plenty of cushions to save us from piles.

I confess that on arrival I did get the impression that I had come to a country where the official personnel were living in a world of their own, out of touch with developments elsewhere on the African continent, and resentful of change.[*] In spite of this I soon realised that, generally speaking, the population of the country of every race and creed, the officials, traders, farmers, miners and tribesmen were some of the very best, and in this community I made many lifelong friends. The Africans, were mainly cattle ranchers, proud and intelligent people, who survived in a tough sub-desert environment, but they too were living mostly in an age gone by. The Victorian era was the first and last real

---

[*] To my amazement, I found that public buildings, the Post Office in Francistown for example, still had apartheid type notice-boards giving separate access to whites and blacks. Without referring this issue to higher authority, I immediately had all such notices removed.

milestone in their history and until recently, when a few enlightened men were beginning to become politically conscious, they had been satisfied to live happily and without question under the protection of the British Flag. There were exceptions, however. One of them was Tshekedi Khama, the most intelligent and farseeing African I have ever met; a great man by any standards. Tshekedi had a very clear and accurate picture in his mind of where Africa as a whole was heading and was far more advanced in his thinking than many of the so-called experts in the country, and for that matter in Whitehall at that time. It soon became clear to me that the key to most of the problems in Bechuanaland was in the hands of this man, and I planned to win his confidence, friendship and cooperation at all costs, but this was easier said than done. Tshekedi, throughout his political life had been at loggerheads with the Administration, and for their part officials had given him a rough ride.

It took me some time to break through Tshekedi's defences and get to know him well. I asked him to come and stay with me and informed the Secretariat in Mafeking of my intention, only to be told that this sort of thing was "not done" (confirming how racial prejudice influenced decision making). However, I went ahead, he came, and an understanding was established between us which was to prove valuable as time went on.

In the beginning, the more I studied the Bamangwato issue the more I realised that I had a problem of extreme complexity on my hands. I was finding it difficult to convince myself that I could handle it without the cooperation and full support of the Bechuanaland Government and, for that matter, the British High Commissioner. In those early days it was obvious to me that I could not expect much sympathy from these quarters, and if it had not been for personal letters received at that time from friends and other well-wishers, I would have been seriously tempted to throw in my hand.

Early on, I had a personal and informal letter from the Colonial Secretary himself which, coming when it did, gave my morale the boost it needed. I still have this letter and another from Sir Ralph Furse, under whom I had worked in the Colonial Office, which gave me further encouragement. Furse said: "I have heard of your new adventure and write to send you my warmest good wishes and congratulations. They could not have picked a better man for this job; but what a job. The most difficult and important task that could have been given in the whole Empire to a man of your age. More power to your elbow." He went on to say, "You will have a difficult time, but you can cope with it if any man can. Remember, if you get troubled, that your Secretary of State – Salisbury – is one of the best and wisest of Englishmen, a real patriot, utterly straight, disinterested, and un-selfseeking."

All this was good high-sounding stuff which helped me a great deal. Fortunately, Furse and others were not aware of my own personal lack of faith in my ability or of the resentment towards me and what I understood to be my terms of reference in the Protectorate, which were that the Seretse and Bamangwato tribal issue would in future be mainly in my hands.

I decided to set up my headquarters in Francistown in the Tati Concession bordering on the western boundary of Rhodesia. At that time Francistown was a rather drab little place in itself, but the Concession had an interesting history dating back to Cecil Rhodes, the early Matabele wars, and gold; in fact gold was mined here before the discovery of the Witwatersrand in the Transvaal. Some of the old men in the town still remembered the rip-roaring days of the gold-rush, and the stage-coaches on the Tati route through to Rhodesia.

From my point of view Francistown was strategically well placed in the area under my control, with Serowe, the capital of the Bamangwato Reserve, to the south, Maun and the Okavango swamps 300 miles due west. Ghanzi, the home of the Bushmen, lay away south of Maun and Lake Ngami. Up in the north-western corner was the Chobe district marching with Rhodesia and with the Victoria Falls only a stone's throw across the border. My kingdom was a vast and rather featureless chunk of Africa, lying between the great Zambezi and its tributaries and the "green, greasy" Limpopo in the far south. All desert and sub-desert areas of the world have a special beauty and fascination of their own, and for me this country and my assignment, in spite of its complexity, soon cast its spell upon me.

For Corinne, too, the country had its attraction and she often accompanied me on my long treks into the interior, promoting the welfare of the female population and the Girl Guide movement. A journey between any two points in Bechuanaland involved hundreds of miles of travelling over rough country and through heavy sand, and for this purpose an excellent vehicle had been developed, the caboose, a sort of mobile home-cum-office on an eight ton chassis, with built-in sleeping bunks, a staff and baggage compartment, long-range fuel and water tanks and big balloon tyres for the sand, and a radio transmitter. You added other knick-knacks to your liking. Corinne and I would go to bed in the caboose after dinner at home, and then, about midnight, old Masunga, our driver, would arrive and we would go bumbling off into the night. One's top speed seldom exceeded 15 mph and once you got used to the movement you slept well. Just before sunrise Masunga would pull up under a flat-topped camel-thorn tree or beside an enormous baobab. Almost immediately tea and shaving water were at the bedside, a mess tent erected, table and chairs arranged under the tree and then breakfast. Normally we worked or rested for a couple of hours and then hit the trail once more, travelling steadily on with a couple of stops for tea or a leg stretch. Towards sunset we would make camp and usually there would be time for a walk with a gun and the chance of picking up a francolin or guinea-fowl. Finally darkness, time for a drink, a bath, and then supper in the caboose or

The caboose: Masunga would pull up under a flat-topped camel-thorn tree or beside an enormous baobab.

more often out under the stars near the fire, with a hurricane lamp hanging from a tent peg driven into the bark of the nearby baobab. Normally, if it was not too cold (the winter nights could be bitter), we preferred to sleep out in the open and be lulled to sleep by the magic sounds of the African night, the yapping of jackals, the whooping of hyenas, the plaintive call of nightjars and often of lions roaring in the distance: combined into a lovely, sometimes eerie music of a remote but beautiful wilderness.

Much as we loved our long treks across the Kalahari in the caboose and our wonderful camps in lonely far away places, I found that travelling in my enormous area was taking up too much of my time, and I decided to get myself airborne. This was a revolutionary idea in Bechuanaland, as single-engined aircraft (all that I wanted or could afford) were as rare as supernovas in the Bechuanaland skies. However, it happened that in Francistown itself were eight or nine Dakotas chartered by the Chamber of Mines in Johannesburg to fly in mine workers from various parts of East and Central Africa. The recruits were brought to Francistown from Nyasaland, Angola, Northern Rhodesia or wherever, and then sent on by train to the Witwatersrand. For a young African in those days a period on contract working on a mine in South Africa was an adventure which gave him esteem and standing in his tribe, almost a test of manhood. He went off as a skinny, ill-fed country bumpkin and came back a year or two later, big, strong and sophisticated with his pockets full of lolly and

I bought a beautiful claret red Tiger Moth for £180.

loaded up with loot for his family and clan. Thousands of mine workers were moved and eventually repatriated in this manner and, as I have said, Francistown was the staging post in their epic journey from some remote village in the bush to the hustle and bustle and bright lights of the great city. One of the Dak pilots, Jimmy Miles, had been a fighter instructor during the war and still had his instructor's licence. I asked him what he thought of the idea - me flying - and how I should go about it. Jimmy said: "Piece of cake, old mate, get yourself a flying machine and I'll teach you."

I said: "How? Where? What sort of flying machine?"

He replied: "Go to Johannesburg with a few bob in your pocket and buy one of those ex South African Air Force Tiger Moths parked behind No 2 hangar at Baragwanath. If you can fly a Tiger properly you will be able to fly almost anything and I will show you how, and what I can't teach you the Tiger will!"

There were only three licensed female pilots in South Africa at this time and one of them was the beautiful Yvonne, wife of one of the Dak pilots at Francistown. I went to see Yvonne and asked whether she would come with me to Johannesburg for two or three days. Not surprisingly she looked at me a bit sideways at this suggestion, but when I explained that the real object of the proposal was that we would buy an aeroplane and that we, or rather she, would fly it back. She stopped looking at me sideways and almost fell out of her chair with excitement and the deal was on.

We got a lift in one of the Daks to Johannesburg, went straight to Baragwanath, bought a beautiful claret red Tiger Moth for £180, filled up with fuel, took off and pointed it in the direction of Francistown. We spent the first night at Beit Bridge on the Limpopo, refuelled at dawn the next morning and finally came roaring in over Francistown. By now the whole district had been alerted and there had been much juicy chatter among the ladies of the town about me and Yvonne, so our arrival back was quite an event! Yvonne did a rather rickety victory roll over the town and a few minutes later we were rumbling along the runway, home and dry. And that was that. The rest was up to Jimmy Miles and myself.

Jimmy was a first-rate instructor, one of the very best, and I could not have had a better training anywhere. He was firm but understanding and at the same time patient. We got to know each other well and our flights together were occasions we both cherished. I think too that he loved flying the Tiger, rather in the same way that a sailor from a huge battle-wagon will spend his off time sailing a small dinghy. Our periods of instruction usually ended with an orgy of crazy manoeuvres and aerobatics, which at first terrified me, but in the end I think increased confidence in myself and my aeroplane. Also, I learned a thing or two in the process.

Finally, one memorable day, without warning Jimmy climbed out of the open front cockpit, shoved his flying goggles up on his head, took off his leather flying helmet, and then shouted above the clatter of the engine: "OK she's all yours, take her away."

Then he turned round, and without even looking back just walked off! I think one's first solo must be an occasion which everyone who flies or has flown remembers vividly throughout his life. Suddenly, the moment of truth in your meagre flying experience has arrived. Suddenly, without warning, you are on your own, overwhelmed by a mixed feeling of doubt, dread and extraordinary exhilaration. I settled down in my seat, tightened my harness and tried to relax, then trundled down to the end of the strip, did my checks and was away. The first landing was a disaster, I went careering down the dusty dirt runway like a bouncing tennis ball and eventually ended up with one wheel in the grass. I am quite certain that the old Tiger Moth had smiled when Jimmy Miles walked away and then said to herself (I think she was a lady!) "I quite like this fellow and after all he saved me from the knacker's yard. However, it is important that he should not be over-confident, and it's important too that he should know who is the real boss in our relationship. But in the end I'll be kind to him and take care of him."

Anyway, the next circuit was very good by my standards, and my third and final circuit that day was also not half bad. And so began 29 years of flying, during which I owned a number of different aeroplanes and flew several thousand

The Bechuanaland section of Africa's Great North Road left something to be desired!

hours in Bechuanaland, South Africa, Rhodesia, East and Central Africa, and once with a friend all the way from our little grass strip on the farm on Kilimanjaro to Surrey in England.

In the course of time our aircraft became very much part of our lives and lifestyle and most of our happiest memories are linked in one way and another with the "Whizzer" and the feeling of independence and freedom it gave us. When we left Bechuanaland and bought a farm on Kilimanjaro, our aeroplane was a sort of airborne farm vehicle, which earned its keep a hundred times over, collecting spares for the tractors and combines, transporting the sick to hospital, searching for lost or stolen cattle, collecting wages and supplies from town, and on one occasion, smuggling a large and very stroppy prize bull calf into the country! Then there were trips to the coast, bird shooting safaris in the bush and camping expeditions with our cook, tents, dogs, guns and food piled in on top of the passengers. In fact our aeroplane was a work-horse par excellence and a great joy to us always. Going back to those early days of flying there were some interesting and unusual occasions. Once for example, after I had been going solo for a couple of weeks, Jimmy Miles suggested that we should have a check-out. "Your spins to the left," he said, "are fine, but to the right they are lousy, so climb up to 3,000 feet and for starters do a few spins to the right."

Meanwhile, he himself settled down in the front cockpit with his head well down and his nose in a paperback. At about 2,000 feet I was in trouble, no

Bechuanaland was a little behind the times in some respects. When I arrived stocks were still used: here being given a trial by a friend, Caroline Combe.

power, in fact I was losing height. I stuck my head over the side and there to my horror was a thin stream of smoke trailing back past my nose. I spoke to Jimmy through the communication tube between the back and front cockpits and said as casually as I could: "Jimmy, when you have discovered whether Lady Chatterley did or didn't, have a look over the port side where there is a dirty streak of black smoke coming out of the front end of this thing."

Jimmy looked. Lady Chatterley and her lover went flying in the slipstream, and like a flash he had the controls and simultaneously cut the engine. At that same moment there was an explosion and the big wooden propeller fragmented into a thousand splinters. It was only Jimmy's instantaneous reaction which saved us, for the build up in engine revolutions without the prop is immediate and so drastic that in seconds the engine is torn from its mountings and one flutters down tail first to a sticky end! Somehow, with a carefully calculated extended glide, Jimmy just cleared the fence at the end of the runway and flopped down safely in the grass on the apron. We managed to fit a tin (I mean metal!) prop from an old "Chipmunk" aircraft and a few days later dear old Yankee Pappa was chugging round the skies again as good as new!

Another time Jimmy said: "Today I'll show you how to wind the old girl up if the engine cuts in flight. All you do is to put her into a dive, the speed builds up to about 120 mph, the prop begins to rotate of its own accord, the engine fires, you pull out of the dive and Bob's your Uncle!"

Happier times: Sir Seretse and Lady Khama, as President and First Lady of the Republic of Botswana, being greeted by King Sobhuza II of Swaziland.

So, I cut the engine and we rocketed earthwards. Unfortunately, the experiment was a flop, the prop failed to rotate and Jimmy had to take over and do one of his famous extended glides back to the airfield. Meanwhile, unknown to us, our antics had been observed and misinterpreted by people in the town, and by the time we got the engine going again and taxied back to the hangars, the doctor, plus ambulance, plus police and an army of good Samaritans had arrived to help pick up the pieces! In fact nearly everyone was there except my dear wife, who assumed, quite rightly – because I was frequently telling her not to fuss – that it was all part of the training! One last word about aeroplanes. Sadly after a year and a half I had to sell the Tiger Moth - the first, best, and most loved of all flying machines. The reason was that distances in Bechuanaland were vast and my range in the Tiger very limited. I did my best to overcome this by establishing fuel and water dumps at strategic points in the Kalahari. But this was a dicey method of getting from A to B, the more so as the maps of this country, though accurate overall, are just blank sheets, brown in colour without contours and almost completely devoid of place names – usually because there are no places to name. And so I bought Oscar Romeo, a Piper Cruiser, and with it, four precious hours of endurance and a bit of extra speed.

Although my time was apt to be dominated by Bamangwato affairs, there was much of interest to occupy me in the districts, and in due course I was able to set in motion a number of other projects of special interest to myself. One was conservation of the wildlife; this involved closer control of the animal skin industry, which was taking enormous toll of the smaller harmless mammals such as cheetah, caracal, jackals, serval cats, leopards and many others.

There was no game department, and never had been in the Protectorate, no national parks as such and poaching, in particular along our borders, was completely out of hand. With a view to regulating these matters, legislation was promulgated which began to have an impact, and, added to this, a game warden, Pat Bromfield, was recruited from Rhodesia, supported by a team of specially selected African game scouts and trackers. The Chobi district, contiguous to the Wankie (today called Hwange) National Park in Rhodesia was gazetted as a protected area and hunting of wildlife generally was restricted. George Silberbauer, one of my DOs, was seconded to carry out a survey and make a study of the Bushmen of the central Kalahari. George did a tremendous job and subsequently became the greatest authority at that time on these fascinating people. I had useful contacts in Johannesburg with the leading banks, Standard and Barclays, and with a bit of prodding they agreed to open branches in Bechuanaland initially in Francistown and afterwards at other centers. This innovation was a success and went from strength to strength. With the cooperation of the Veterinary and Agricultural Departments, DCs were encouraged to put farmers' associations on a proper footing to involve Europeans and Africans more closely with this movement and to hold annual agricultural shows.

Meanwhile, the Seretse Khama/Ruth controversy was hotting up. There were riots in Serowe, the Bamangwato capital. Two African policemen were killed. An administration officer was nearly chopped up, but was rescued by a gallant colleague who was decorated for his bravery. Teams of oxen were hitched to the telegraph and telephone lines and whole sections, poles and all, were dragged off into the bush. The church in the person of Canon Collins and others of his ilk, got their fingers into the Bamangwato pie, and newspaper reporters came in from every direction. Members of Parliament from both sides of the House turned up in droves like eager carpet-baggers, each with some new remedy for sale, and parliamentary questions were as common as Christmas cards in December. In fact, a jolly good time was being had by one and all at the expense of those of us who were battling away under great pressure on the spot!

By now Tshekedi and I had got to know each other well and we had a number of meetings at his place at Pelikwe and in Francistown. Unfortunately, I am unable to refer to the correspondence that passed between us, as when Seretse became President I sent these papers to him for his archives, but I have found one of Tshekedi's long letters which ends rather nicely as follows:

> Like you, I have many ideas running through my mind, and you are the only official at present with whom I can discuss my views openly and frankly.

There were not many people in Government who Tshekedi liked or trusted.

Seretse's marriage to an English girl had come as a terrible blow to him. I think it had always been his dream that some day the great name of Khama would be carried forward when finally the Protectorate gained its independence, and that Seretse, the true heir to the Bamangwato throne, would automatically be President of a new sovereign independent state of Bechuanaland. However, all of this was now in doubt.

In his brilliant way, Tshekedi had a tremendous flair for political juggling, and any policy decision made by ourselves or HMG seemed to hinge on whether it conformed with Tshekedi's reading of the situation. Tshekedi had played this game before on a number of occasions. Indeed, as far back as 1946 he had been influential in preventing General Smuts from annexing South West Africa, the ex-German colony, and perhaps a very brief flashback to that period will give an idea of the sort of man with whom we now had to deal.

What happened was this. In 1946 just after the end of the Second World War, the future of the Mandated territory of South West Africa was uncertain. Smuts, a great man with dreams as to the shape of things to come in Africa, was obsessed with the concept of a greater South Africa made up, possibly, of Rhodesia, the High Commission Territories and South West Africa, but South West was his primary objective. At the time it was generally recognised, even by the Labour Government in England, that South Africa had a priority claim to this territory, having been the Mandatory power since its conquest by the South Africans in the First World War, but more as a reward in recognition for the part played by South Africa military forces in both World Wars. It is probable too that if Smuts had taken matters into his own hands at that time and annexed South West Africa the whole thing would have been accepted as a fait accompli, and South West Africa would have become an integral part of the Union. There were so many other momentous international problems under review just then that Smuts would have achieved his objective without question, for, as I have said, his claim to the sovereignty of this huge and sparsely-populated territory was generally regarded as legitimate. But Smuts was an honourable man who preferred to see the transfer done properly through the medium of the newly-formed United Nations body, of which he himself was one of the architects.

Tshekedi, however, the other man with dreams as to the future of South West Africa, was entirely ruthless. He claimed that his objective was a rail link via the Kalahari to Gobabis and on to the Atlantic ports on the West Coast, but it is also probable that he himself had designs on South West Africa as an ultimate greater Bechuanaland. Possibly if he had not died as a comparatively young man, he would have won out on his other objectives as well. Tshekedi left no stone unturned to achieve his ends. He was the first African leader to see and make use of the United Nations to speed up decolonisation in Africa, and in the process he involved, as his allies bodies such as the Anti-slavery Society, the Colonial Office, the London Mission Society and the press, and very soon built up a formidable lobby of individuals and organisations in Europe, America, and even in India. With Tshekedi, absolutely no holds were barred. This was a tough and fascinating struggle, but the fact remains that where South Africa was concerned, Smuts lost the contest and Tshekedi won on points. Smuts himself once said of Tshekedi that he was the greatest African he had ever met. I agree entirely and in my view this man, with his amazing vision, energy and aggressiveness would, if he had lived longer, have had an influence on events in Africa over and above all other leaders during the decolonisation period. Even a body such as the Organisation of African Unity may have prospered under his guidance and leadership.

Tshekedi could see far beyond tribalism and parochial nationalism, and although he would not hesitate, if he saw fit, to be critical of and even contest issues involving HMG he valued his links with Britain above all others, and it is probable that he would have resisted the acceptance of Marxist ideologies or influence in any African state. So this was Tshekedi Khama, an exceptional personality and a man who, in one way or another, influenced most of our decisions and policies at that time in Bechuanaland.[*]

Somehow I have allowed myself to be side-tracked. I have drifted away from Bamangwato affairs and the stalemate which now existed over Seretse and Ruth. It was becoming very important that some solution or compromise be found.

In my meetings with Tshekedi, I began to detect in him a slightly more flexible attitude towards the problem as a whole. My own view, shared by some of my colleagues, was that Seretse and Ruth should be invited back to the country, allowed to settle down in Serowe, as an ordinary private couple, and that for the time being everything connected with Seretse's hereditary rights in the country be forgotten.

Tshekedi eventually agreed in principle that Seretse's return to the Protectorate on this basis was feasible, and he assured me that if by chance this came about he would see to it that the operation be permitted to go through without incident. There were those in London, and in the Protectorate itself, who were convinced that Seretse's return would result in a major factional conflict, but I was prepared to accept Tshekedi's assurances that it would be peaceful. Furthermore, I was convinced that in the course of time, if Seretse and Ruth cooperated, kept a low profile, and distanced themselves entirely from politics

---

[*] David Stirling, the Phantom Major of wartime days and an old friend was staying with us in Francistown. He was promoting a movement at that time known as Capricorn Africa. David was confident that he could win the support of Tshekedi. With his tremendous personality and power of leadership, David would normally succeed in a mission such as this, but I was aware of Tshekedi's doubts about Capricorn and warned David that he would not succeed. He didn't.

and the chieftainship issue, the problem would burn itself out and that some day, in a more settled political climate, it would be possible to view the whole affair reasonably and without the pent-up tensions currently existing.

Tshekedi once said to me that it was inevitable that one day Seretse would be president of an independent Bechuanaland. This did not surprise me, as elsewhere in Africa attitudes towards race and colour were changing rapidly and it seemed possible that ultimately, when the independence of the country came about, the mixed-marriage aspect of Seretse's status would have ceased to be a significant deterrent to his election as president.

Anyway, at long last I was given the green light. Seretse and Ruth would have a comfortable new house in Serowe, where they could reside as ordinary people. Seretse would fly back to Rhodesia, and be channelled from Bulawayo through the back door as it were to Francistown, the arrangements for his reception being in my hands. Ruth would follow at a later date. There was always the chance that the whole experiment would blow up in my face, and no doubt if this happened I would be the fall guy, and have to carry the can! Obviously the flash-point had to be the arrival at my headquarters in Francistown, but I was not unduly anxious. As I have said, Tshekedi had given me his personal assurance that the homecoming would be peaceful and without incident, and I had complete faith in his appreciation of how things were likely to go.

However, the press were there in force, clamouring for blood and thunder, and a very considerable crowd assembled in the big square outside my office. Security and the control of the crowd was efficiently and tactfully handled by Capt Taylor with his small but well disciplined contingent of European and African police, all of them unarmed.

Seretse arrived, speeches of welcome were made, there was a certain amount of singing and some cheering, and rather to my amazement the whole ceremony was a push-over. One newspaper man in his dispatch reported that armed uniformed troops were evident, strategically positioned round the perimeter of the gathering, and this was mentioned the next day on the BBC news. I was furious. I sent for the culprit and carried out a rehash of the gathering with markers showing the position of the various sections of the crowd and police. While engaged on this exercise, a prison warden emerged from the prison gates on the far side of the square with an old unloaded single-barrelled Greener shot-gun over his shoulder, and with him 20 or 30 dejected-looking prisoners dressed in their brown smocks, smartly decorated with large broad arrow markings.

"There they are" yelled the reporter.

"There they are what?" I asked.

"The soldiers," he retorted.

Now I was really angry. I paraded the prisoners and walked him up and down the ranks in the hope that in the future he might be able to distinguish between paratroopers and convicts, and then made him apologise for his stupidity and see to it that his error was corrected. He did, and it was! Afterwards, I did remember that in order to give the prisoners a bit of fun I had agreed that they could watch the ceremony on the previous day from the prison gates!

Seretse handled his side of the arrival superbly, and in the months that followed he and Ruth settled in quietly, and with their tolerance, patience, and tact, won the respect of everyone, including the rather rugged Afrikaner farmers and miners in the Tati Concession and the surrounding districts.

Our second daughter, Caroline, arrived in 1958 while we were based in Francistown. Corinne was rushed across the border for the event to Bulawayo where medical services were more advanced, and was cared for by Catholic nuns. On the morning after Caroline was born, Corinne asked if a cable could be sent to her family in Ireland to notify them of the birth. "I've already seen to it," came the reply in the thickest of brogues, "I don't know what your married name is, but I cabled your mother and gave her the news as soon as she was born yesterday. She will have got it by now." To Corinne's amazement the nun came from Naas in County Kildare and knew her parents well.

For me, the return of Seretse and the winding up of that saga was rather like the end of a chapter. In the New Year's Honours List of 1st January 1958 I was awarded an OBE, which increased a feeling, which I had experienced on a few other occasions, that I had reached a milestone, a crossroads. What to do now? Where to go? What next? The Colonial Service, the war, and all the wonderful experiences and adventures of recent years were a period now completed; ahead lay another phase, and I had a gut feeling that I should launch forth on something new while I was young enough to make a go of it. I dreaded getting into a rut. It would be entirely wrong to suggest that the Colonial Service was rutty; on the contrary, it was one of the most rewarding careers a man could wish for. At the same time, there was still so much else to live for, so much to do, so much to achieve, and not that much time.

To be frank, the easy way out, and probably the correct course to follow was to continue with the life I loved and understood, but here the pattern of things was changing and much of what one had lived and worked for in the past was being caught up in "the wind of change". No doubt, in view of one's training and experience, this was a vital time in which to serve, but the horizons were becoming limited, independence throughout the colonial empire was inevitable, just over the hill in fact; what then? If one decided to attempt something new it should be done now or never.

Another thing, for Corinne's sake, and that of our two daughters, there was a great deal to be said for having a firm base, a real home of our own at last, and an end to the nomadic character of service life. Decisions such as this are not easy. Those who have had the experience of service life will know how splendid it is to live and work with men and women with whom you can share your interests and ideas, you have the same outlook, the same background and ambitions, and a great deal in common. To serve and to do the job well becomes something of an obsession, you are part of a team, a club, it's your life, and the thought of breaking away from it is an awful wrench.

It happened that about this time I was approached through a semi-official channel and asked whether I would be prepared to go with Sir John Maud when he took up his new appointment as British Ambassador in South Africa. I had met Sir John only once before, but he was a man I had always admired and I knew full well that to serve under him would be a privilege, and a fascinating experience.

There was yet another option: Con Benson was a merchant banker of renown, a man who during the war years became one of my greatest friends. At that time Air Commodore C.E. Benson CBE, DSO was on the staff of the 8th Army. I had joined up with him in Cairo and served under him in Sicily and Italy. Just after the Sicily landings I was in Syracuse, and Con came there to see me. The harbour and the town were being heavily bombed by the Luftwaffe from nearby Catania, mostly at night and, as I had not slept very well for two days, I suggested that we throw our bedrolls into his jeep and find a nice little olive grove in the country, away from all the noise and mess of Syracuse. We chose a tree on high ground overlooking the sea shining below us like silver in the moonlight, and that night we lay on our blankets and talked of many things.

Con told me that after the war what he longed for almost more than anything else in the world was a small stake in Africa, in some remote and beautiful place. He had set his heart on this and made me promise that some day, if I found something which fitted his dreams I would let him know.

Many years later, while I was in charge of the Kilimanjaro district, I opened up Ol Molog on the northern slopes of Kilimanjaro for farming. One of the farms surveyed and pegged out was Unit No 8, rather remotely situated and a difficult unit to develop, but superbly beautiful, with almost limitless views to the east and northwest, and just behind, very close and towering above the forest and bleak windswept moorlands was Kilimanjaro itself, the snow and glaciers glittering in the sun, or enveloped in enormous cumulus clouds, always spectacular and awe inspiring. I remembered Con, our talk that night in Sicily, and my pledge to him, and without a doubt this was the place for him. Con and his delightful wife, Lady Morvyth came out immediately and were allocated Unit No 8. Lady Morvyth (Dickie) was a great lady and Con was one of the best of men and for their sakes I was delighted.

Soon after this I was transferred to Bechuanaland, but before leaving and with an eye to the future, I made a deal with Con, namely that should he for some reason decide to abandon his Kilimanjaro project he would give me first option on Legumishira Farm, as it was called.

As time went on, the possibility of acquiring a farm and a home on Kilimanjaro kept on cropping up in my mind as I mulled over our future. It was at this very moment of indecision and doubt that out of the blue came a cable from Con. He said that for various reasons it was becoming increasingly difficult for him and his partners (Sir Rex Benson and Trevor Beer) to devote sufficient time and energy into the development of Unit No 8 on Kilimanjaro. He reminded me of his agreement to inform me if for any reason they were forced to abort on the farm project. Was I still interested?

Arriving just when it did, this cable from Con was like a message from the gods, a sort of oracular decision which I was bound to follow, a good omen which I could not disregard. Anyway, it tipped the scales and for me the course to follow was now crystal clear. I would ease out of the service and at last, as a family, we would have a permanent home situated in one of the most beautiful and spectacular areas of Africa. We would farm and live happily for ever afterwards; and perhaps make a few bob in the process!

And so it was that I resigned from the service, I bought an old 8-ton Bedford lorry, piled our furniture and possessions into it, and while Corinne, Philippa and little Caroline travelled northwards by air, I set off in the truck, accompanied by Hamisi, my old and faithful servant and companion and Dickie Dixon, a good friend and one of the best police officers I have ever known. Dickie, off his own bat, decided to take a couple of weeks local leave and come with me to help with the driving and for company on the long 2,000 mile journey to Kilimanjaro, and I was grateful.

Our elderly Bedford truck had spent its entire lifetime grinding through the sands of the Kalahari and was bone tired and desperately slow. On the comparatively good roads of Southern Rhodesia we made fairly good progress, but in due course we crossed the Zambezi at Chirundu and spent three days on the Northern Rhodesian section, which in those days was not much more than a sand track wandering, seemingly forever, through the flat, featureless Mopani forest. We had lashed a big easy chair behind the cab and on top of the beds, chests, tables, books and other clobber, and this was Hamisi's throne, a sort of crow's nest facing backwards, and he was linked with us in the cab by an electric bell salved from the front door of our previous Francistown home. A single tinkle from the crow's nest meant slow down, vehicle overtaking. Two bells for stop, minor problem, loads rattling, time for a brew-up of tea or something. Three bells, this was an emergency, puncture, exhaust fallen off, elephants crossing the track ahead.

Each evening we pulled well off the road, found a big tree or outcrop of rocks and made camp. This was Hamisi's big moment. As if by magic, a table, chairs, canvas water bag, glasses and whisky appeared. Soon the camp-fire blossomed in the evening light, basins of hot water, soap and towels were placed by our bedrolls, a splendid three course supper followed, then finally, the three of us would spread our blankets on the soft sand, feet to the fire and roll up for the night.

There is something quite different about this Mopani country, quite unlike the Kalahari. Apart from the familiar plaintive call of the nightjars, it is quiet, perhaps the sounds of the night are deadened by the trees. After darkness in the Kalahari the world seems to come to life. Not so here, though it is true that on one occasion, near Mpika we had lions roaring in the immediate vicinity of our camp, but mostly it seemed quiet. Maybe, too, we just slept like logs, as we were always dead tired at the end of each day. At first light Hamisi was there with steaming cups of tea and mugs of shaving water. Breakfast followed, then refuelling, checking the vehicle and loads and finally away, beckoned on by memories of Kilimanjaro still far away to the north.

Eventually we reached Tunduma police post on the border between Tanganyika and Northern Rhodesia. We were getting on well, only 850 miles to go. Tunduma is on high ground and in addition to being the entry point to Tanganyika, it is the gateway to the beautiful Southern Highlands Province. It was a relief to be clear of the Mopani forest at last; ahead were high hills and great escarpments. Rain forest crowned the nearby hills and every so often we rumbled across bridges spanning rushing mountain streams and threaded our way through forested gorges. This was a country I knew well, as before the war as a junior DO based at Mbeya, this section of the district had been my special responsibility. Now we were getting towards the end of our long journey, and two days later, as we approached Arusha on the rolling Maasai plain near Monduli, there in the distance was the mountain, Kilimanjaro at last, its lower slopes already in semi-darkness as night was falling, but the snows and glaciers of the summit still glowing pink in the last rays of a sun now below the western horizon.

Late that night, unannounced and in pitch darkness, we churned our way up the final escarpment to our farmhouse on the slopes of Kilimanjaro. Since breaking camp that morning we had been travelling continuously for 16 hours, and this, at last, was the end of the road and the beginning of a new life.

For me our arrival was something of an anticlimax. I had given up a fascinating way of life and a profession I understood and loved, and had distanced myself from friends and a job that maybe I should have seen through to the end. The road ahead was full of pitfalls and a tremendous challenge, as we were desperately short of capital and I lacked farming experience.

That first night, as we groped round in the darkness, dead tired, trying to set up some sort of a camp in the empty house, was one of the bad moments in my life! I suppose we undressed, I can't remember, all I know is we lay down and slept like logs.

The next morning just as the sun was rising, we took our mugs of tea out on the verandah - there 3,000 feet below us lay the Amboseli plain covered by a blanket of ground mist, the high hills in the distance rising above the cloud base and views for one hundred miles and more to the north and the west. To the south, very close, was the mountain towering above the forest and purple moorlands, the snow and glaciers gleaming brilliantly clear in the morning light. It was a moment I shall never forget, and my gloom of the previous evening faded into the distance. This was 'it' at last, our new home and I was happy. The date was 1st March 1959.

CHAPTER 11

KILIMANJARO

AND so it was that Corinne, Philippa, Caroline and I began a new chapter in our lives. The war and many years of service life now belonged to another world. This was something entirely different and no doubt we had much to learn and much to enjoy. Now at last we had a permanent home in a beautiful locality, something we had always wanted and missed, among a happy band of dedicated farmers, most of them old friends, who were prepared to accept us into their community. All the same, I suppose it was only natural that on occasions we would look back over our shoulders and perhaps miss, but not regret unduly, a way of life which had meant so much to us in times gone by.

To the south, very close, was the mountain towering above the forest and purple moorlands.

Corinne, who had gone ahead of me with the girls, had already arrived on the mountain and was staying with my sister Joan and her husband Brian awaiting my arrival, and great was the rejoicing and jubilation that followed on that our first day on our farm.

Between times we started off-loading the old lorry and made a beginning at establishing ourselves in the house, but there were continual and very cheerful interruptions as farmers from the little community, such as Robin Johnston, Piet Hugo, David Read, Dick Soames, Derek Bryceson and others from further afield dropped in to welcome us.

These old-timers, the pioneers on the Ol Molog scheme, had been there from the very beginning and had developed their units from scratch the hard way. We on the other hand got away to a flying start for Con Benson, assisted by his European manager and his mate had gone quite a long way towards taming Unit No 8, but the task ahead of us was still prodigious. We were fortunate too in that we had a ready-made house to move into.

In the early days the original settlers had a pretty rough time; they lived for a year or more mostly in tents and in temporary thatched shelters made of timber felled in the forest. They worked 16 hours a day and subsisted mainly on game meat and such vegetables as they were able to purchase in the nearest African markets. They were desperately short of capital for development and the purchase of farm machinery and spares and almost daily there were problems. Labourers were gored by rhino and buffalo, there were mechanical breakdowns, and cattle were taken by lions. Water too was scarce, grass fires destroyed acres of precious wheat and buildings, and fences were flattened by giraffe and eland. In short, it was very tough going indeed, but gradually the stands of iron-hard olive trees were felled and the roots dug out. Three days work for four men was the normal task on a big brown olive tree. Every day new ground was broken, and fields, small at first but expanding rapidly, were ploughed, harrowed and planted and slowly but surely acres of wheat, barley and pyrethrum were carved out of the great expense of sage, scrub and forest. Step by step houses were built, mostly of timber from a small sawmill in the forest, and gardens with roses and many other flowers blossomed in the rich virgin soil. Out of what was an untamed wilderness the beginnings of any ever expanding paradise was created.

We ourselves lost no time on settling in, for there was much to be done. I was not entirely satisfied with my already installed resident manager, and anyway he was lonely and had never really adapted to the remoteness and isolation of Ol Molog. So he moved on, and I searched around in Kenya for a suitable replacement.

Right away I hit the jackpot in Ben Hogan and Jackie his attractive young wife. Ben had come out to Kenya early on in the Mau Mau emergency and had immediately been incorporated into a special unit recruited at that time to deal with the terrorists, an ever-growing force of fanatical freedom fighters - to use a more polite title - who were engaged in promoting a reign of terror and mayhem in the Colony. The story of the Mau Mau rebellion, the horror of it, the rights and wrongs of it, and its sadness is well known and I won't expand on this period. Ben had done exceptionally well in the Mau Mau campaign and when he decided to join us in Tanganyika I was more than pleased.

Apart from being a first class mechanic, Ben was a good administrator, got on well with labour and worked like a Trojan. This was at a time when I needed just such a man as Ben and he became a loyal and trusted friend and companion; everyone liked Ben and Jackie. From the start, we, as a team, set about putting the farm on its feet and making it pay its way. This, the financial aspect I mean, was vitally important as the only capital Corinne and I could muster between us at that time was £11,000 and somehow we had to pay off the balance of £19,000 over and above this figure to offset the total overdraft accumulated by the previous owners. We were given five years in which to clear our debt. By modern standards £19,000 is not a very large sum, but in those days for us it was a hell of a lot of money and the task ahead of us a real challenge, but we did it; indeed we paid it off to the last penny in two and a half years. Without Ben's loyal support and dedication I could never have achieved this, and I will always be grateful to him. The Hogans remained with us for several years and then moved on to Southern Rhodesia, where he did extremely well, and they were happy.

We divided the work on the farm, Ben and I. He took on the machinery and the livestock, with myself concentrating mostly on the development plan, fencing, pipe laying, contour construction, agriculture generally, and on our pyrethrum project of 90 acres, a tremendous money-spinner at that time. However, when under pressure during harvesting, cultivating and planting, we mucked in together.

At that time none of us could afford the individual ownership of an aircraft, so four of us shared Kilo Golf Oscar, a splendid little work-horse which earned its keep a hundred times over. As I was the Unit No 8 pilot, I handled the town trips 80 miles to Moshi, 90 to Arusha and 120 to Nairobi.

We borrowed money and introduced a small but exceptionally good herd of high-grade in-calf Friesian heifers from Kenya. Soon we began to earn substantial profits from the pyrethrum and milk, and as we expanded our acreage the wheat crop also began to pay its way. We learned a lot from the successes and obvious mistakes of our neighbours and were gradually able to launch forth on new schemes. The machinery, the combines, tractors, implements and electrical plant thrived under Ben's tender care. Every spare penny went back into the farm. We were in business and Legumishira Farm Limited, our farm, began to sing.

We grew first class wheat.

On the farm was an extinct volcano that rose 500 feet above the wheat fields and paddocks. The deep gullies on its flanks were heavily wooded, the rim was a perfect circle with a uniform diameter of 1,000 yards and sometimes, after a good rainy season, a small lake formed on the floor of its crater. Scrub and stunted forest clung to the almost vertical walls, and it was obvious that the area within had been the haunt of elephant, buffalo and wildlife of every variety throughout the ages. Even in our times we would often see eland, bushbuck and Chanler's reed buck. There were leopard too and other smaller predators. A herd of buffalo lived there for a while and on one occasion a pack of wild dogs. We treated the crater as a sort of sanctuary, but used it also for grazing our cattle when there was a shortage of grass in the paddocks.

Great herds of elephant and other animals had visited this place in search of water and grazing, and a well defined perfectly graded elephant roadway leading up to the rim had been cut into the side of the hill by the feet of countless marching feet, going back no doubt for thousands of years. More recently, nomadic pastoral tribes used the same animal made roadway to the rim and down to the water below. There is only one narrow single-file track down the cliff-like inner face and this too had been carved into the hard lava wall by the constant tread of animals.

The hill is known to the Maasai as Legumishira (hence the name of the farm), a word relating to the branded incisions this tribe makes on the neck or flanks of their cattle for identification purpose, or perhaps for drawing blood to mix with their milk. The scar made by the elephant road on Legumishira hill is visible for fifty miles and was always a welcoming beacon to us as we approached in our aircraft, tired and longing for home.

It was here on Legumishira, most likely within the crater itself, that the greatest of all elephants was hunted and shot about the middle of the last century by the freed slave of an Arab slave trader. The exact spot is not known, but many years ago a German writer, telling the story of this legendary elephant, stated categorically that it was killed at a place called Legumishira. The records in the British Museum are less specific and say merely that it was shot by an Arab hunter on the northern slopes of Kilimanjaro.

It was the custom in those times for slave traders to drop off hunters along their route into the interior to hunt and trade for ivory; then, on the return journey to the coast, they would pick up the hunters and their accumulated ivory, which would then be carried on by the newly-acquired gangs of slaves and sold, usually in Zanzibar.

The massive tusks of the great Kilimanjaro elephant are now lying in an obscure vault in the British Museum (Natural History) and one day, a few years ago, I made a pilgrimage to see them.

I had some difficulty in penetrating the ranks of a regular Gestapo of museum attendants and security men, but eventually found a friendly curator who took me down into the depths of the building. There, lying on the floor of a dark cell-like room together with a pair of world record Indian tusks, were our tusks, the Indian specimens, 161 and 169 lbs respectively looking like a couple of toothpicks by comparison! I say "our tusks", for we have always had a kinship for this old elephant, we knew his previous habitat so well, and had often pictured him when he was the unchallenged monarch of the territory in which we ourselves lived for sixteen years. I have no doubt that during his lifetime he dominated the great herds that roamed the forests above our farm and the dusty plains below.

The two tusks are the heaviest ever recorded. They were sold in Zanzibar in 1896 and there is every reason to believe that they are a pair. The heaviest was bought by the British Museum for £350. This massive tusk, 10 feet 2½ inches in length and 24½ in girth weighs 226½lbs. The other was purchased by William B. Hatfield, ivory buyer for Joseph Rogers and Sons Ltd, (cutlers) of Sheffield and was exhibited in the firm's showrooms at Norfolk Street, Sheffield. In 1932 it was sold to another firm, W.B. Wolstenholme Ltd, who in turn sold it to the British Museum in 1933. This tusk, 10 feet 5½ inches in length, 32½ inch girth, weighs 214 lbs. The heavier tusk, the shorter of the two shows signs of wear and was probably the digging and working tusk; the longer of the two curves inwards to its fellow and it is probable that in life they nearly met at the tip.

I believe that at one time one of the pair, or perhaps both, were exhibited in

Legumishira farm as seen from our aeroplane. The Legumishira crater, from where the world's record African elephant tusks came and after which the farm was named, is in the background.

the main entrance hall of the museum, and it is sad that they now languish in the darkness of a strong-room. I took the curator to task over this, but he held that the public generally were not really interested in them. I doubt this, as no one – even if he lacked a knowledge of or interest in elephant – could avoid experiencing a feeling of wonder, even awe, at the sight of these huge teeth. To me, and I am sure to thousands of others, they conjure up a vision of the times gone by when vast herds of animals, large and small, roamed the forests, the deserts, and the limitless savannas of the African continent, and there would have been elephants as large as, and maybe even mightier, than this Kilimanjaro giant.

In those far away times the only enemy would have been prehistoric man armed with his stone hand-axe and perhaps a shaft, bone headed, or with the point hardened by fire. He alone was the ultimate enemy, the sole predator, and a cunning and ruthless killer. Strange to say, that situation is still much the same as it ever was, except that now in these modern and so-called civilised times, man is still nature's greatest predator and destroyer, the only difference being that with his four-wheel drive vehicles, his high-powered rifle and his telescopic sights, he is a thousand times more efficient and deadly, and the African elephant, this majestic and fascinating animal, is, like the black rhinoceros, in grave danger of extinction.

A superb crop of pyrethrum.

We were being troubled by lions – we all were from time to time – and recently Ati de Beer, an Afrikaner farmer further down the line, followed a wounded lion into his wheat and had been killed. This was a sad business, we all liked Ati, and it was tragic that he should go in this manner. On the whole we had been more fortunate than most, but every so often, usually at the height of the dry season, lions in small prides, or loners, moved up from the plains and raided our cattle bomas.

I well remember one occasion. It was a pitch-black night and we were fast asleep when suddenly, at about 0200 there was a frantic banging on the ploughshare suspended from the branch of a thorn tree near the dairy and cattle pens. This was the normal alarm signal on the farm and could mean one of two things, a raid by Maasai moran, or by lions. I pulled some clothes over my pyjamas and called Ben Hogan on the field telephone between our houses. "Bring your rifle and the old stripped down Land-Rover," I shouted. "We have problems at the dairy. Action stations and step on it."

A few minutes later Ben skidded to a stop at the back door and we tore down the hill to the cattle boma, where there was much ado and beating of drums and buckets behind firmly-locked doors. There was no sign of the night watchman with his bow and poisoned arrows, as he too was holed up in one of the houses. Dead, and dragged halfway through the fence, was one of our best in-calf heifers. Of the lions, for it was obviously lions, there was no sign.

(a) Philipa with her mother. Giving Corinne and the girls a decent home was among the foremost of my reasons for resigning from the Colonial Service and becoming a farmer. *(b)* Caroline, *(c)* Philipa.

Experience had shown that the key to success at times like this was an immediate counter attack, and I was satisfied that once the racket and dust settled the lions would be back.

We placed the car facing the dead animal, about 20 paces, and then tossed up for the first watch. I won, and so Ben was on guard and I dozed off. A short time later I was roused by rumblings and grabbed my rifle only to find that it was Ben snoring away with the muzzle of his rifle tucked under his chin! Clearly this was no good, so we went to the hay shed, stripped off about 30 yards of strong bailing twine, tied one end to Ben's ankle and the other to the leg of the dead beast. We knew the drill well, the Land-Rover had no doors, no roof and no windshield and we could both leap out immediately there was a tug on Ben's ankle; then on would come the headlamps and we would shoot the lions. Ben continued his watch. Suddenly there were fearful screams and shouts. I switched on the lights, and there were two lions dragging the dead beast at speed through the fence with Ben firmly tied by the ankle at the other end, hopping along on one leg trying to keep pace with the drag. There was no chance of a shot, as, what with the dust and general confusion and Ben in my line of fire, and me laughing and Ben yelling, and the lions growling and grunting, we were getting nowhere. Anyway, I fired a shot to one side of the procession and the lions made off, and that was that!

Next morning two lions, two big females, were spotted lying up in a patch of sunshine in the centre of a very dense clump of thorn bush on the slopes of our crater.

We decided against crawling into the thorn thicket on hands and knees and instead sent some men round the rim of the crater with instructions to roll down big stones to flush the lions. This worked like a charm, except that the lions turned up the slope and out of range instead of down in our direction. They made straight for the stone-rolling party and this little band of stalwarts took off like long dogs and only reported for work two hours later, and that was that. Not a very professional lion hunt!

Robin Johnston, who shared Unit No 6 with Archie MacIndoe*, had a better idea for dealing with marauding lions, or thought he had. He welded together two empty 44-gallon petrol drums, cut a loop hole for his rifle in the bottom of the second drum, made a strong trap door at the open end and then pointing the contraption in the right direction, he climbed in, rolled up in his sleeping bag, and waited for the lions to come to a dead cow a few yards from the muzzle of his rifle. In due course the pride arrived all right, but led by a couple of half-grown cubs who were far more interested in this strange-smelling tube of metal than competing with the rest of the pride for their supper.

On gently patting their new toy, the cubs found that it moved slightly accompanied by strange noises from within. Better still, if they gave it a good push it began to roll down the gentle gradient below the carcass. The game of patting to get noises and pushing to get still better noises (an avalanche of filthy language they did not understand) went on for quite a while and very soon Robin's secret weapon, with him inside, was some considerable distance from the kill and facing in the wrong direction. By the time he felt he could safely leave his armour-plated capsule, the breakfast bell was ringing, Robin was in a flaming temper, and the pride had polished off the cow and gone for a snooze.

Generally speaking the wild-life which was prolific on our farm, had a free run, provided it stuck to the rules. Ours was the very end farm, beyond which we marched with Maasailand and the great rain forests of Kilimanjaro between the 6,000 and 11,000 foot contours. However, because of our situation, flanked on two sides by the forest, we were more exposed than our neighbours to the dwellers of the forest, in particular, elephant, buffalo, and rhino. We succeeded to some extent in keeping out most of the big stuff by a deep ditch along the forest perimeter with an electric fence above it, but in spite of this, sometimes we had to deal with individual herds of elephant and buffalo. The devastation caused by 30 elephants in a 40 acre wheat field has to be seen to be believed: a valuable stand of ripe wheat has every appearance of a tank battle-ground following an invasion of elephant or buffalo. Rhino were plentiful in those days, but being browsers they did little damage to crops and were tolerated.

As for the predators such as leopard and lion, they were protected provided they kept clear of the dairy herd, as they earned their freedom by keeping down the pig and baboons.

---

* Sir Archibald, world famous for his plastic surgery and the amazing work he did during the War reshaping the faces of numbers of the Forces, suffering from terrible burns and other injuries.

In the 18 years we were farming on Kilimanjaro, I had to shoot only one rhino and one leopard. The rhino was shot in self-defence and the leopard was a calf killer. There is quite a story attached to the leopard. This was a big beast, full of guile and cunning. For months we tried to get him without success. Then, early one morning, he was spotted lying up in the fork of a huge isolated wild fig tree near the homestead. Using every bit of available cover and moving with great caution I managed to get within about 30 yards. I knew that every move I made, every step taken, every flick of an eyelid, was being registered by the leopard, but, because he was in an isolated tree he was reluctant to give away his position by making a dash for the nearby forest. Anyway, by now I was placed for a rather difficult shot. Only the head and neck were visible, partly covered by an overhanging branch. To have advanced a step further would have put me in the open and no doubt the beast would then have abandoned caution and streaked for the forest.

Meanwhile, unknown to me, I was being followed by a large, shaggy, yellow mongrel dog, the property of one of the cattle herdsmen, and my stalk was being watched by about 30 labourers grouped outside their houses in the nearby labour lines. I had to do something and soon, for any moment the leopard would make his bid for freedom. The shot registered, I was unable to say where, but to my satisfaction he seemed to drop like a stone from his perch as if dead. This was where I was mistaken, however, for simultaneously with hitting the ground he was coming straight for me. I had reloaded my .375 magnum and was ready, but nothing it seemed could stop this charge. It was during this split second that the dog behind me flashed by and tangled with the leopard giving me the chance as they rolled over, of putting a bullet into the leopard's brain. Maybe this great old mongrel saved my life. He was badly mauled, but recovered, and during his life time on our farm "Pombe", for that was his name, and I were very special friends. It transpired that my first bullet had taken the leopard in the fleshy part of the neck and had merely made him rather angry!

At midnight on December 8th 1961, Tanganyika became independent. The new President Nyerere went out of his way to assure us white farmers that we were welcome to stay and contribute to the country's development. On April 23rd, 1964, Tanganyika and Zanzibar became a United Republic which, at the end of October 1964 adopted the name Tanzania, by which it has been known ever since.

It was March, and with us at that time were old and dear friends, Terence and Jane Mayo from 'Doon' their lovely home in the west of Ireland. In addition to a safari to the Serengeti we decided, off the cuff, to fly to Cape Town. Terence had been a member of the Fleet Air Arm aerobatic team and had seen action during the Suez affair in 1957, so we could share the flying.

We took off for the Cape refuelling in Tanzania at Dodoma and again at Mbeya, and then set course for Lilongwe, the capital of Malawi, on a track which took us over the spectacular Southern Highlands of Tanzania and then, leaving Lake Malawi on our left, by way of the high plateau which forms the western wall of the Great Rift in those parts.

By late afternoon we were within 100 miles of Lilongwe and were now in radio contact. I asked for landing instructions and gave details of our party: myself, Corinne, and Lord and Lady Mayo. There was a rather surprised sounding "Roger" from the Lilongwe control tower followed by the usual landing instructions and procedure.

In due course we rolled to a standstill on Lilongwe airfield, where, to our utter amazement, we were met by a group of high-ranking Government officials and a red carpet welcome. We were whisked off to the leading hotel, where a High Court Judge on his circuit had been persuaded to give up one of his rooms as it was urgently needed for the Lord Mayor and his Lady. Being St Patrick's day, the hotel was booked to capacity with Irishmen and others from every corner of the territory. Corinne and I were guests of the Airport Controller and his wife, a delightful couple.

We never really got to the bottom of the Lord Mayor mix-up, maybe they thought Terence was a defecting Mayor from a neighbouring state! The fact remains that we were given a royal reception by Europeans and Africans alike and the party that night had all the features of an event to be remembered. The presence in their midst of a real Irish Earl, and, in Corinne, the daughter of a Master of the 'Killing Kildare' fox hounds gave a special added Irish flavour to the evening, an occasion which is no doubt still talked about by those who were there.

It was a rather jaded foursome who climbed into Oscar Foxtrot the next day and headed southwards on a beautiful crystal clear autumn morning, rather later than planned. We decided to have lunch at Meikel's Hotel in Salisbury, Southern Rhodesia, but Terence and I were in our bush jackets, no neckties, so no lunch in the main dining room! However, we were given a very good meal, served to us as a special favour in the children's nursery dining hall! That night we clocked in at a very comfortable lodge near the ancient Zimbabwe ruins. Here we delayed a day, and then pressed on to stay with friends in Johannesburg. More great junketings and many old friends. Then the final 1,000 miles on to the Cape.

Our return trip was several days later and went according to plan. We spent a night at Umtali on the Mozambique border. While we were loading up the next morning, a chopper landed nearby and a dozen or more superbly fit-looking young men spilled out. Armed to the teeth and camouflaged, they seemed to melt into the neighbouring forest, soundlessly and at speed. This was our first sight of the now world-famous Selous Scouts. It was the time of UDI and the Rhodesian war, and Umtali was a hot-spot operational area. These men were clearly disciplined and tough, and we were impressed.

The same day we ran into weather and were forced to climb through the murk to over 14,000 feet, really too high for us without oxygen, and bitterly cold, but all was well, as three long rather anxious hours later we broke out into glorious sunshine. Finally, far in the distance the snow-capped summit of Kilimanjaro appeared on the horizon and within an hour we were on the farm again, safe and sound, with just over 8,000 miles on the clock. That was a very good safari.

I made two further flights to South Africa while we were on the mountain, and one great old jog up the Nile and all the way to Surrey, England. George Carr, an Ol Molog farmer, was my companion and we used his aeroplane, a new and very smart little machine but desperately slow and rather under-powered: our average speed over the ground was only 119 statute miles to the hour, but we got there in the end, taking it easy in nine days!

Mostly on the long flight up the African continent we maintained an altitude of about 10,000 feet. Up there it was pleasantly cool and free from turbulence, and usually the Nile was visible, sometimes close but sometimes just a thread of green and silver in a desolate featureless landscape.

As we progressed northwards, the character of the terrain changed to stark desert with vast expanses of treeless sand-covered wasteland, lion-coloured and forbidding. Visibility was reduced to ten miles due to the dust and heat haze and the friendly Nile was no longer to be seen, but we were making steady progress in spite of stops for refuelling and the occasional night's rest. Juba, Malakal, Khartoum, and Atbara were behind us, and finally we reached Wadi Halfa with the luxury of a good hotel and a memorable visit the next morning to the Valley of the Kings.

Then came Alexandria, good restaurants, belly dancing at the rather sleazy night club, a comfortable bed at our hotel and then a very early start the next day to fly westwards towards Tunis by way of El Alamein, Mersa Matruh, Benghazi and the great Western Desert battlefields of the early forties. Sadly I had come in for only the final chapter of that era. My posting from the East African Command to 8th Army HQ in Cairo took place just after the commencement of the El Alamein contest, but I had the good fortune to be in Tunis in time for the final collapse of Rommel's Afrika Korps and the end of a Nazi presence on the continent of Africa.

That day, the day we left Alex, in a remote and hidden depression or wadi somewhere south of Mersa Matruh, we flew over and then circled what must have been the site of a lonely and desperate battle between three German Tiger Tanks and two British anti-tank guns. The tracks of the tanks, their approach and manoeuvres had written a story in the hard-baked earth which was still clearly visible and could be read like a book from our aircraft two or three hundred feet above. Only three enemy tanks were involved and they were completely destroyed. As for the two anti-tank guns (they looked like six-pounders), one, including the whole gun position, was shattered and the other gun lay on its side. There was no sign of this place having been visited after this incident or ever again till the day we spotted it, and it is probable that this was a fight to the bitter end when all involved were destroyed and that there were acts of great bravery on both sides on that day, never to be heard of or recorded.

For some reason what we had seen in that remote and lonely place made a profound impression on us, and as we flew on George too was lost in his own thoughts. Maybe we were not concentrating, for suddenly we became aware of the fact that directly ahead of us on our track was a vast wall of yellow sand from ground level to thousands of feet above. This was clearly the dreaded Khamseen, a sandstorm of proportions greater than either of us had seen before in Africa. To turn back would have been fatal, as there was insufficient fuel in our tanks; our only hope was to battle on, hold as steady a course as possible, and hope for the best. The next hour was a nightmare. We bucked around in the sky like a piece of straw in the wind and sand hissed against the windshield and fuselage, the sound clearly audible above the beat of the engine. At last, very faintly, we picked up Benghazi control tower on the radio and from then on and with their help were able to steer a course which finally put as directly over the end of the only serviceable runway in a storm such as this. Somehow we taxied a zig-zag course to a hangar where a gang of men was needed to manhandle the aircraft into the hangar, which was rapidly filling up with wind-blown desert sand. After this adventure the rest of our journey via Tunis, Sicily, Italy, France and on to little old England was a piece of cake!

* * * *

In the late sixties the elephant population of the great Tsavo National Park in Kenya had increased to such an extent that the park's ecology was under pressure and the habitat of the plains animals in danger.

A great controversy raged among conservationists far and wide. Many held that the huge herds should be culled, others favoured the normal procedure in situations such as this, namely to leave it to nature. I favoured the latter course, as on occasions in other parts of Africa when certain species became too numerous diseases, debility, and other natural processes take over and thousands of the weaker and infected beasts fade out, with the result that the pressure on the environment is once again balanced. This is exactly what happened. There were two desperately dry seasons, the park became nothing more than a dust bowl and several thousand elephants were eliminated. However, before this happened, and while the problem was prominent in everyone's mind, we decided to make a count of the existing herds, and those of us who had aeroplanes offered our machines and services. In addition, the British Army, who had a presence in Kenya at that time, provided two helicopters together with their crews and maintenance staff, mostly young aircrew men on their first venture into the African wilderness. The operation was to be administered by David Sheldrick, the park's warden, based near Voi.

On the appointed day, I arrived at the Park headquarters airstrip, just as dark was falling, parked my aircraft under a big lone thorn tree adjacent to the chopper's vehicles and crews, laid out my bedroll on the ground under the tree and then joined the lads round their lorries. As it was so late I decided to remain with my aircraft and to meet up with pilots for the briefing at 0600 hours the next morning. I shared my bottle of whisky with the lads and they reciprocated by inviting me to supper.

It had been a long hard day on the farm, and I turned in early. Soon the moon rose, so bright that the whole camp area was clearly visible, the nearest truck only 30 yards from where I lay. It was hot and most of the men dossed down for the night on the canvas tops of their vehicles.

Sometime during the night, it must have been about 0200, I woke suddenly and sensed that something unusual was afoot. What had happened was that a herd of about 30 elephants had wandered in and were silently grazing and moving peacefully among the parked lorries. This is not unusual, as one often finds while on safari that elephants have passed through a sleeping campsite on their way to water or some favourite pasture nearby.

Anyway, as my eyes adjusted to the scene, there, very close, was one old jumbo interested, but not aggressively, in the vehicle nearest to where I lay. Maybe the men sleeping on the canvas top had some oranges or paw-paws up with them, and the elephant was feeling around with its trunk among the sleeping forms above him. The next few minutes were a pantomime! There was a voice clearly audible in the still night air. "Alfie stop that will yer." "Alfie" (this time with a certain amount of venom) "take yer bloody 'ands off of me will yer", a short pause, then "Alfie unless you cut out that sort of bluddy crap…"

At this moment all hell was let loose, men shouting and screaming and dropping to the ground like apples from a tree as they abandoned the top of the trucks and made for the cabs of their vehicles or dived under them, elephants trumpeting and plunging off in every direction, fuel drums knocked down and rolling, dust, pandemonium and complete panic – a sudden and dramatic end to what I had been enjoying as a peaceful Africa on a lovely moonlight night!

In due course normality of some sort returned amid great chatter and some rather nervous laughter. The show over, I settled down for the remainder of the night. Someone came over to see how I had fared – I pretended to be asleep!

In those faraway days farming in Africa was quite a challenge. You were on your own, no subsidies, no compensation for crop failure, no special technical assistance or privileges and very little in the way of marketing arrangements or advice. So, you became a Jack-of-all-trades – mechanic, ploughman, carpenter, builder, vet, water diviner, fencer, road-maker and a hundred and one other things. In my view this was half the fun of the game and, depending on how good a Jack you were, you won or you lost out.

Most of us had outside interests as well. Soon after Tanganyika gained its independence, I was asked by the Europeans in the Northern Region to stand as an Independent member to represent their interests in the new Parliament. Reluctantly, for this sort of thing is not my line of country, I agreed. The symbol allocated to me for the build-up to the election was a "motor car", and I journeyed round the area selling my wares. My manifesto was full of good cheer and great things I would do for one and all, supported by the background of a life spent mostly among Africans and dating back, in Tanganyika, to my arrival in the country as a junior DO in 1936, then as a soldier fighting for King and country, and finally as a farmer and the friend of the people!

Frankly, I knew that our chance of success was minimal, but in the end was surprised and flattered at the number of votes that came my way from the African sector in addition to the Europeans and at least I did not have to sacrifice my deposit.

There were other things outside the business of actual farming in which I became involved such as Chairman of the Pyrethrum Board, the Wild Life Society of East Africa, the Farmer's Association, on the Board of the Outward Bound Mountain school on Kilimanjaro with Sir Donald MacGillivray, Kenneth Matiba and James Foster, Chairman of a big game fishing syndicate on Mafia Island south of Dar es Salaam together with Robin Johnston, Bill Stirling, Tufton Beamish (Lord Chelwood), Susan Pretzlik, and others. This was an intriguing venture, which prospered up to the time of independence, as it became the Mecca for fishermen from Rhodesia and South Africa. However, when they were debarred from entering the country, and tourism was regarded by the Tanzanian President, Julius Nyerere, as detrimental to the culture of the people of Tanzania, business declined and finally we were forced to sell out to the new Government for an absurdly low price or be nationalised.

As for farming itself, you worked hard, you had to, for we harrowed, ploughed, planted, and harvested twice in every year. If in the brief interim period between crops you were overtaken by the rains you could very easily go to bed with thousands of pounds sterling worth of unharvested wheat and barley, and at the same time miss the chance of a successful planting to catch the vital first rains of the next rainy season. During these critical periods a day's work added up to twenty four hours, with every machine going full-blast day and night. Finally, you had to cope with the evacuation of thousands of bags of grain over 90 miles of appalling roads to Arusha.

To all of us, this was a home of beauty and splendour.

At last, when all this was over and the pressure eased off, there was time for a well-earned visit to the coast, a safari to the Serengeti, sand grouse shoots on the plains, climbs on Kilimanjaro, and friends from abroad.

The focal point for some 40 farms on the mountain was the West Kilimanjaro Country Club. This was a rather grand title for an old and rather dilapidated farm house 25 miles away, but it was here that we got together for parties, birthdays, church services, weddings, tennis, dances, St George's Day dinners and similar occasions. If you were lucky, Annabel from Simba farm would dance the cancan for you on the bar counter. Or if it was a beautiful moonlight night you could perhaps take part in a revolver shooting contest beyond the tennis court where the lads were blasting off at empty beer cans. I think our visitors from England found our club nights somewhat unusual, and were intrigued!

Nearby was the West Kilimanjaro police post, the post office and store run by Eric Brown (ex Royal Navy) and his wife Edie. In the early days Eric, his post office and the store were the hub of our little universe. Eric with his P.O. and telephone was a key man and our sole link with the outer world. If your wife or girlfriend wanted a hair-do in the nearest town, or you wanted to borrow £1000 from the bank manager, Eric Brown was your man, and Eric could be relied upon to fix it.

As time went on, a second telephone was installed in a little corrugated iron shed on the nearby grass airstrip, and when some of us got flying machines we would nip down off the mountain to make our calls. One day Corinne and I had to fly to Arusha for a meeting. It was an awful cold grey day, with low cloud, wind and mist, and eventually, because of lack of visibility, we turned back and landed at the West Kilimanjaro strip to telephone Arusha and explain our delay. We battled our way through driving rain to the dreary little telephone shed and opened the creaking door. It was dark and gloomy, the rain drummed down and the corrugated iron roof rattled in the wind. As our eyes became conditioned to the semi-darkness within, there, hunched up on the wooden stool, the receiver tied to his wrist and glued to his ear was an almost complete human skeleton! This ghastly apparition with its black, empty eye-sockets regarded us with a sly grin on his half open mouth as we recoiled and then recovered from the initial shock. Finally we were able to untangle the receiver from our ghostly friend's hand and make our call. We never did discover who was responsible for this superb joke.

Jokes and leg-pulls were regular features in our community. One day I flew over the farm of an old friend and neighbour. He was a first rate farmer, his crop was perfect and quite rightly he was proud of it. When I got back to our farm I rang him on our new party-line telephone. "I have seen some lousy wheat in my time" I said, "but never, for so long as I can remember have I seen such an amateurish sight as yours – weeds, smut, rust, the whole works, in particular that 40 acre field adjacent to your workshop."

The phone slammed down accompanied by some extremely rough language! Next day I had reason to fly over the same area and found that my old friend had succeeded in getting his own back, he had gone into the field with a 12 foot cut combine and had written in huge 30-yard letters "Piss Off"!

The saga of Ol Molog and our time there, and in the West Kilimanjaro area as a whole, covered a period of approximately two decades, and the events, the adventures, the friendships, the successes and the setbacks of our closely-knit community is in itself a story that could fill a book.

Never in my experience has there been an environment quite like this. We were individuals, each with his own approach to life, often with entirely different backgrounds and interests, but somehow we achieved the status of a community having trust, loyalty, and companionship between ourselves, a group of people who pulled together as a team, sharing each other's successes and failures and helping each other in times of need. Children were brought up and great friendships made. Guests and relations came to stay from the four corners of the earth and were embraced into the pattern of our life on the mountain; we gained from their presence, and I believe many went away enriched by what they experienced and by the spirit of the people they met and got to know. To all of us on the mountain, including our children who grew up there, this was a home of beauty and splendour and a period never to be forgotten.

Our life on Kilimanjaro ended in great sadness, cut short in the mid-seventies by a policy decision of the Tanzanian government of that time to take over and occupy the privately-owned property of most Europeans and Asians. This was a strange move by a President believed to be a man of compassion and free of prejudice. The decision was all the more inexplicable in that at the time of independence we had been told by the President himself, and repeatedly by Ministers and high officials of Government, that existing titles would be honoured, and that those of us who wished to live in Tanzania would be more than welcome to do so.

All of those who elected to stay on accepted absolutely and wholeheartedly the situation as we found it when the country gained its independence, and I do believe that almost everyone who suffered as the result of Nyerere's nationalization program were committed to making their contribution, each in his own manner, to the country of his choice. Many applied for Tanzanian citizen status but were refused.

The land occupied by people of non-Tanzanian origin by birth was a minute percentage of the great land mass of the territory as a whole, and in productivity, whether it was coffee, sisal, wheat, tea, cattle or any other commodity, was on the whole, developed to capacity and with extreme efficiency.

For many this was the end of a lifetime of sweat and toil, with everything lost and no other home. For others it was the end of a way life in a country they loved and among people they knew and respected. There were setbacks when great schemes for the future came to nought, but that is farming life, and the lasting and overwhelming memory is and always will be one of exceptional happiness and contentment.

We were the last family to vacate the farming area at Ol Molog on Kilimanjaro following President Nyerere's devastating ethnic cleansing experiment, and for the first time in our lives we were homeless. Everything we had worked for and built up during eighteen years on the mountain was gone forever, the house, the garden, our horses, dogs, friends and plans for the future.

There was an abandoned farm house under the shadow of Meru mountain (14,979ft) on the perimeter of Arusha National Park in an area called Momella. The house had been vandalised, but was beautifully situated and had been built by Hardy Kruger, the German actor, who for some reason had been declared a prohibited immigrant and left the country. We moved into this house with all our remaining possessions and set about knocking it into shape. The living room was 60 ft long with an enormous fireplace in which one could roast an ox, the floor was tiled with cedar blocks, the roof thatched, and the ceiling beautifully constructed with interwoven banana fronds. Always there was the sound of rushing water from a nearby mountain torrent, and buffalo, giraffe, elephant and other animals grazed to within fifty paces of the front door.

Our bank account had been blocked and rather than let it lie fallow we formed a safari company, "Tanzania Game Trails Ltd", took on a young German, Bert von Mutius, as manager and launched forth in tourism.

Our venture prospered in spite of the fact that Nyerere disapproved of tourists and gave the industry no support. Finally the President fell out with the Kenyan government and closed the border for several years. The negative pressures brought to bear on us became so intolerable that we decided to sell the safari company and bought an attractive property on the outskirts of Nairobi. Bert moved into the Momella house and established his own safari business, but sadly, after a few years he was killed together with his clients and the pilot in an air crash on an island in Lake Victoria.

As for the rest of the old Kilimanjaro community, each went his own way, some to Kenya and others to South Africa, Australia or England. Elsewhere in Tanzania, British settlers and businessmen, Greeks and Asians, lacking capital and with nowhere to go, suffered extreme hardship. Some were evicted from their homes at gunpoint by heavily-armed police and given only an hour or so to leave. This was a desperately sad end for all of us who loved the country and its people.

And so it was that for Corinne and me a new life lay ahead. It is said that "Change is never a loss, it is a change only." All the same we were desperately sad to leave Tanzania where we had spent so many happy years of our married life. I confess that I did think maybe this was meant to happen and that now we should settle down to a quiet retired existence. Happily these thoughts were soon cast aside, all sorts of new horizons, new opportunities lay ahead.

Someone wrote about age, Ruskin I think it was:

Age is a quality of mind.
If you have left your dreams behind,
If hope is gone,
If you no longer plan ahead.
If your ambitions all are dead,
Then you are old.

But if you make of life the best,
And in your life you still have zest,
If you love to hold,
No matter how the years go by,
No matter how the birthdays fly,
You are not old.

Now at last we were able to travel, to visit far away beautiful places. India, Nepal, Kashmir, and to fish. There were never to be forgotten expeditions to Chile, Labrador, British Columbia, Scotland and elsewhere.

Now too we could more easily keep in closer touch with Philippa and Caroline, and were better placed to liaise with those concerned with the family business in the Republic of Ireland and our Connemara property and Fishery.

Life goes on, and all is well.

I am not afraid of tomorrow, for I have seen yesterday, and I love today.

INDEX

Aachen, 157
Abalti, 107
Aberdare mountains, Kenya, 41-2
Aberdeen, Scotland, 26, 28
Abyssinia, 54, 137, 143
Abyssinia, under Italy, map, 87
Adama, 132
Addis (a horse), 86, 100, 132
Addis Ababa, 85ff, 100ff, 108, 110, 113, 129, 131, 132; Addis Ababa-Jima road, 92
Adwa, 122
Afmadu, 83-4
Afrika Corps, see Rommel
Alamata aerodrome, 130
Alanbrook, Field Marshal Viscount, 78
Albany Museum, Grahamstown, 31
Alexander, Fiona, 54
Alexandria, 218
Ali, Fitewerari, 110
Aliwal, 9, 11, 16
Allia Bay, 51n, 52
Amba Alagi, 89
Amba Mariam, 118, 124
Ambararata Bay, 137
Amboseli plain, 206
Amonaya, Barambas, 111
Amundsen, Capt Roald, 32n
Angola, 192
Antarctic, the, 23, 32n
Antsirabe, 138
Anti-slavery Society, the, 200
Antwerp, 153
Araya Galla tribe, 129-131
Ardennes, the, 157
Arrow, the 138
Arctic, the, 32
Arnhem, 153, 154, 155, disaster of, 155n, 156
Arran, Isle of, 29
Arusha, 205, 209, 221, 223
Arusi, 50
Asmara, 130; Asmara-Gondar

road, 123
Asosa, 126, 128
Atbara, 218
Atlantis, the, 137
Austin, Major Herbert, 35
Australia, 11, 23
Austria, 30
Awash River, 85
Azebo Galla tribe, North-Eastern Ethiopia, 89n, 129ff

Bagamoyo, 175
Bagnold, Major, 32
Bakala, Sheykh, 111
Balcha, Akim, 111
Ballyglunin, 24
Bamangwato Reserve, Bechuanaland, 185
Bark-Jones, Raymond, 28
Bark-Jones, Raymond, 30
Beamish, see Chelwood
Barlow, Col Hilary, 153
Bastogne, German assault on, 157-8
Basutoland high country, 58
Basutoland, 9, 11, 18, 56ff; Civil Administration of, 56; mounted police, 57
Bayeux, 148, 149
Bechuanaland, 64, 182, 185ff
Beer, Trevor, 204
Begemder province, 88
Belas Gugani, 84
Benghazi, 218
Benson, Air Commodore C E, CBE, DSO, 203, 204, 208
Benson, Lady Morvyth, 203
Benson, Sir Rex, 204
Bernhard, Prince of the Netherlands, 155
Bettington, Col, of GHQ East African Command, 133, 133n
Biddle, Lois, 30
Biggs, Maj Michael, 126-7
Biru, Fitewerari, 113, 116, 117, 118,

125
Biru, Fitewerari, 122
Blue Nile, the, 23, 115
Blumenthal, Andy ('Bloom'), 26, 28
Blundell, Sir Michael, 6, 123
Bottego, Vittorio, 35
Boyd, Lord (Alan Lennox-Boyd), 169
Brava, 85
Breuil, l'Abbé, 30, 32
British Antarctic Survey, 33n
British Association for the Advancement of Science, 30
British Association, the, 34
British Columbia, 226
British invasion routes of Italian-held Abyssinia, 87
Bromfield, Pat, game warden, 198
Brown, Eric and Edie, 223
Browning, Lt Gen Sir Frederick ('Boy'), 155
Brussels, 158
Bryceson, Derek, 208
Buchanan, John, 28, 31
Bulawayo, 201
Bullet (a dog), 70, 132
Bulo Erillo, 84
Burgersdorp, 9
Bushmen of the Kalahari, study of, 196
Buttagiari, 111
Buxton, David, 36

Caen, battle for, 151
Cairo, 202, 218
Cambridge, 12, 22ff
Cambridge African Great Lakes Expedition, 32
Cambridge University Artillery Battery, 23
Camels, 47
Campbell's Scouts, 114
Canada, 23

Cape, the, 9, 186, 216
Cape Province, 61, 62
Cape Town, 22, 63, 186, 216
Capricorn Africa movement,
    199n
Carr, Barbara, 24
Carr, George, 218-9
Carr, Maj, 106
Carr, Maj Fred, of the Galway
    Blazers, 24, 25
Catania, Sicily, 202
Cavendish expedition of 1897, 35
Chagga people of Kilimanjaro,
    177-180; traditional enemies of
    Maasai people, 188
Chamala, 79
Champagne (a horse), 58-9
Charles the 'tame Italian', 120
Charlie Brown's pub, 26
Chelwood, Lord (formerly Sir
    Tufton Beamish), 221
Chile, 8, 226
Chobi District, 190, 198
Chobi River, 64
Chobi River, Bechuanaland, 65
Chunya, 71-2, 73
Churchill, Sir Winston, 78
Churundu, 203
Clare-Galway River, 24
Clarendon, Lord, 61
Clark, Diana, 61
Clark, Sir William, KCSI,
    KCMG, 59, 60, 61, 62, 68
Cleves, Anne of, 158
Cobbo Village, 130, 131
Colchester, (17th Field Brigade
    camp), 23
Collins, Col Gilbert of Southforce,
    120, 122
Collins, Col Gilbert, 118, 121,
    122, 123, 124
Collins, Canon John, 197
Colonial Office, the, 200
Combe, Caroline, in the stocks,
    196
Connaught Rangers, 9
Connemara, 166
Copenhagen, liberation of, 163;
    166
Corsica, 30
Costock, 11
Coulson, David, 6, 54
Crichton-Miller, Dr, letter to
    Joan Millard after her father
    died, 161
Crisp, Bob, DSO, 147

D-Day landings, 144ff
D-Day, planning of, 143
Danakil, 131
Dar-es-Salaam, 34, 73, 133, 219

de Beer, Ati, killed by lion, 213
de Gaulle, Charles, 152
de Klerk, Lavinia, 68n, and see
    Struben
de Klerk, Stephen, 68n
de Klerk, Theo, 63, 64, 66, 67,
    69
de Klerk, Theo, 66, 67
de Paula, Capt Clive, 133, 134
Debenham, Frank, 23
Debre Birhan, 114
Debre Sina, 114
Debre Tabor, 114, 115, 118, 120
Debre Zeit, 120
Degoma, 116, 117
Delamere, Lord, 35
Delia the maid, 168
Dempsey, Gen, 141
Denk'ez, 123
Deresa, Ethiopian orderly, 125
Dese, 114, 130
Diego Suarez, 134-5, 137, 138
Dinant, 157
Dixon, Dickie, 203
Djibouti, 54
Dodoma, 214
Dominion students' teams, 23
Douglas, Maj, of the Highland
    Light Infantry, 113, 116, 117n,
    118, 120, 121, 123
Dover, Straits of, 146
Drumnadrochit, 28
du Toit, Sarel, 104
Dublin, 165
Duki, Ras Fitewerari Garusa, see
    Garusa
Duncan, Jos, 67
Duncan, Lt, 101, 102, 111
Dunkirk, 128
Durban, 14, 56, 133, 134, 137
Dyson, Dr Bill, 36, 40, 41, 43,
    44, 45, 46, 47, 48, 49, 51;
    disappearance of, 53
Dyson, Dr Bill, 38

Eagles Club, Cambridge, 23, 29
Eagles Club, Cambridge, 29
East Griqualand, 57
Egeland, Leif, 61
Eileen of the Free French, 139
Eindhoven, 155
Eisenhower, Gen Dwight D, 157
El Alamein, battle of, 81n, 139,
    218
El Molo, 52
Elbe River, 160
Eldoret, 81
Elephants, 174; Kilimanjaro ele-
    phant, Natural History
    Museum, 211-2
Emanuel, Wolde, guerilla leader,

117
Endeber, 89n, 97
Engushai River, 181
Erroll, 22nd Earl of (Josslyn
    Hay), 82
Eritrea, 120
Ethiopia, 8, 34, 35, 37, 39, 116,
    129, 132
Evans, Adml, 60
Everest, 23

Falaise Pocket, Falaise plain, 151
Falaise, 156
Falkland Islands, 32n.
Fanta Forts, 127, 128
Far East, the, 11
Fenners sports ground,
    Cambridge, 23
Ferguson's Gulf, 35, 39-40, 41, 48,
    49, 53
Fisher, Col, of the Gold Coast
    Regiment, 83
Fleming, Launcelot, 23
Foster, James, 183, 221
Foster, Roger ("China" Foster),
    12, 13
Foster, Ursula, 11, 12; and see
    Millard, Mrs Philip
Fowkes, Brig 'Fluffy', 105, 107
Francistown, Bechuanaland, 187,
    189, 191, 192, 194, 196, 197, 203
Freyburg, Brian, husband of Joan
    Millard, 161
Friedeburg, Adml Hans Georg,
    161
Fuchs, Joyce, 38
Fuchs, Joyce, 40
Fuchs, Sir Vivian (Bunny), 32-3,
    35, 36, 37, 38, 39, 40, 46, 47,
    48, 49, 52, 53, 54
Fuchs, Sir Vivian (Bunny), 38, 39
Furse, Sir Ralph, 68, 164, 189, 190

Gabris, Gyula, 54
Gage, Connie, 138
Gage, Jack, 59, 60, 137, 138
Gage, Mrs (Jack's mother), 138
Gage, Sandra, 59, 137-8
Galway Blazers, the, 24
Galway Blazers, 25
Garissa , 82, 83
Garusa (Ras Garusa Duki), 93,
    94, 95, 106, 107, 108, 110, 112,
    132
Gay Prince (a horse), 67
Geldof, Bob, 176
Geological Society, 34
Geto village, 95, 104
Gilib bridge, 84
Gillman's Point, Kilimanjaro, 182
Gobana, see Jabi

Gog Magog Hills, 29
Gogetti, 101
Gojam province, 88
Goldfields Hotel, Chunya, 71-2
Goldsmiths' and Silversmiths'
  Ball, 23
Gondar, 89, 106, 113, 115, 117, 118,
  121, 126, 127, 128
Gorgora, 118
Gort, Lord, 78
Goss, Charlie, 73
Graaf, de Villiers, 61
Grahamstown, 16, 17, 19; Albany
  Museum, 31
Graziani massacres, 126
Great Barranco split, Mawenzi
  peak, Kilimanjaro, 184
Great Karroo, the, 16
Great North Road, Bechuanaland,
  195
Greenland, 23
Grenfell, Pasco, 17
Guinness & Company, 169
Guraghe 110
Guraghe Plateau, 109
Guraghi plateau, 89n, 92, 97

Haile Selassie, Emperor of
  Abyssinia, 88, 89, 108
Haile, Lij, 111
Hamisi, African driver, 186, 204-
  5
Hampshire, Keith (fighter pilot),
  163
Hancock, Lt Cmdr Wilfred, RN,
  133
Handeni, Tanga Province, 170ff
Happy Valley mores, 42
Happy Valley murder, 82
Harar, 85
Harar, Duke of, 108
Harris, Wyn, climber, 41, 45
Hartigan, Alf, 104
Hatfield, William B, ivory buyer,
  211
Hawks' Club, Cambridge, 23
Hay, Josslyn, see Erroll
Heaton, Tom, 6
Henfrey, Tom, 105, 106
Herschel, 9, 11, 14, 17, 31, 61, 62,
  74
Hetchel, 153
Hitler, Adolf, 74, 153, 159
HMS Arrow, 138
HMS Shropshire, 85
Hogan, Ben, 208-9, 213-14
Hogan, Jackie, 208-9
Holmes, Lt, 50
Holmes, Sir Maurice, Permanent
  Secretary to the Ministry of
  Education, 164

Holyhead, 24
Hook, Raymond, 42
Hopkins, Col, of the 2nd
  Nigerians, 105
Horn of Africa, the, 175
Horrocks, Lt Gen Sir Brian, 154,
  156, 160
Hosaena Hill, 102
Hosaena, 89n, 102, 103, 105, 111,
  132
Hughes, Gervas, husband of
  Barbara Millard, 161; shot and
  killed, 161
Hugo, Piet, 208
Hunger, Herr, 76
Huri Hills, the, 50
Hurran Hurra, 51
Hwange National Park,
  Rhodesia, 196

Iceland, 8
India, 11
Indibir, 93, 95, 104, 106, 132
Inver, Ireland, 166, 168, 169, 184
Ipswich top security camp, 143,
  144
Iridibida, 127

Jabi, Basha Gobana, village head-
  man at Geto, 95, 104, 132; his
  wife as cook, 95
Jacob, the African assistant, 13,
  61, 62
James, Brig, 123, 125, 127
Jijiga, 85
Jim the Etonian, 72
Jima, 103-12
Johannesburg, 17, 36, 191, 192,
  193
John the Baptist, 172
Johnson, John, CMG, 54, 163
Johnston, Robin, best man, 166
Johnston, Robin, DFC, DSO,
  78-81, 151, 163, 164; best man
  at author's wedding, 166; 167,
  208, 215, 221
Jones, 'Ropesole', 73
Juba, 218
Juba River, 84, 85
Jubaland, 82, 144
Jumbo, 84

Kaalgat, 66
Kabaku Village, 99
Kabid Ali, Fitewerari, 110
Kachikau village, 65
Kalacha water hole, 50, 203-4
Kalahari Desert, 54, 63, 185, 191,
  203, 204
Kapsiliat, 81
Kasani, Bechuanaland, 63

Katungi, African cook, 95, 99,
  108, 132
Kebede, Balambaras, 111
Keckwick, James, 28
Kelly the driver, 140
Kelly, Ned, 12
Kenya, Mt, 41-5
Khama, Sir Seretse and Lady, 186,
  197
Khama, Lady, 197
Khama, Sir Seretse, marriage of,
  185-201; see also Williams,
  Ruth
Khama, Tshekedi, 185, 186, 188,
  197, 198-200
Khama Tshekedi, 189
Khamseen, the (sandstorm), 219
Khartoum, 35, 218
Kibanga, 175
Kigoma, on Lake Tanganyika,
  176
Kikuyu people, 181
Kildare, County, 165
Kilimanjaro, 177ff; climbed, 182-
  3; farm bought, 194; in charge
  of Kilimanjaro district, 202;
  Kibo, 182; see also
  Legumishira; Kilimanjaro ele-
  phant, the, 211; rainforests of,
  215
Kilimanjaro, 207
Kilimanjaro, 207
King's College chapel,
  Cambridge, 29
King, Lt, 115, 116
Kingstown, County Dublin, 24
Kipling, Rudyard, 9; parody of
  'If', 141
Kismayu, 85
Kleinboi, 19
Kleve (Cleves), 158
Koitherin 38; mountains, 39
Kondoa Irangi, 170
Koroli desert, 45
Kruger, Hardy, German actor,
  225
Kulal, Mt, 45
Kulkabar Hill battle, map, 119
Kulkabar Ridge, 120
Kulkabar, 115-24

La Trobe, Charles Joseph, 12
Labrador, 8, 226
Lake Baringo, 34
Lake Naivasha, 36, 41, 82
Lake Ngami, 185, 190
Lake Nyasa, 77
Lake Rudolf, 32; expedition, 34-
  55, 56
Lake Rukwa, 71

Lake Stefanie, 51n
Lake Tana, 113, 115, 116, 118
Lake Tanganyika, 34, 170, 176
Lake Victoria, 34, 53, 223
Lamprey, Hugh, 54
Lapurr mountain range, 38, 39
le Brocq, Capt Alan, 133, 134
Leach, Capt 'Bulgy', 84, 85, 105
Leach, Gerald, 19
Leakey, Louis, 31, 32
Leakey, Mary, 30
Legumishira, 210
Legumishira Farm, 204,
Legumishira Farm, 212
Leicester, 12
Lenteni, 140
Leslie-Moore, Latham, 77, 172, 172n
Lewis Glacier, 41, 43, 45
Lewis Glacier, 44
Libyan Desert, 32
Lieching, Percy, 60
Lilongwe, capital of Malawi, 216-7
Limpopo River, 185, 190
Lindi, the, 134
Livingstone, David, 175
Livingstone Mountains, 77
Loch Ness, 28
Lodwar, 36
Loiengalani, Kenya, 46, 50n
London Mission Society, the, 200
Longondoti, Mt, 51, 52
Lorimer, Guy, 28
Losodok Hills, 37
Lotagipi swamp, the, 39
Love, Chris, 31
Lovelock, Jack, 23
Lueneburg Heath, 161
Luftwaffe, 140, 145, 147, 155, 202
Lunn, Arnold, Mountain Jubilee, 145
Lupa, 72, 75
Lupa Lill, 73, 75
Lupa River, 71
Lush, Brig Maurice, 86, 139
Lutheran missions, 74, 75

Maas River, 156
Maasai people, 179ff
Maasai Steppe, 174
Mababi Depression, the, 63
MacDonald, Lady, of the Isles, 23-4
MacDonald, Paddy, 31
MacGillivray, Sir Donald, 184, 221
MacHugh, 73
MacIndoe, Sir Archibald, plastic surgeon, 215, 215n

MacInnes, Dr Donald, 36, 48, 49, 53
MacInnes, Dr Donald, 38, 40
Mackinder, Sir Halford, climber, 41, 45
McLean, Lt Col Billy, DSO, 113, 117, 117n
Macoun, Michael, CMG, OBE, Tanganyika Police, 134
McQuirk, Joe, 167, 168
Madagascar, 133ff, 139, 144
Mae West (lifejacket), 146
Mafeking, South Africa, 185
Magdeburg, 160
Maginot Line, 78
Majunga, 134
Makuyuni, 80
Malakal, 218
Malangali, 79
Malawi, 216
Maldabar fort, 128
Maletsunyane Falls, 57
Malta, 140
Malmedy, 157
Mangis (Chagga chiefs), 178
Mangoakay Village, 135
Marangu, 183
Marealle, Thomas, 178
Marealle, Thomas, 179
Mariam, Engide Work Gebre, interpreter, 95, 107, 112
Market Garden (military operation), 154-5, 155n
Marsabit, 45, 47, 48, 49, 52
Marshall, Col, 94
Martin, Mrs, 54
Martin, William 'Snaffles', 36, 38, 45, 46, 47, 48, 49, 51; disappearance of, 53, 54
Martin, William 'Snaffles', 38, 53
Maruma, John, 181
Marwick, Brian, 68
Maseru, 56, 60
Masunga, African driver, 192
Matabele Wars, the, 190
Matiba, Kenneth, 184
Mau Mau, 182; oath-taking, 181
Maud, Sir John, British Ambassador in South Africa, 203
Mayo, Lord and Lady, 216; Lord Mayo, 217
Mbeya, 69-77, 205, 216
Mbozi, German club at, 74
Megech River, 126
Meikel's Hotel, Salisbury, Rhodesia, 217
Mekele, 130, 131, 132
Mekonen, guerilla fighter, 95, 97, 98
Mengesha, Balambaras, guerilla

fighter, 104, 111
Menzies, Ken and May, 71
Merca, 85
Mersa Matruh, 218
Meru, 225
Meskel, feast of, 115, 115n
Messina, Straits of, 140
Meuse-Escaut canal, 153
Meyer, Percy, 139
Miles, Jimmy, pilot, 192-3, 194-5
Milio, Gen Bisson, 106, 107
Millard, Barbara (Mrs Hughes), 11, 13, 16; death of, 161
Millard, Barbara, 21
Millard, Caroline, 54, 55; birth of, 202; 203, 206, 207
Millard, Caroline, 214
Millard, Charles, 11, 12
Millard, Corinne (Mrs John Millard), wedding of, 166; 168, 170, 171, 175; riding accident, 183; reunited with husband and daughter, 184; welfare and Girl Guide movement, 190; birth of second daughter, 201; 207, 208, 217-8, 225
Millard, Corinne, 176, 214, 222
Millard, Dr Maurice, 12
Millard, Dr Philip, 9, 10, 11, 12, 14, 18, 30
Millard, Dr Philip, 10, 15, 20
Millard, Joan, (Mrs Brian Freyburg), 11, 13, 161, 175, 208
Millard, Joan, 20, 21
Millard, John, 13, 20, 27, 30, 31, 47, 57, 61, 64, 66, 120, 122, 150; wedding picture, 167, 169; with wife and daughter, 176
Millard, Mrs Philip (Ursula Foster), 11, 12, 13, 14; death of, 73-4
Millard, Philippa (Pippa), (birth of), 175; nurture after mother's accident, 183-4; 204, 207, 208
Millard, Pippa, 176, 214
Millard, Ursula, 10, 20
Millard's Scouts (Milcol), 90
Millard's Scouts (Milcol), 91, 97

Mitchell Gen Sir Philip, Governor of Kenya, 85, 182
Mogadishu, 85
Moiben, 82
Molloy, Maj Peter, MC, 117, 118, 124, 127
Mombasa, 56
Momella farmhouse, 225
Monduli, 204
Montgomery of Alamein, Field Marshal Viscount, 155, 156, 157, 161

Mopani Forest, 203, 204
Morogoro, 171
Morrison, Alexander, 28
Morrow, Sgt, 116, 117, 118, 124, 125, 127
Morrow, Sgt, 118
Morvyth, Lady, 203
Moshi, 108, 177, 181, 209
Moss Bros, 24
Mosteyn, Sir Piers, 48
Mountains of the Moon, Uganda, 40
Moyale, action at, 80
Mozambique border, 76, 217
Mperoto Mountains, 69
Mpika, 204
Mpishi, 175
Muggo, 89n, 95, 96, 99, 100, 102, 105, 110, 111, 132
Mussolini, Benito, 82, 106, 114, 120, 128
Mwakatumbi, 134
Mwayo, 76

Naas, County Kildare, 201
Nabuyatom, 54
Nairobi, 36, 47, 48, 49, 78ff, 82, 110, 132, 165, 209, 225
Nakuru, 81
Nanyuki, 42
Nasi, Gen, 106, 113, 117
Natal, 137
Nazis, 74
Neumann, Arthur, 35
New Zealand, 23
Newman, Cdr Max, Fleet Air Arm, 164
Newtown, Ireland, 24
Ngorongoro crater, 80
Nijmegen, 155, 156
Nile, the, 34, 35, 218
Njombe district, 75, 76, 77
Normandy beaches (D-Day landings), 144-156
North Africa, 140ff
North Horr, 50, 51, 55
Northern Rhodesia, 14, 170, 191
Nurk, Karl, 113, 124, 127, 128
Nyasaland, 191
Nyerere, Julius, president of Tanzania, 110, 216; ethnic cleansing policy, 221; 224-5
Nyeri, 41, 42
Nyiro mountain, 54
Nzega district, Sukumuland, 176
Nzonzwa, son of Ndolombo, 16
O'Rorke, Molly, 25
O'Rourke, Joy, 165
Oder River, 159
Odlum, Claude, author's father-in-law, a Governor of the

Bank of Ireland, 168-9
Odlum, Corinne, 165, 166; wedding picture, 167
Odlum, Corinne, 165-6; marriage to author, 166; see also Millard, Corinne
Okavango swamp, 65, 185, 191
Ol Molog, 180, 202, 208, 224
Omo River, 34, 35, 62, 93, 95, 103, 106, 110; river gorge, 103; bridge, 103; river valley, 105
Orange Free State, 9
Orange River, 9, 17, 57 58, 62
Organisation of African Unity, the, 199
Ormsby, Lt Col John, 126-7
Ortona, 143
Orwell River, 144

Page-Jones, Mr, Provincial Commissioner, Tanganyika, 181
Palmer, Mr, 22
Pangani, 34
Pangani River, 177
Papadopoulos the Greek, 73
Pare Mountains, 177
Parker, Chris, 6
Parker, Ian, 6
Pelikwe, 197
Penelope, 143
Percy Sladen Trustees, the, 34
Persian Gulf, winds from, 175
Phoney war, 78
Pienaar, Brigadier, 84
Pilkington, Mark, 113, 117, 121, 124, 125, 126
Pimple Hill, 124
Platt, Gen Sir William, 89
Polder, the, 158
Pole, Sir John Carew, 60
Pombe (a dog), 216
Poole, Guy, 50n
Pretoria, 63
Pretzlik, Susan, 221
Pritchard, Derick, climber, 184

Qachas Nek, 57
Queen of Denmark, the, 163
Quetta, 82

Rametsana Group, Bechuanaland, 185
Rank, Arthur, 166
Rasbistos, 73
Raiya, 129
Rashid, Fitewerari, guerilla fighter, 96, 97, 98, 110
Raven, Canon Charles, 22, 26
Read, David, 208
Reese, Idwal, 28

Reitz, Deneys, 61, 62
Reusch, Revd Dr Richard, 182
Reusch, Revd Dr Richard, 183, 184
Rhine, the, 158, 159
Rhodes, Cecil, 17, 190
Rhodes University, 19
Rhodesia, 190
Ridley, Mervyn, Mr and Mrs, 81
Rift Valley, the, 37, 54, 76, 81
River Elbe, 160
Rogers, Alec, magistrate, 181
Rogers, Joseph and Sons Ltd (cutlers), 211
Rombo sub-district, 181
Rome, fall of (World War II), 145
Rommel's Afrika Corps, 81n, 139, 218
Rosmead, 16
Royal Geographical Society, the, 34, 47
Royal Society, the, 34
Rudolf, Crown Prince of Austria, 34
Rudolf Expedition, 37, 38
Rungwe District Commissioner, 76
Ruskin, John, 226

Sadani, 175
Salisbury Plain, 23
Salisbury, Southern Rhodesia, 189
Sandbostel concentration camp, near Bremen, 159
Sandford, Col (later Brigadier) Dan, DSO, Legion d'Honneur, British Consul in Abyssinia, 88, 89n, 96, 108, 110, 113, 129, 130, 131, 132
Sangro, 143
Sarah, the Millards' ayah, 13
Sciola, 103, 104, 111
Scotland, 8, 27, 29, 226
Scott Polar Institute, Cambridge, 23
Scott, Capt R F, 32n
Serengeti National Park, Tanzania, 155n, 216, 222
Serowe, 185, 190, 199
Seyfu, Fitewerari, 110, 132
Seyoum, Ras, Ethiopian chief, 130, 131
Shackleton, Lt, 33
Shaka Bakala, 97

Sheldrick, David, game warden, 220
Shipton, Eric, climber, 41, 45
Shropshire, the, 85
Sicily, 140, 143

Silberbauer, George, 196
Simon, the author's driver, 157
Sirima, 45
Slade art school, 11
Smallwood, Brig of 3rd
    Nigerians, later Gen, 106, 138
Smith, Arthur Donaldson, 35
Smith, Ian, 161
Smith, Mr (a dog), 15
Smuts, Lt-Gen Jan C, 14, 60, 61,
    62, 198, 199
Smuts, Lt-Gen Jan C, 60, 61
Soames, Dick, 208
Sobieski, the, 136
Sodo, 103, 112
Sodo-Jima road, 103, 110, 111, 112
Somaliland, 144
Sondra, the, 134
Sorbonne, the, 30
Spitzbergen, 23
St Andrew's College, 18
St George, the, 134
St John's College, Cambridge,
    22, 33
St Lo, 151
Stanford, 'Doc' (fighter pilot),
    163
Stavelot, 157
Stigand, Mr, explorer, 35
Stirling, Bill, 221
Stirling, David, the 'Phantom
    Major', 200n
Stockwell, Col Hugh, 134-5, 136
Stone Age Man, 32
Stormberg Mountains, 9
Strong, Peter, 58
Struben, Capt, 67
Struben, Lavinia, (later de
    Klerk), 67, 68
Sudan, 39, 116
Sukumuland, 176
Surrey, England, 218
Symington, Noel, 28
Syracuse, Sicily, 202

Table Mountain, 61, 162, 170
Tabora, 170
Tada Ridge, 127
Talakea Glades, 181, 182
Tambaro, 103
Tana River, 82, 83
Tanga, 175
Tanganyika, 134, 163ff, 170ff
Tannerhill, Sgt, 134
Tanzania, 216, 155n, 225
Tanzania Game Trails Ltd, 225

Tarleton, Ben, 113
Taylor, Capt, 201
Teleki, Count Samuel, 34, 35, 46,
    51n, 54, 55
Teleki volcano region, 47
T'ereg Iman, 115, 116, 117, 118
Thika, 83, 182
Thomas, Ipogolo, 73
Thomas, "Smelly", 73
Tiger Moth, author's first aircraft,
    193
Tigre province, 89n
Tito, bull terrier, 186
Todenyang, 38
Tony, 'brave but straitlaced', 158;
    teased by Gretl, 159
Tsavo National Park, Kenya, 219
Tunduma, 204
Tunis, 140, 218
Turkana (formerly Lake Rudolf),
    34-55
Turkana desert, 36
Turkwell River, 35, 36
Twining, Sir Edward, 179
Twining, Sir Edward, Governor
    of Tanganyika, 178, 180

Uganda, 40
Ukinga escarpment, 79
Ukinga plateau, 71
Umtali, 217
Urbaragh, 110, 111
Urquhart, Maj Brian, 155, 155n
Usangu, 69

Valkenwaard, 154
van Staden, Mrs, 63, 65
van Veen, Belgian patriot leader,
    113, 124, 133, 134
Vandelour, Col 'Joe', 153
Vereeniging Peace, the, 61
Victoria Falls, 170, 190
Victoria, Queen, 172
Voi, Kenya, 220
von Höhnel, Adml Ludwig, 36,
    46, 51, 54, 55
von Mutius, Bert, 225
von Rundstedt, Field Marshal
    Karl Gerd, 157
Vorbeck, Lt-Col Paul Emil von
    Lettow, 14, 75
Waal, 155
Wajarat/Azebo Galla uprising in
    Tigre province, 89n
Wajirat tribe, North-Eastern
    Ethiopia, 129

Wakefield, R C 'Jumbo', 36, 38,
    53
Wakefield, R C 'Jumbo', 38
Wakwavi village, 171
Waldblott, Baroness Marie
    Theres, 54
Waller, Jocelyn, 29-30, 33
Waller, Jocelyn, 30
Wallinger, Geoffrey, 61
Walso, 95
Wankie National Park, see
    Hwange
Webe River, 93
Welby expedition of 1899, 35
Welega province, 88
Welo Banda, the, 120
Wembere Steppe, the, 172
West, Mae, actress, 146
Western Desert, the 19
Wheat, 210
Wickenburg, Count E, 35, 54
Wilkins, District Commisioner,
    69
Williams, Col, 133
Williams, Ruth (Lady Khama),
    185, 200
Williams, Ruth (Lady Khama),
    186
Wilson, Bruce, 104
Wilson Report, the, 178
Winchester Castle, the, 33
Wingate, Orde, 100, 113
Wittebergen, 11
Witwatersrand, 191
Wolff, Whisky, 73
Wolters, Lt Cdr Arnoldus, 153
Wordie, Sir James, 23, 33n
Worthington, Dr Barton, 35, 40
Wostenholme, W B Ltd, 211

Xanten, 159
Xinodo range, 11
XXX Corps HQ staff, Belgium
    1944, 154

Young, Francis Brett, 68
Yvonne, pilot, 193-4

Zambezi River, 19, 65, 170, 185,
    203
Zanzibar, 211, 216
Zimbabwe ruins, 217